Teaching Law by Design

Teaching Law by Design

Engaging Students from the Syllabus to the Final Exam

Michael Hunter Schwartz
PROFESSOR, WASHBURN UNIVERSITY SCHOOL OF LAW,
CO-DIRECTOR, INSTITUTE FOR LAW TEACHING AND LEARNING

Sophie Sparrow
PROFESSOR, FRANKLIN PIERCE LAW CENTER

Gerald Hess
PROFESSOR, GONZAGA UNIVERSITY SCHOOL OF LAW,
CO-DIRECTOR, INSTITUTE FOR LAW TEACHING AND LEARNING

CAROLINA ACADEMIC PRESS
Durham, North Carolina

Copyright © 2009
Michael Hunter Schwartz, Sophie Sparrow, and Gerald Hess
All Rights Reserved

Library of Congress Cataloging-in-Publication Data

Schwartz, Michael Hunter.
  Teaching law by design : engaging students from the syllabus to the final exam / Michael Hunter Schwartz, Sophie Sparrow, Gerald Hess.
      p. cm.
  Includes bibliographical references and index.
  ISBN 978-1-59460-497-3 (alk. paper)
  1. Law—Study and teaching—United States. 2. Law teachers—United States—Handbooks, manuals, etc. I. Sparrow, Sophie. II. Hess, Gerald F., 1952- III. Title.
  KF272.S37 2009
  340.071'173—dc22   2009013705

Carolina Academic Press
700 Kent Street
Durham, NC 27701
Telephone (919) 489-7486
Fax (919) 493-5668
www.cap-press.com

Printed in the United States of America

This book is dedicated to

My mother, Alice Gokkes, whose unfailing belief in continuous self-improvement—
even at age 80—has inspired my own efforts to grow
~Mike

Layne, Mike, and Amanda—my family of teachers and writers
~Gerry

Kai, Silas, and Chris, three of my best teachers
~Sophie

Contents

Preface	xiii
Chapter 1 · What It Means to Be a Teacher	3
What we know about effective learning	3
Introduction	4
Cognitive Learning Theory	4
Constructivist Learning Theory	7
Adult Learning Theory	8
Self-Regulated Learning Theory	9
What we know about effective teaching	12
Subject matter expertise	12
Respect	13
Expectations	14
Support	15
Passion	16
Preparation and organization	16
Variety	17
Active learning	18
Collaboration	19
Clarity	20
Formative feedback	21
Chapter 2 · Student Perspectives on Teaching and Learning	23
Students want to be treated with respect	24
Treat students as colleagues	24
Include different perspectives in class	25
Create a positive and welcoming environment	25
Use students' names	26
Students want to be engaged in their learning	27
Use a variety of teaching methods	28
Give students an organizational structure — provide context for learning	28
Provide ways for students to be actively involved in class	29
Make class preparation assignments reasonable and meaningful	29
Provide opportunities for students to work with others	30
Be aware of students' concerns about the Socratic method	31
Students want to become good lawyers	32
Connect what students are learning to the practice of law	32
Be explicit — tell students what you expect	32

Give students opportunities to practice meeting expectations	33
Give students feedback on their progress	34
Allow students to show their progress in multiple ways	35
Parting shots—students' general advice to us	35
How to hear *your* students' perspectives.	36
Checklist for considering the students' perspectives	36

Chapter 3 · Designing the Course — 37

Introduction	37
Initiating the design process: setting course goals	38
Know your students: assessing the learners	42
Plan assessment: how will you know whether your students are learning?	43
Introduction	43
The three uses of student assessment	44
Finding the book of your dreams: sifting the morass to find the right textbooks for you	45
Broad principles of textbook selection	45
Some points of textbook comparison we regard as significant	46
Converting goals to results: designing the course to increase the likelihood students will learn what you want them to learn	47
Introduction	47
Designing learning units and synthesizing those units in an overall course design	47
Writing your syllabus	54
Introduction	54
What topics should be addressed in your syllabus?	55
Tone, high expectations, communicating your attitude about student learning, giving students a role in constructing your syllabus	58
Course web page design	61
Evaluate the design and plan for the future	63
Checklist for course design process	64

Chapter 4 · Designing Each Class Session — 65

Context	65
Course context	66
Student context	66
Teacher context	67
Class objectives	68
Learner centered	68
Professional knowledge, skills, and values	68
Clear and concrete	70
Instructional activities	71
Opening	71
Body	72
Closing	75
Feedback	76
Materials	77
Evaluate and Revise	82
Sample class designs	83

  Checklist for class design process   85

Chapter 5 · Student Motivation, Attitudes, and Self-Regulation   87
  Introduction   87
  Motivating students   88
   Introduction   88
   Specific techniques   89
  Teaching for attitude or value change or development   94
   General principles of attitude learning   94
   Techniques for producing attitude change   95
   Conclusion regarding motivational teaching strategies and attitude learning   98
  Engaging students to become expert self-regulated learners   98
   Persuasion   99
   Role modeling   99
   Experiencing: getting students to take their "metacognitive pulse"   100
  Checklists   104

Chapter 6 · Teaching the Class   107
  Create a positive learning environment where students feel that it is safe to take risks.   108
   Know and use students' names.   108
   Be conscious of the messages you send.   109
   Be enthusiastic.   110
   Model taking risks and acknowledging weaknesses.   110
   Envision yourself less as the "sage on the stage" and more of a "guide on the side."   110
   Be transparent.   111
   Be authentic.   111
  The Nuts and Bolts   111
   Pre-class: the fifteen minutes before class starts   112
   Openings: the first five minutes of class   112
  Body—the heart of the class session   115
   Instructional activities   116
  Lectures   119
   Use mini-lectures.   119
   Add valuable content.   119
   Surround mini-lectures with other activities.   119
   Include visuals.   120
   Deliver mini-lectures effectively.   120
  Questioning Techniques   120
   Prepare students in advance.   121
   Ask clear questions.   122
   Ask one question at a time.   122
   Ask a range of questions.   122
   Elicit different levels of thinking.   122
   Allow sufficient wait-time (at least three to five seconds) after you ask a question.   123
   Encourage and promote effective responses.   123
   Respond appropriately to ineffective answers.   123

Use the "live discussion" course webpage tool to engage students in
law school, Socratic-style discussions. ... 124
Discovery sequence instruction ... 125
Using real-life experiences ... 125
Using simulations to promote deep learning ... 126
Address controversial issues ... 126
Visuals ... 128
PowerPoint and other visuals ... 128
Dress ... 129
Timing ... 130
Closings: the last five minutes of class ... 131
Summarize key points. ... 132
Give students time to consolidate their learning. ... 132
Allow students to reflect on their learning. ... 133
Closing modification: the very last class. ... 133
Final notes on teaching the class ... 133
Checklist for teaching the class ... 134

Chapter 7 · Assessing Student Learning ... 135
Introduction ... 135
The Assessment Cycle ... 136
Assessing students to improve their learning during the course ... 137
Step one: Identify learning objectives ... 138
Step two: Prepare the assessment instrument ... 139
Step three: Give feedback to students ... 143
Assessing students to improve your teaching—using classroom
assessment techniques ... 149
Minute Papers ... 150
Student Surveys ... 152
Analysis Charts ... 153
Evaluating students to assign grades ... 154
Use multiple assessments ... 155
Use a variety of assessments ... 157
Evaluate fairly ... 158
Talking to students about grades ... 160
Designing and using rubrics ... 161
Checklist for assessing student learning ... 163

Chapter 8 · Developing as a Teacher ... 165
Sustaining a teaching practice ... 165
Instructional awareness ... 166
Formative feedback ... 166
Pedagogical knowledge ... 167
Implementation ... 167
Assessment ... 167
Types of teaching development activities ... 167
Self-Assessment, Reflection, and Study ... 169
Benefits of reflective practice ... 169
Self-Assessment ... 169

Teaching portfolio	170
Teaching journal	170
Print and electronic resources	171
Formative feedback from students	172
Student evaluations	172
Feedback from students during the course	173
Collaborating with colleagues	176
Discussions with colleagues	176
Peer observations and feedback	176
Team teaching	178
Small group instructional diagnosis	178
Consultants	179
Individual coaching	179
Videotape	180
Teaching workshops and conferences	181
Fostering a culture of teaching	183
Criteria for appointment, tenure, and promotion	183
Separation between development and evaluation	183
Administrative support	184
Faculty leadership and motivation	184
Institutional reward structure	185
Community, collegiality, and collaboration	185
Scholarship redefined	186
Continuous process	186
Appendices	**189**
Appendix 3-1: Course Goals	191
Course Goals for Civil Procedure I Course	191
Course Goals for Torts Class	192
Appendix 3-2: Lesson Objectives	194
Objectives for a Lesson on Express Conditions	194
Appendix 3-3: Syllabi	195
Torts Syllabus	195
Environmental Law Syllabus	201
Appendix 4-1: Charts, Tables, and Diagrams	206
Dismissal under FRCP 41 Chart	206
Chart Depicting Restitution in the Context of a Contracts Course	207
Common Contract Terms Chart	208
Personal Jurisdiction Analytical Framework	209
Partially Completed Graphic Organizer Synthesizing Contract Interpretation Principles	210
Appendix 5-1: Role Plays	211
Civil Procedure I Oral Argument Role Play	211
Oral Argument Problem - Fall 2008	212
Client Counseling and Insurance Policy Analysis Exercise	214
Example Sections of a Client Letter	218
Environmental Law Role Play — Philosophical Perspectives	220
Appendix 5-2: Experiential Professionalism Instruction	221
Lucy Lockett Professionalism Problem	221

Handout for Small Group Public Service Experiential Learning Exercise	223
Professionalism/Values Exercise Arising out of a Class Incident	224
Identifying Criteria for Successful and Positive Interactions with Classmates	225
Appendix 5-3: Time Management/Self-Monitoring Log	226
Appendix 5-4: Post-Assessment Reflection Exercises	227
General Post-Assessment Reflection Exercise	227
Cognitive Protocol	230
Appendix 6-1: Discovery Sequence Exercises	231
Duty to Disclose Discovery Sequence Exercise	231
Binding vs. Persuasive Authority Discovery Sequence Exercise	234
Appendix 7-1: Assessment Instruments	235
Peer Feedback Formative Assessment Exercise	235
Midterm/Peer Feedback, Reflection Assessment	237
Guidelines for Phase III: Reflection	240
International Environmental Law Quiz	243
Civil Procedure – Reflections on Civil Litigation	245
Appendix 7-2: Rubrics	247
Torts Rubric	247
Rubric/Scoring Sheet	248
Remedies Peer Review Rubric	250
Client Letter Rubric	251
Clinical Rubric –Performance Competencies	253
Appendix 8-1: Principles for Enhancing Student Learning – Faculty Inventory	256
Appendix 8-2: Reflection Prompts	260
Selected Resources – Books, Articles, Newsletters, Videos, and Websites	263
Books	263
Articles	264
Newsletters	265
Videos	265
Websites	266
Index	267

Preface

In this book, we seek to apply the enormous body of research on teaching and learning to legal education. Our goal is to provide concrete suggestions about how to design and conduct all aspects of teaching law students, from sequencing a course to grading an exam. While new and experienced teachers can apply the book's principles to any law school class, we have primarily focused on translating nuts-and-bolts teaching and learning techniques to doctrinal classes.

We invite you to read the chapters and appendices sequentially or individually, depending on your interests, competing demands, and students. We hope the book helps you and your students enjoy teaching and learning in law school. At the same time, we caution you not to feel compelled to adopt every suggestion in this book. Not only have none of us adopted every suggestion in this book, but we doubt anyone could do so. Instead, make small rather than wholesale changes, evaluate the effectiveness of every new practice you try, keep doing the things that work, discard the things that don't work, and, above all, aspire to continuous improvement.

The first chapter provides a legal education-focused overview of the research on teaching and learning. The second chapter captures the student perspective on law teaching and learning. Chapters 3 through 7 focus on fundamental elements of teaching: course design, class design, teaching methods, and assessment. Chapter 8 focuses on things law teachers can do to systematically improve themselves as teachers.

In writing this book, we are fortunate to benefit from the vast research on teaching and learning in higher education and studies of law students and legal education. A list of teaching and learning resources is at the end of the book; we encourage you to explore these further.

While we wrote this book in an effort to share what we believe to be core principles of teaching and learning, the book also is sort of a white paper for the "Context and Practice Casebook" series from Carolina Academic Press. The series is designed to apply the principles from this book, as well as other insights and recommendations from BEST PRACTICES IN LEGAL EDUCATION (CLEA 2007) and EDUCATING LAWYERS (Jossey-Bass 2007), to the creation of law school course materials.

We wish to thank the many people who made this book possible. We appreciate the support of our respective law schools and the patience of our families. We are grateful to our many students, who had no choice but to help us learn from our mistakes.

Michael Hunter Schwartz
Sophie Sparrow
Gerry Hess

Teaching Law by Design

Chapter 1

What It Means to Be a Teacher

This chapter explores what we know about effective learning and effective teaching. In this short chapter, we cannot possibly provide a graduate level exploration of either topic, and we do not purport to aim so high. Instead we are aiming for an only-what-you-need-to-know treatment of these topics. As a result, if you are familiar with the learning and teaching research, this chapter will not offer new, earth-shattering insights but might provide a useful review. If you have not encountered these ideas before, however, the discussion will provide necessary background. For both the teaching and learning theory novices and even for you experts, we cannot help but kibitz a bit about your learning process as you read: find the echoes of the ideas introduced in this chapter in our recommendations throughout the rest of the book. You are more likely to remember and be able to use the ideas in this chapter and the rest of the book if you discern for yourself the relationship between these ideas and the teaching principles.

What we know about effective learning

We have chosen to start a book on teaching with what we know about effective learning. That choice is deliberate. From our perspective, teaching is effective *only* if it produces significant learning.

And there's a lot of stuff out there about learning. While we think of ourselves as peer teachers in this field, we also recognize we always will be students. Educational psychologists and instructional designers have produced literally thousands of books, studies and papers addressing learning, and there is a growing cadre of authors from every other discipline, including law, who conduct their own, discipline-specific studies of student learning. Because the field is so vast, we cannot cover it all. Instead, we have chosen to focus on the four theories we believe are most salient for law teachers: cognitive learning theory, constructivist learning theory, adult learning theory, and self-regulated learning theory.

Some might see the ideas explored in this section as conflicting. Because we have no intellectual or professional investment in any particular set of ideas, we feel free to be reconciliatory. Thus, while we have divided the discussion of what we know about learning into five sub-topics: an introductory discussion and an explanation of each of the four theories, we present the ideas as a synthesis and not as a set of competing viewpoints.

Introduction

All learning theories assume a similar goal. Whether that goal is labeled "mastery" or "competency" or "transfer," the basic idea is the same. Students have learned something significant when they can apply what they have learned to solve a previously-unseen problem. Translated into the law school context, we would say our students have developed competency when they are able to solve a legal problem (analyze a hypothetical or real set of facts) by articulating arguments competent lawyers would make and predicting how courts would resolve the issue. In other words, they must be able to transfer what they have learned by analogizing previously-seen cases and problems to the new problem they encounter in law school and, more importantly, in law practice.

Cognitive Learning Theory

To transfer learning from an old setting to a new one, students must store their learning in an organized, meaningful and useable way. The processes of storing new learning and retrieving stored learning occur according to the sequence described and depicted below in Illustration 1-1. Although the sequence may appear linear, moving from one place to the next and then to the next and so on, the process probably is more circular and interactive. Although we describe this "cognitive processing" as a model, there is considerable research supporting its accuracy.

Hundreds of pieces of information reach our students' senses every moment. At any point during a class session, students are hearing what we and their peers say but also are

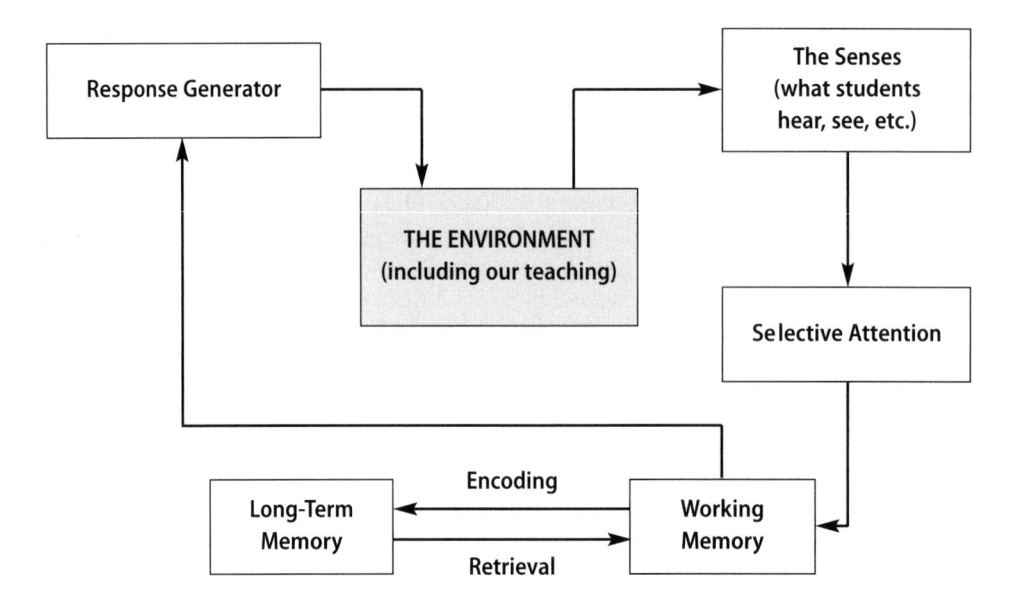

Illustration 1-1: A Model of Cognitive Processing

hearing each others' clicks on their laptops or scratches on paper, seeing what's on their computer screens, feeling how hard or soft their chairs are and how cold or hot the classroom is (all three of us have taught in many classrooms that seem only to have two temperatures: uncomfortably hot or agonizingly cold), and, perhaps, even smelling their each others' colognes and soaps. The information registers in our students' senses for a brief moment. Humans can attend, however, to only a few of these pieces of information so our students must decide: which stimuli warrant attention? The process of choosing a focus is known as "selective attention." Thus, the learning process is over at the spigot if our students decide to pay attention to their e-mail, their e-bay purchases, their social interactions, their breakfasts, the hardness of their chairs, or their doodling instead of attending to learning the skills and knowledge we are teaching. Of course, all we hear is, "What was the question?"

If our students do pay attention to their learning, it passes into their working memory. Students' working memory can retain only a small amount of learning and only for a limited time. Most of us have noticed we usually can remember a new phone number for only 10 or fewer seconds unless we do something to help us remember it, such as saying it out loud several times. When our students do something *active* to store their learning in a meaningful way, the information becomes a part of their long-term memory.

For this reason, cognivitists were the first to emphasize the crucial importance of engaging students in active learning activities. Active learning activities are those in which students cannot simply sit and listen but must do something to mentally process the concepts we want them to learn. If students are writing about the concepts, discussing them with a peer, figuring out how they relate to each other and to what they already know, students are engaged in the necessary active learning.

The most common way students store new learning is by making connections between the new learning and what they already know. For example, a student learning promissory estoppel might recognize the similarities between carelessness in actions, which we call negligence, and carelessness in promising, which we call promissory estoppel. There are, however, many ways to store new learning. These techniques include a wide range of techniques including mnemonics, rehearsal (practicing recall, such as self-testing using flashcards), and elaborations (which include paraphrasing difficult concepts). The more deeply students think about what they are learning, the more likely they are to remember and use it.

If students learn material so well that they can retrieve it with minimal attention, a process known as "overlearning," they have developed "automaticity." For example, most adults have developed automaticity with respect to reading; they can process the meaning of sentences and paragraphs without sounding out the words used or the meanings of unfamiliar words. Because they can read words so readily, they can focus on learning the concepts the author has used the words to express. To be able to apply the high level intellectual skills we teach our law students, the students need to have developed automatic knowledge of the rules of law, case holdings, and public policies, and of the skills involved in applying all three. This automaticity allows students to focus mental energy and effort on the more challenging skills involved in developing and sifting through facts and analyzing the complex combinations of issues students encounter on exams and lawyers encounter in law practice. Experts possess well-organized and deep wells of automatic knowledge.

The brain organizes long-term memories in hierarchical structures called "schemata." Think of a schema as being a little like the folder systems provided for users of computer operating systems, such as the folders users can create with Windows or with the Apple operating system. To a person who is familiar with schema theory, both operating systems appear to assume the existence of schemata because they allow users to create folders and sub-folders and sub-sub-folders. These hierarchical systems allow users to readily remember where they can find any document they need. For example, Mike stores his contracts I course syllabus in a folder labeled "handouts." The "handouts" folder, as well as folders labeled "teaching notes," "powerpoint slides," and "student evaluation," are in a folder labeled "contracts I." The "contracts I" folder, in turn, is in a folder labeled "courses" (along with folders for each of the other courses Mike teaches—contracts II, remedies, and insurance law). Finally, the courses folder, as well as folders for presentations, committee work, scholarship, and many others are in a folder on the Washburn system labeled Mike Schwartz.

Humans can store a single concept or set of concepts using more than one schema. For example, law professors can recall the process of applying and distinguishing cases both in abstract, generalized terms as a set of mental steps (involving, among others things, identifying the key facts in a precedent and identifying and explaining the legal significance of factual similarities and differences between the precedent and the new problem). Law professors also can recall the process by the myriad contexts in which they themselves have performed the skill or have read cases or briefs in which others have applied it. Storing learning in multiple schemata improves recall—either because it strengthens the memory trace (the mental processes involved in gathering previously-learned concepts)—or because it creates more mental paths to the learning.

Based on this initial discussion, it is easy to develop a misperception that cognitive theory focuses on acquiring and not on applying knowledge. Schemata, however, are not only analogous to operating system folders. Schemata also are like entire computer programs in that the organized material includes structures that reflect how to perform skills. Thus, most adults who can play a musical instrument, such as the piano, have developed a schema for performing all the mental and physical steps involved. These steps include identifying each mark on the sheet of music, knowing what each mark means and understanding the relationships among: the marks, the black and white keys, their hands, the necessary fingering to reach all the keys, the pedals below the keys and their feet. In addition, schemata are like theories in that they allow us to make predictions and to draw inferences.

But storing learned skills and knowledge in schemata isn't enough. To analyze a problem, students must recall ("retrieve") what they have learned and use that learning to interact with the environment in some way. In law school, this last step involves recalling cases, rules, and policies, and then generating an oral answer to a classroom hypothetical, writing a full analysis to a legal writing problem, or answering a timed essay test. In law practice, it includes interacting with a client, a judge or another attorney, and drafting pleadings, briefs, contracts, wills and other legal documents.

One final example may help. Imagine you have been assigned the task of teaching your colleagues cognitive learning theory. Your own process would include:

- learning the concepts explained in this section by seeing and reading about them;
- focusing on the concepts so they entered your short-term memory;
- using a technique to help you store the model in your long-term memory (such as drawing Illustration 1-1 yourself from memory, making connections between your understanding of the world and this new theory, or creating a mnemonic to remember each of the parts);

- retrieving the encoded model from long-term memory by thinking about it; and, then,
- using that recollection to direct the body movements needed to do the teaching.

Constructivist Learning Theory

Constructivists focus less on the sequence of learning and more on the process required for new learning to become a more-or-less permanent part of who the students are. Three crucial learning principles derive from constructivist research. First, learning is a matter of constructing an interpretation from an experience. When students engage with materials in an active, effortful way and reflect on the process, they develop personal understandings. And those personal understandings, having been entirely generated within the student's mind, stay with the student. Thus, significant law student learning only can happen if the law professor provides the students with opportunities to develop such interpretations, to figure things out for themselves.

Teachers in all fields (and many law teachers in our experience) frequently complain that they can tell their students some things over and over again and yet their students don't recall those things on the day of their exam. Why don't the students remember? A constructivist would explain that merely "telling" the students did not allow them to develop a personal understanding. In other words, a law professor who wanted her students to understand illusory promise would subject them to such a promise (hopefully as to a minor issue—such as letting students out of class early one day), and a law professor who wanted her students to understand personal jurisdiction might tell students they had to attend an important hearing in an inconvenient location.

Constructivists also emphasize the importance of real-world experiences, both in learning activities and assessment. Students learn when their opportunities to construct understandings are authentic, such as when their learning is anchored in a realistic context. Thus, law professors who situate even their doctrinal teaching in law practice problems, whether simulations or actual client issues, provide students the authenticity they need to construct meaningful understandings.

Finally, constructivists emphasize the role of social interaction in learning. Students engage in crucial mental activity when they negotiate meaning and seek to synthesize their personal understandings. The hundreds of studies demonstrating the superiority of cooperative learning groups compared to all other teaching methods support this assertion. While reading a textbook or interacting with a professor in a Socratic dialogue involve some social negotiation (between author and reader in the first case and between student and teacher in the second), neither method places all students in the class in both a teaching and a learning role in the way that a cooperative learning experience does. These groups are so effective because they allow students to obtain access to multiple perspectives with respect to a problem or issue and thereby to develop the more complex approaches and understandings required to address complicated problems.

Any law professor who has graded a set of exams has had the experience of reading some exams that argued an issue only could be resolved one way and others arguing the issue only could be resolved the exact opposite way. Cooperative learning experiences in class could have helped students see other perspectives on the final exam. And most of us have participated in a meeting or discussion during which the group as a whole developed a better understanding of a problem or a better solution than any individual had been able to come up with on his or her own.

Of course, such results are the product of groups who know how to work together, how to subdue ego in service of the goal of obtaining the best results possible, how to develop "positive interdependence," where each member of the group invests in the success of every other member of the group, and how to develop "accountability," where each member of the group holds every other member of the group responsible for performing her or his share of the group work. Groups who do not develop these qualities may be dysfunctional, and dysfunctional groups are no more productive or valuable than dysfunctional families or working on one's own. When constructivists talk about the learning that comes from social negotiation, they are referring to effective groups.

Finally, a constructivist would encourage a law professor to conceptualize law teaching more as coaching and less as lecturing. As the coach, the professor plans the sessions, organizes opportunities for practice, delivers explicit, corrective feedback, and encourages teammates to help each other improve.

Adult Learning Theory

Adult learning theory has considerable overlap with both the cognitive and constructivist theories but provides important points of emphasis. The application of adult learning theory to law students, however, is more complex. Law students vary greatly in age. While some, second-career law students undoubtedly fit the adult learner classification, others, those who have just finished a four-year college sequence they started at age 18, have characteristics of adult learners and characteristics of younger learners. Also, much of adult learning theory focuses on professional development of practitioners in a field; legal education involves, for the most part, novice lawyers. In fact, some second-career adult law students struggle in law school because the ego aspects of being an adult learner makes them more resistant to reconciling the differences between their own, non-practitioner experiences in the legal field and how lawyers should practice. Nevertheless, adult learning theory is useful to a law teacher, not only because it allows law teachers to reach their more mature students, but also because it offers useful touch points from the previously-discussed theories.

For example, like constructivist theory, adult learning theory emphasizes the importance of real world experiences, but adult learning theory takes this idea one step further: not only must the experience be authentic, but the students must see the experience as authentic *and* as important to their personal and professional needs.

Moreover, while adult learning theory and cognitivist theory share an emphasis on articulating learning goals, adult learning theory suggests students not only want to know what they need to be learning and how what they are learning relates their career goals, but also want to understand the relationship between the learning goals and the methods the teacher has chosen to achieve those goals.

Adult learning theory, like cognitive theory, emphasizes the importance of connecting new learning to the students' prior knowledge. Because adult learners have a much wider base of prior knowledge, they need their teachers to recognize and draw out their relevant prior knowledge.

Like both cognitivism and constructivism, adult learning theory emphasizes the need for students to be in control of their own learning process. Students must have a role in deciding what and how they will learn.

Finally, and related to the previous point, adult learning theory emphasizes the importance of teachers showing respect for their students, a principle that applies to all students. Adult learning theorists would suggest that law professors find opportunities to treat law students as equals with respect to subjects about which the students have as much or even greater expertise. In addition, it is useful for law professors to communicate an understanding that the singular way in which they, as law professors, are superior to their students — their ability to read, understand and apply law — is not a matter of inherent ability but, rather, derives solely from the professors' experience as lawyers and with the materials.

Self-Regulated Learning Theory

Cognitivist learning theory, constructivist learning theory, and adult learning theory implicitly assume students possess the skills, knowledge and values necessary to take control over their own learning by organizing or at least facilitating their cooperative groups and making the links between experience and the personal understanding that are necessary to store new learning in long-term memory. Many students, perhaps even most new law students, do not. Mike's research suggests that law school forces nearly all students to improve their self-regulated learning skills, but students taught to self-regulate learn to do so faster and easier, and, according to Mike's research, do better in law school.

Self-regulated learning, which is sometimes called "expert learning," is the process by which successful students manage their learning process.

> **Thinking exercise**: Think about the students you have most enjoyed teaching. What are they like? What do they do? List the characteristics of the students you most enjoy teaching.

We suspect any law teacher who was asked to list the qualities of the students she most enjoys teaching might include many of the following personal qualities commonly attributed to self-regulated learners:

- The student actively controls the student's behavior, motivation and thinking process when engaging in academic tasks;
- The student views academic learning as something the student does rather than as something that is done to or for the student
- The student believes academic learning is a proactive activity, requiring self-initiated activities;
- The student is interested in the subject matter, well-prepared for class, and ready with comments, questions, ideas, and insights;
- The student looks for problems and tries to solve them;
- The student not only seeks opportunities for practice and feedback but creates them; and

- The student is unafraid to fail or to admit a lack of understanding, and the student is driven to rectify failure and to construct understanding.

Self-regulated learning is best understood as a cycle involving three phases: a planning phase, in which the student decides how, what, when and where to study; an implementation phase, during which the student executes her plans; and a reflection phase, during which the student thinks back on her results and efforts, soberly evaluates her learning process and plans how she will learn even better the next time. Each of these phases involves a few mental processes, all of which we explain below. Illustration 1-2 depicts the self-regulated learning cycle.

The Planning Phase. The planning phase consists of all the thinking the student does before engaging in a learning task. It is the preparation phase, although the term "preparation" misleadingly makes it sound as if the activities are not as important or as demanding as the tasks in which the student will later engage. In fact, educational researchers have studied each of the activities involved in the planning phase and found that each independently improves a student's educational results.

As Illustration 1-2 reflects, the forethought phase includes four principle activities: deciding what to learn, setting mastery goals, predicting success, and planning how, when and where the student will study. We explain each of these tasks below.

Only a very small percentage of law students get themselves in trouble by incorrectly deciding what they need to learn; students who decide to ignore class discussions and in-

Illustration 1-2: The Self-Regulated Learning Cycle

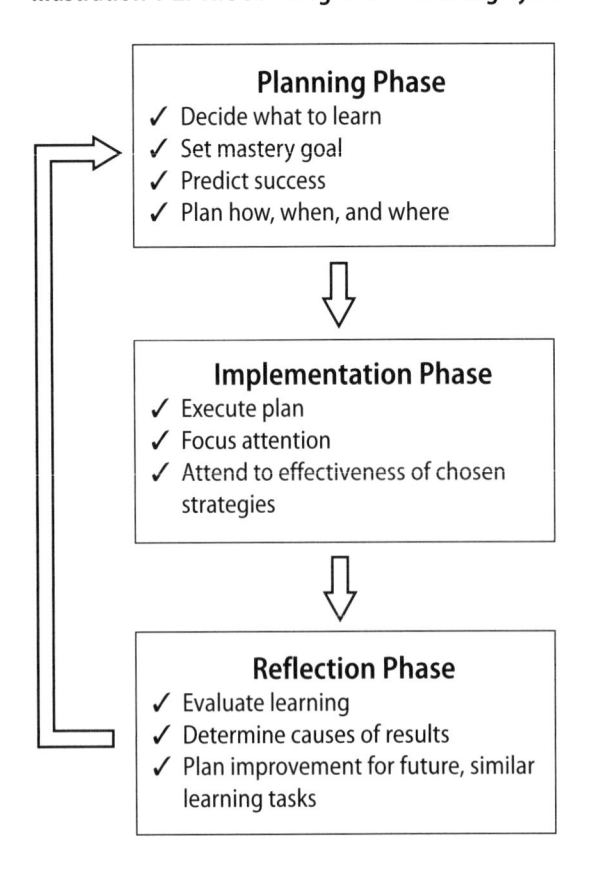

Planning Phase
- ✓ Decide what to learn
- ✓ Set mastery goal
- ✓ Predict success
- ✓ Plan how, when, and where

⇩

Implementation Phase
- ✓ Execute plan
- ✓ Focus attention
- ✓ Attend to effectiveness of chosen strategies

⇩

Reflection Phase
- ✓ Evaluate learning
- ✓ Determine causes of results
- ✓ Plan improvement for future, similar learning tasks

stead rely exclusively on the class notes or outline of a peer or former student or on a supplemental resource, such as a commercial outline, have, in most law school classes, made an erroneous choice about what to learn.

In some instances, the choice to rely on another student's work or an authoritative-looking book actually reflects an error in performing the second task—predicting success. Students who doubt themselves are more likely to rely on someone else's efforts. The belief that one can succeed in learning a difficult skill is called "self-efficacy." Self-efficacy is up there with active learning and cooperative learning groups in terms of its correlation with student learning success. Students with high self-efficacy do better on academic tasks because their belief that they can learn causes them to persist when they encounter difficulty, their persistence increases the likelihood of success, and those successes increase the students' self-efficacy. Thus, self-efficacy, itself, operates cyclically—high self-efficacy predicts persistence which predicts success which increases self-efficacy. The most successful students, therefore, consciously invoke self-efficacy.

The self-regulated learner then sets a goal, a specific, desired outcome, for the task. Expert self-regulated learners generally set mastery learning goals, goals that emphasize learning the material as well as possible rather than on grade implications. In fact (and, perhaps, somewhat perversely), students who set mastery goals get higher grades than students who set grade goals and students who set grade goals get higher grades than students who set no goals or whose only goals are to complete assignments.

The final and crucial step of the planning process involves devising and tailoring a strategic approach to achieving the goal. The student identifies possible strategies most appropriate to the goals, reviews the student's own learning preferences, predicts outcomes based on the various options, and then chooses how to learn. Strategy selection also includes planning how the student will stay focused and where, when, with whom, and for how long the student will study.

The Implementation Phase. This phase is much simpler. Principally, the student just executes the plans the student made in the planning phase. One key to a successful implementation is maintaining focused attention. Nearly all of us have had the experience of reading a book and discovering, an hour later, that we cannot recall what we have been reading for the last hour. You may be having that experience right now (although we certainly hope you are not).

The other key to successful implementation is called "self-monitoring." Successful students continually monitor whether they understand what they are supposed to be learning. When a legal reader chooses to re-read a paragraph of an opinion to make sure he understands the author's point or tries to brainstorm a hypothetical that either proves the author wrong or confirms the author's assertion, he is engaging in self-monitoring.

The Reflection Phase. The reflection phase of the cycle guides the students' future learning endeavors. The student reflects on what she did and how effective it was and then considers the implications of her experience for future learning activities. The student begins by evaluating how well and how efficiently she learned. Expert self-regulated learners evaluate how they are doing accurately and engage in this evaluation immediately after they have completed their learning activities. Thus, in a traditional, Socratic-style law school class, a self-regulated law student would evaluate how well the student would have been able to answer the professor's questions.

Having evaluated their performance, self-regulated learners develop attributions about the causes of their results. An attribution is an explanation for why the student performed well or poorly. Self-regulated learners are much more likely to attribute failures to correctable causes, such as insufficient effort or incorrect selection of learning technique(s), and to attribute success to personal competence. These attributions lead self-regulated learners to try again and to try harder when they fail; in contrast, novice self-regulated learners are more likely to attribute their failures to ability and, therefore, are more likely to give up and stop trying.

Finally, the attributions influence students' future adaptations to their learning strategies. Having identified the correctable causes of any errors, the students brainstorm adjustments to their learning processes. In this way, self-regulated learners are more adaptive than their novice learner peers because they recognize both that learning difficult skills may require multiple practice cycles and that systematic variations in approaches will help them overcome learning difficulties.

What we know about effective teaching

What does it mean to be an "effective" teacher? What elements contribute to teaching excellence? How do teachers create healthy teaching and learning environments? Where do we find answers to these questions?

There is a vast literature on teaching effectiveness in higher education, including legal education, in books, web sites, and journal articles. Much of that literature is based on empirical studies of instruction and learning. Researchers approach the task of describing teaching excellence through several avenues—asking faculty members to assess their colleagues' teaching, reviewing student ratings of their teachers, directly observing teachers in their classrooms, analyzing student achievement in courses, and interviewing teachers about their educational philosophies and practices.

The first lesson we draw from the education literature is our definition of teaching effectiveness. For us, teaching excellence is measured by significant student learning. To what extent do students leave our courses with deep understanding of legal doctrine and theory, competence in analytical and other lawyering skills, and internalization of appropriate professional values?

The second lesson is our synthesis of what faculty members can do to facilitate significant student learning. We have identified eleven elements for effective educators and environments. (OK, we got a bit carried away with the "e"s.) These elements are the focus of the rest of Chapter 1.

Subject matter expertise

An essential foundation of good teaching is subject matter expertise. To teach well, we need to know our subjects well. We should understand the subject's organizational scheme, the important details, the relationships among concepts, and the nuances. Subject matter expertise includes doctrine, theory, policy, practical application, thinking skills, performance skills, ethical issues, and professionalism. That is a lot to know and is one of the reasons teaching a new course so difficult. Each time we teach a course, we should strive to deepen and broaden our subject matter expertise. Our scholarship can play a vital role in enhancing our knowledge.

Illustration 1-3. Eleven Elements of Effective Educators and Environments

1. Subject matter expertise
2. Respect
3. Expectations
4. Support
5. Passion
6. Preparation and organization
7. Variety
8. Active learning
9. Collaboration
10. Clarity
11. Formative Feedback

Subject matter expertise alone will not make an effective teacher. We could spend all of our professional time expanding our knowledge of our subjects. For example, Gerry teaches environmental law courses and could devote every waking moment to learning more about that enormous, ever-changing topic. The same is true for most courses. Instead, to maximize our effectiveness as teachers, we must devote serious effort to the other ten elements of effective educators and environments.

Respect

Mutual respect among students and teachers is fundamental to a healthy teaching and learning environment. Respect should go in three directions: teacher to students, students to teacher, and students to students. Classrooms that feature humiliation, intimidation, or denigration lead many students to withdraw from participation and learning. In respectful environments, students and teachers feel free to explore ideas, solve problems creatively, and challenge one another to grow.

Although a precise definition of respect is difficult to articulate, most students and teachers know it when they see it and feel it. We can begin our courses by articulating the critical role that mutual respect will play in our classrooms. Then, students and teachers need to act in ways to maintain a respectful environment throughout the course. Here's a brief list of behaviors that foster respect.

- Learn your students' names. Call students by name in and out of the classroom. Do not allow students to go through your course anonymously. Is it hard to learn students' names in large classes? You bet. Seating charts and pictures can help. The bottom line is that everyone from students to educational researchers tell us that it is well worth the effort.
- Learn about your students' experiences and goals. Have students introduce themselves by completing a short questionnaire in class or on line. The information about students' education, work, goals, hobbies, and families allows us to appreciate and draw upon the tremendous human resources we have in the classroom.
- Value students' time. Law students, like their teachers, lead busy lives. Time is at a premium. Start and end class on time. Be in your office during office hours. Keep appointments with students. Respond to email from students.
- Be inclusive. Students come to law school with diverse backgrounds and perspectives. We motivate students when we make them feel welcome and when we

try to tie their learning to their personal and professional interests. We can include diverse perspectives in our courses by choosing material that reflects a variety of viewpoints and by validating students who raise divergent views in the classroom.

- Model respect. Respect is more about what we do than what we say. It is how we treat students, colleagues, and staff on a daily basis. Many of the other elements of effective environments also demonstrate respect, including collaboration with students and high expectations for each student.

Expectations

Teachers' expectations affect students' learning. High, realistic expectations lead to more student achievement; low expectations result in less student learning. Extensive research supports these simple statements. But the implementation of these principles is more complex.

> **Thinking exercise:** What expectations do you have for student preparation, behavior, and performance? How do you communicate your expectations to students as the beginning of the course? Throughout the course?

Five attributes of teacher expectations affect student motivation and learning: clarity, quality, achievability, uniformity, and credibility.

Clarity. Before a course begins, we need to think through our expectations for student preparation, participation, behavior, and performance, to clarify those issues for ourselves. At the beginning of the course, we should clearly communicate those expectations, and our rationale for those expectations. We should communicate our expectations to our students orally and in writing. Throughout the course, we can continue to clarify our expectations through our actions; for example, giving specific directions for our assignments, articulating goals for each class, providing feedback on student performance in class and on written assignments. Lack of clarity in our expectations can occur because either we fail to communicate them to students or we act in ways that are inconsistent with them.

Quality. The focus of our expectations for student learning should be on quality rather than quantity. Piling on more work, giving overly long reading assignments, and covering more content are unlikely to enhance students' motivation and learning. Instead, we can maximize student learning by focusing our students' attention and effort on the knowledge, skills, and values critical to the subjects we teach and to our students' professional lives after graduation.

Achievability. Our expectations should challenge students to stretch themselves and to do their best work. Expectations that are unrealistic and unachievable by even our best students are counterproductive. Our expectations for student preparation for class should be at a level that a diligent student can attain, day after day, in light of all the demands of the student's other courses. Our expectations for student performance in class, on assignments, and on exams, should be based on our students' current level of development and the requirements of professional practice after law school. What constitutes "high, achievable, realistic" expectations differs as students progress through law school.

Uniformity. Effective teachers believe that every student can attain a high level of achievement. We communicate our expectation that every student can succeed by seeking participation from every student and by spreading difficult questions and assignments among all the students - men, women, and students with diverse backgrounds. However, individual students are at varying stages of professional development. It is important for us to challenge all students throughout the course. We can do so by building various levels of difficulty into our assignments, questions in class, and exams.

Credibility. Perhaps the best way for teachers to inspire students to excellence is through modeling. We should have high expectations for ourselves. Our high, realistic expectations for student preparation, participation, behavior, and performance are most credible when we demonstrate our commitment to meeting those expectations in our teaching. It does not mean we need to model perfection—that is not an achievable expectation for us or our students. Instead it means that we show, day after day, that we are diligently seeking continuous improvement in our professional practice.

Support

A supportive teaching and learning environment should accompany high expectations. We should demonstrate our commitment to helping each student succeed in law school. A supportive environment is built upon teachers' attitudes, availability, and trust.

One set of common descriptors of exemplary teachers focuses on their attitudes toward students—"helpful," "caring," "concerned," and "encouraging." Our attitudes have strong positive effects on students' motivation, level of engagement in the classroom, willingness to take risks, and openness to new ideas and perspectives. Conversely, the quickest way to fail as a teacher is to communicate our lack of care about our students and their learning.

Another group of attributes of effective teachers is "available," "accessible," and "approachable." Student-faculty contact outside of formal class time is associated with students' motivation, satisfaction, and active involvement in their own education. We make ourselves available, approachable, and accessible in a variety of ways:

- arriving early and staying after class to talk with students,
- welcoming students when they come to our offices, rather than resenting the interruption,
- attending law school events,
- responding to student email messages,
- sharing a meal with students, and
- holding conferences with students.

Most students trust us and respond positively to our trust in them. Personal attitudes tend to produce reciprocal attitudes in others. An operating assumption that reflects our trust is that "there is a good faith explanation for students' behavior." When we make ourselves available to students, we give them the opportunity to validate this assumption on a regular basis. When we communicate our faith in students, most will reciprocate with faith in us.

Passion

Students regularly identify teachers' passion or enthusiasm as the most important ingredient of effective instruction. Our passion can inspire, energize, and motivate our students. Students take their cues from us. If we appear bored and disengaged, they will too. But when we convey our delight in teaching and love for our subject, many students will share our positive attitudes.

We communicate our enthusiasm for teaching and passion for our subjects by what we say, how we say it, and how we act. We should tell students directly what we love about teaching at this school, our joy in working with students, and our fascination with the subject matter. (If we do not feel passionate about any of those things, we should look for other jobs—many other people are eager to take our position as law teachers.) Of course, revealing our feelings to students entails some risk and makes us vulnerable. But many students will appreciate our passion, identify with our vulnerability, and be more willing to take their own risks in the classroom.

Celebrate success in the classroom. Provide positive reinforcement when students produce insight, solid analysis, or creative thinking. Call attention to students who demonstrate professional skills and values. Congratulate students on significant personal and professional success (getting married, placing in a moot court competition).

Research has identified verbal and nonverbal behaviors that convey passion and enthusiasm. Verbal behavior includes speaking expressively, using humor, and not reading from notes. Teachers' nonverbal behaviors associated with enthusiasm include movement (away from the podium and out into the classroom), gestures, facial expressions, and smiling. These behaviors seem painfully obvious and simple, but, together, they reinforce our direct statements to students about our joy in teaching and passion for our subjects.

Preparation and organization

Thorough preparation and transparent organization contribute to teaching effectiveness and student learning. We believe this principle so strongly that we devoted several chapters of this book to those topics! Why? Because teachers and students benefit when they are clear about what should be learned, how that learning will take place, and how students will demonstrate their learning.

Course design. Comprehensive course preparation requires us to think through a series of design issues. Then we should inform students, through the syllabus and throughout the course, of our plan for the course. Course design issues (explored in detail in Chapters 3 and 7) include:

- Needs assessment - what strengths and weaknesses do students bring to the course, what aspects of the course do students learn readily, and with which skills, knowledge and values do students struggle?
- Course goals - what should students know and be able to do at the end of the course?
- Policies - what are the expectations for student attendance, preparation, participation, behavior?

- Teaching and learning activities - what methods, exercises, assignments will take place in and out of class?
- Materials - what print and electronic resources will support the teaching and learning activities?
- Pacing - what will happen on the first day of the course? The last day? In between?
- Feedback - how will students receive feedback throughout the course?
- Evaluation - how will student performance be assessed and graded?

Class design. A parallel set of issues inform our design of individual class sessions (addressed in Chapters 4 and 7):

- Where are students at this point in the course in terms of their understanding and skills?
- What are the two, three, or four concepts or skills that students should learn or practice in this class?
- What should students do outside of class to prepare (read, write, synthesize, etc)?
- What will students do during the class (discuss, listen, write, collaborate, argue, perform)?
- How will the class begin? End?
- How will students and teachers get feedback about the class and the students' learning?

Preparation. A prerequisite to successful teaching, learning, and professional practice is thorough preparation. Successful teachers engage in two types of preparation for class. First, teachers need to understand at a deep level the concepts and skills that will be the focus of the class. Second, teachers should make conscious choices about all of the class design issues listed above. The first time we teach a course, much of our time is devoted to attaining an appropriate level of expertise in the subject and less time goes into design. As we become more comfortable with the subject, we should give more and more attention to class design and delivery. Finally, we should be thoughtful about how we can facilitate thorough student preparation for class (*see* Chapters 3, 4 and 5).

Flexibility. Effective teachers are not only prepared and organized; they are flexible too. Planning need not lead to rigidity. In every course and many individual class sessions, opportunities present themselves to explore a concept in more depth, weave in professionalism, and build on students' insights and skills. On our best days, we achieve a balance between doggedly pursuing the objectives for the class and seizing "teachable moments."

Variety

A characteristic that cuts across the design and delivery of courses and classes is variety. We can inject variety into many aspects of our teaching—objectives, teaching and learning methods, materials, and evaluation.

Course and class objectives should not be one-dimensional. Every subject can include goals for student learning of concepts, skills, and professional values. Teaching and learning activities in and out of the classroom can come from an extensive menu, including Socratic dialog, large group discussion, small group work, problem solving, lecture, simulation, experiential learning, electronic discussions, student presentations, writing, etc. Materials appropriate to support wide ranging teaching and learning activities include casebooks, statutory supplements, articles, computer programs (such as CALI), websites, pictures, and videos. Evaluating students can occur through exams, papers, and performances.

Variety is an important contributor to effective legal education for several reasons. First, the extensive literature on learning styles makes clear that students prefer to learn in different ways. Students have different strengths and weaknesses as learners. Throughout a course, a variety of teaching and learning methods, materials, and evaluation methods can maximize learning and give each student an opportunity to excel. Second, different types of teaching methods and materials are appropriate to achieve different objectives. For example, a Socratic dialog dealing with appellate opinions may help students develop their case analysis skills, a contract drafting assignment may be a good vehicle for developing students' writing and strategic planning skills, and a simulation exercise may raise professionalism issues. Third, variety can keep students' interest and sustain their motivation throughout a course. Finally, different methods lead to different depths of learning. For example, students' learning of the law, policy, and strategy relating to filing a complaint in federal court will deepen as they read the relevant federal rules of civil procedure, brief a Supreme Court opinion on the sufficiency of a complaint, review sample complaints, and draft a complaint.

Active learning

Students learn from active and passive methods. Students learn passively when they listen to a presenter who organizes and conveys information. Active learning occurs when students engage in more than listening.

Student learning can be put on a continuum of increasing levels of activity.

Illustration 1-4. Learning Methods Continuum

PASSIVE

Listen
Read
Take notes
Formulate questions
Answer questions
Organize and synthesize
Discuss
Write
Perform skills
Make presentations
Apply content and skills (simulation or real-life)

ACTIVE

Law teachers employ many types of active learning techniques: Socratic dialogs, discussions, writing exercises, simulations, computer exercises, and real-life experiences in externships and clinics. However, active learning goes beyond a set of techniques. It includes a way of viewing education on the part of students and teachers. It assumes that legal education should facilitate student learning of concepts, theory, critical thinking, lawyering skills, and professional values.

Active learning is not "better" than passive learning. Effective teachers choose different methods to achieve various goals in their courses. Researchers agree, however, that active involvement by students enhances their learning. Active learning is particularly effective in achieving four types of core goals of legal education.

- **Thinking skills.** Active learning methods can foster critical thinking (making informed judgments about facts, law, policy, arguments) and higher-level cognitive skills (analysis and synthesis).
- **Understanding concepts.** Active learning helps students learn content at a deep level. As students articulate their understanding and work with concepts in new settings, they are more likely to retain their knowledge and be able to apply it on an exam or in real life.
- **Lawyering skills.** Students learn skills such as interviewing and negotiation through simulations and experiential learning. Ideally, those methods allow students to have practical experiences, receive feedback, and refine their skills.
- **Professional values.** Complex, nuanced problems, simulations, and real-life experiences often raise professionalism issues. Student reflection, discussion, and writing about those issues can help students develop a healthy set of professional values.

Collaboration

Two types of collaboration enhance teaching and learning in law school. The first is cooperative learning, where students work in pairs or small groups in or outside of class. The second is teacher and student collaboration in course design decisions.

Cooperative learning. A large body of research in higher education and legal education documents the effectiveness of cooperative learning. In college education, cooperative learning fosters the following: (1) more student learning and better academic performance, especially when the task is complex and conceptual; (2) development of problem solving, reasoning, and critical thinking skills; (3) positive student attitudes toward the subject matter and course; (4) closer relationships among students and between students and teachers; and (5) students' willingness to consider diverse perspectives. Legal educators note additional benefits of cooperative learning. Cooperative learning enables students to learn to work in a team and develop collaborative approaches to negotiation and mediation. Moreover, cooperative learning helps students build community in and out of the classroom and to develop greater respect for one another. Given the substantial benefits of cooperative learning, effective law teachers look for ways to incorporate small group learning in their courses. (Chapters 4 and 6 describe the design and delivery of small group exercises.)

Collaborative course design. Course design involves decisions about objectives, materials, assignments, teaching and learning activities, roles and responsibilities of teachers and students, and an evaluation scheme. Typically, teachers make all of the design decisions. However, teachers can involve students in some or all of those decisions. The benefits of teacher/student collaboration in course design is supported by the literature on learner-centered teaching, adult education theory, and empirical research on motivation and performance in college and law school. Student involvement in the design of their own education can increase students' intrinsic motivation and positive attitudes toward the course, the teacher, and law school. Ultimately, student engagement in course design can enhance the classroom environment and student performance.

The teacher's level of comfort with the notion of sharing design responsibilities with students will vary from person to person. Further, students' ability and willingness to participate meaningfully in design decisions changes during law school as students become more self-directed in their learning.

> **Thinking exercise**: Do you currently involve students in course design decisions? Are you comfortable doing so in the future? If not, why? If so, in what aspects of course design are you willing to collaborate with students?

Teachers and students who are ready to engage in collaborative course design can do so in a variety of ways, from small to large. For example, we can build student choice into assignments—students can select their topics for writing assignments, choose from a menu of supplemental readings, or find relevant pictures and news stories from the Internet. Student options in assignments can allow them to build upon their strengths and interests. Or we can work with students on the first day of class to make basic course design decisions. We could ask students to weigh in on all or some of these questions: (1) What are your goals for the course? (2) What roles and responsibilities do students have to achieve the goals of the course? (3) What roles and responsibilities does the teacher have to achieve the goals of this course? (4) What teaching and learning activities should we use in the course? (5) What evaluation methods should be used to assess student performance?

Clarity

Clarity is an important aspect of our expectations, course design, and evaluation scheme. We need to think through and clearly communicate to students our expectations for student preparation, participation, behavior, and performance. Likewise, systematic course design leads to clarity through organization; for example, explicit course objectives, well-defined reading assignments, and focus questions guide students in preparing for class. Clarity in the evaluation scheme is especially important—students need to get our grading criteria in writing before the exam, paper, or performance (see Chapter 7 for more detail).

The present focus is on clarity in the classroom. Clarity in the classroom is *not* about "spoonfeeding" or "dumbing-down." Instead, it is about effectively communicating complex ideas, skills, and professional values. Several practices can help us communicate more clearly in the classroom.

- **Roadmap.** At the beginning of class, articulate the objectives for the class. Put concepts, skills, and values in the broader context of the course as a whole.
- **Closure.** At the end of a topic or unit, include an activity, problem, exercise, or brief lecture that provides synthesis and summary.

- **Examples.** Illustrate concepts, skills, and values with examples. We can find applicable, appealing examples from our own experience, from our students, from cases, and from current events.
- **Visuals.** Most students learn more when abstract ideas are supported with visuals. Handouts, slides, charts, and the whiteboard can foster organization and understanding. Pictures, videos, documents (contracts, complaints, deeds) can provide clarity that most of us cannot convey with words alone.
- **Questions.** Effective teachers consistently monitor student understanding. How? Pay attention to nonverbal cues during class. Ask for questions—and really mean it! Give students time to generate questions in class before moving on. Have students articulate questions in writing at the end of class, via email, or on electronic discussion boards.

Formative feedback

Feedback is a critical, and often overlooked, element of teaching and learning. Law school challenges students to learn a complex set of doctrine, theory, professional values, and analytical and performance skills. Law school challenges teachers to strive to continuously improve their teaching effectiveness. Formative feedback helps law students and teachers meet those challenges.

Formative feedback is an essential part of the learning loop—students engage in learning activities, perform in writing or orally, and get feedback on how their learning and performance can be improved. Effective formative feedback has four characteristics: specific, corrective, positive, and timely. Feedback is most effective when teachers articulate specific criteria for student performance and give students feedback based on those criteria. Corrective feedback points out weaknesses in student work and provides strategies for improvement. Positive feedback identifies the strengths upon which students can build. Timely feedback comes relatively soon after student performance and gives students an opportunity to improve before their performance is evaluated. (Chapter 7 details types of formative feedback appropriate in law school.)

Formative feedback is essential for teachers' continued development as well. To make appropriate adjustments during a course, we need to get feedback from students about their learning. A variety of Classroom Assessment Techniques (discussed in Chapter 7) can give us that feedback. Further, for continuous improvement of our teaching practice, we can engage in self-reflection and gather input from students, consultants, and colleagues (the focus of Chapter 8).

Chapter 2

Student Perspectives on Teaching and Learning

You may be tempted to skip this chapter and get right to the basics—Chapters 3 through 7—where we give you concrete suggestions about how to design your courses, teach students and assess their learning. We might be tempted to do the same. But we urge you to read this chapter. It is different from all our other chapters in that it focuses on the words of students, our audience, not the "educational experts." The words here are in the students' voices, spoken passionately and from the heart. Given our perspective—that good teaching focuses on student learning—we would be remiss if we didn't include students' views.

As noted in Chapter 1, we now know a great deal about how to maximize student learning; you could spend weeks reading publications on the topic. But it's also amazing what you learn when you ask the resident experts attending your law school—the students. These adults have been in school for at least sixteen years. They have over two decades of experiential learning. Many of them don't have the same law school experience we had. As one student stated,

> *I don't think that a lot of professors go through what the majority of students go through. The majority of professors graduated at the top of their class and unfortunately that makes them least equipped to assess the validity of the three-hour examination as a measure of your intellectual capacity and your potential as, you know, a budding lawyer.*

Students are generous and articulate about what we can to improve their learning. All we need to do is ask. If you want to be a good teacher, don't hesitate to ask your students for help.

Who are our students? From the science of teaching and learning (Chapter 1), we know that each class is comprised of complex humans who all process and learn things in different ways. They come with their own elaborate sets of preconceptions, experiences, learning preferences, and cultural backgrounds. Even with all their diverse experiences and backgrounds, students share a number of perspectives when talking about law school. From surveys, articles, interviews and our collective five-plus decades of teaching and conducting focus groups with students attending our own and other law schools, we have heard similar themes from many students, regardless of the students' year, race, gender, background, class standing, or chosen law school. **Overall, students want us to treat them with respect, engage them in learning, and help them become good lawyers.**

Many of the comments students make about their learning in law school overlap with the elements identified in Chapter 1 as indicators of effective teaching—with a couple of exceptions. Almost never do students say that their teachers don't know the material or are not prepared. Instead, they talk about how much respect, high expectations, compassion, empathy, excitement, active learning, varied teaching methods, collaboration, practical application, and feedback help them with their learning. In this chapter, we offer you students' words; we believe these words reflect the sentiments of most law students. Some of these are direct statements from our students; most are excerpts of students' comments taken from sixteen hours of videotaped interviews with sixty-seven students from seven different law schools. For concrete suggestions about how to implement the students' suggestions, refer to Chapters 3, 4, 5, 6 and 7.

In this chapter, we limit students' comments to things teachers can do. Students repeatedly note that eliminating the negative influence of grading curves, reducing class size, increasing the number of clinical opportunities, and improving classrooms' physical attributes would help their learning, but few of us have control over those factors. If, however, your school is considering making changes in its physical plant, grading system, staffing, or curricular choices, we encourage you to invite students to contribute. They have much to offer.

Students want to be treated with respect

When asked about the most important characteristics of effective law teachers, "respect" hits almost every list. Respect encompasses a wide range of behaviors—students want us to treat them with compassion, welcome their different perspectives, create a positive and welcoming environment and use their names. Treating students with respect helps them learn.

Why is respect so important? From the way students talk about teachers' influence, it is clear that our voices are very powerful. As one student said about a particular law professor, the teacher was not "a vindictive nasty person, but sometimes they just don't understand the impact of what they're saying or the way that it's coming across." Compounded with the stress of law school, our seemingly innocuous slips can feel degrading and demoralizing to our students. Our one slip can make a student want to give up—on the course, on the teacher, and on ever being a lawyer. A positive comment may correspondingly boost a student's confidence and help a student decide to stay in school and devote herself to her law studies. Because of the disproportionate power in the classroom, respect—important in any effective relationship—is especially critical in the law school classroom. As one student said,

I learn better from professors that I feel talk with me and not down to me.

Treat students as colleagues

Students frequently note that they learn more effectively from teachers whom they feel treat them as novice colleagues and teachers who acknowledge their own humanity and fallibility. Students appreciate it when we are available to meet with them, have a sense of humor, and are enthusiastic about helping them learn. From their comments, students show that our humanity empowers and motivates them; it does not, as we might fear, make us appear weak.

> [W]hen a professor exhibits an air of humaneness toward his or her students it just goes a long way in the student's heart, especially a first-year student, toward feeling like the professor is in the classroom not only to teach the students the law but to welcome them into the legal profession. And the professors that exhibited that air by and large motivated me to work the hardest in their classrooms.

> [I]t's not necessary for the professor to impress me by speaking in a mysterious language.... I'm already in awe of the professors. But I want to learn from a human being, a fellow human being.

It doesn't take much to show our humanity. Being able to laugh at ourselves, admit mistakes, and acknowledge emotions help our students connect with us.

Include different perspectives in class

Students want us to acknowledge and respect their differences. Students want us to encourage their classmates to share their views in class discussions and to be willing to talk about difficult issues of race, gender, sexual orientation, religion, and politics. Above all, students want us to recognize how many different perspectives there are in the classroom, and seek to learn more about them.

> Oftentimes I think the culture here is dominated by white males... you get this feeling of being excluded. I had a professor who came into class and he would begin class with a few minutes of interesting anecdotes, and they usually involve things like golf and skiing and rock-and-roll music that were not part of my cultural experience.... [T]here were three African-Americans and one Native American in class... [W]hile this was going on we would just sit and look at each other and try to figure out why, why this was so funny to everyone else but us and we just felt like we weren't part of it.

> [M]y understanding has been that racial and sexual orientation minorities feel terribly, terribly alienated here. And I think to a degree that is perhaps not even recognized or fully appreciated by the faculty.

> I'm in Criminal Law class where being one of two minority students in the class it seemed that every time that an issue of race came up that for some instant the professor always called on me as if I was the answer, you know, to everything. And sometimes I didn't mind it but then sometimes I did mind it because I didn't feel as though my purpose for being in that class was to answer all race issues that came up within that class.

> I would advise a new professor [to] remember that he is teaching a group of people with varying cultural experiences and to actively solicit varying opinions so that the class is not dominated by a single culture.

Create a positive and welcoming environment

Students seek a healthy classroom environment. Teachers' and classmates' negative comments threaten students' confidence in their ability to grasp difficult material. They want us to maintain an enthusiastic, encouraging, and professional atmosphere where their learning can thrive, regardless of their learning style, background or views.

> *[The teacher] set up an incredible atmosphere ... you have a dialogue in that class. People talked to each other, people talked to the professor, he valued your opinion, we discovered avenues that we all were confused about.*

> *Create an environment where [the students] will feel comfortable, where they will feel validated and not made to feel small, like they're not worth being in an institution.... I tend to learn better from professors that I respect and create that environment and make me feel that I can contribute to the profession. [W]hen [teachers] don't check a student that is talking out of line ... or if they don't maintain that kind of decorum ... it's very distracting to others ... since this is a professional environment ... there is a duty that teachers have of maintaining that.*

Creating a positive environment means that we also need to be careful about the assumptions we make about students.

> *I would definitely say that at least 99% [of us] try our hardest to make sure that we get it because we don't want to look foolish in class.... [I]t's very important that a teacher realize that ... we wouldn't ask the question in class ... if we just honestly didn't understand it.*

Using different teaching techniques to address different learning styles also helps build a positive learning environment.

> *[E]ven though this is law school, you still have students who learn differently and who have different capabilities as far as learning skills are concerned.*

> **Thinking exercise**: How might you include different perspectives in class? What steps might you take to make create a positive learning environment? How might you show your humanity to students?

Use students' names

Using students' names goes a long way to showing respect. Students are delighted when teachers know their names and pronounce them correctly. Sophie and Mike both have colleagues who teach large sections of civil procedure. Within the first two weeks, both teachers begin class by looking at and naming each student. Students spontaneously applaud, and, even when the professor makes a mistake using their names that day or later, students graciously help the professors out.

> *[W]hen you raised your hand, it was not you in the back or you with the shirt, it was Ms. So and So or Mr. So and So. And it absolutely made you feel like all right the focus is on me and this professor wants to hear what I'm about to say.*

> *[The teacher] engages the students. He calls them by their first names.*

> *I guess it's my age. If feel a little older and if you're going to call me Millie then I should be more comfortable in calling you Bob.... A few professors came right out and said ... I'm calling you by your first name, I am Bill to you or I am Sandra. I like that.*

[T]hroughout the rest of the class he said, "and the rule as articulated by Ms. Paul was...." He did that four times and I go, well, gee, I got that rule, and I felt so good, you know. It was a very effective way of him to say that here's an individual who is learning.

Referring to a first-year class where the student had a Japanese-American classmate:

[T]he professor wasn't able to get his name right. And finally one day he slipped and said ... Mr. Hiroshima, and then asked him a question.... [T]hat was kind of an uncomfortable moment in class.

Even if we can't learn all the names of our students in class, we can still have them available, on a seating chart for example, and use them in class discussions.

> **Thinking exercise**: Whom do you call by name? Colleagues you respect? Your dean? Friends? How might you react if a respected colleague forgot your name?

Students crave our respect. Each of us has talked to students who have had professional careers where they have been highly successful and worked hard to resolve complex problems. These smart, competent, and previously-confident professionals are distraught to find themselves confused, stressed out, isolated, and constantly in doubt about their ability to succeed in law school. If students feel that we genuinely care about them, they will be more willing to talk about their concerns and forgive us when we make mistakes. But first they have to believe that we do care and respect them.

Students want to be engaged in their learning

The vast majority of students come to law school excited about becoming lawyers. They are eager to engage in learning the law. They want to have assignments that relate to what happens in class. They seek to understand where the class is going and what they should take away at the end. They want to be challenged and inspired. They have many suggestions about how they can be more engaged in class. As one colleague said, "the student corollary to 'publish or perish' is 'engage or enrage.'" If we respect our students, we will seek ways to engage them. Because each class is composed of different personalities, backgrounds and learning preferences, asking students what works for them helps us figure out how to maximize their learning in and out of the classroom.

Students' behavior may suggest that they are not interested in engaging in class, but we each have learned—sometimes the hard way—not to make assumptions about the reasons why students seem disengaged. One early September, Sophie was frustrated to see that a student hadn't prepared for several classes in a row; when she talked to him, she learned that he had just moved across the country, was trying to help his wife and sell their home in Texas, and was still looking for a suitable place to rent. He wanted to do well but at that moment he had too many pressing demands to devote sufficient time to studying. He had a good reason not to be prepared or engaged. Most students, if they have the time, want to be prepared and engaged. They have many suggestions about how we can help them do this—we only need to ask.

Use a variety of teaching methods

Students repeatedly talk about the value of variety. Having a variety of teaching methods allows students to learn things in different ways, reaches students' diverse learning preferences, helps students solve legal problems from new angles, and mixes up the usual class performance patterns. Students' interest surges and they frequently talk about those teaching methods that break the usual mode of law school teaching.

> [A] mix of lectures, discussions and group work is effective for me because the class is broken up and not as monotonous. Too much of one method makes my mind wander and I don't think it stimulates me as much as a class that is unpredictable.

> [I]f you can bring in any sort of outside materials or handouts or overheads or just something to liven up the discussion, it really helps keep my interest as opposed to just a strict lecture format.

> [T]he more variation you can bring to class the more interested ... I stay. When it's just strictly lecture I tend to have a habit of drifting in and out.

> [What] really helps in the process of the day-to-day going to class and getting something out of every class ... are varied, like workshop-type things.... Every day [one of my teachers] would [do] different types of exercises with the work.... getting involved in activities ... actually engaging in the classroom, you know, is a huge help.

> [G]ive your students as many opportunities to learn in different ways as you can.

For suggestions on different kinds of teaching techniques and how to apply them, refer to Chapters 3, 4 and 6.

Give students an organizational structure—provide context for learning

Many students comment on their need to understand what is going on in class and why it matters. Students highly value having a detailed syllabus and learning how a particular class fits into the course as a whole. It helps them to learn **why** they are studying a particular case, statute, theory or set of facts. In addition, previewing the class goals and materials at the beginning of class and summarizing them at the end help students stay on track and focus their learning.

> [A]nything a professor can do to ... bring back the big picture ... "You know, there's a reason why we're discussing this detail today" ... that would be huge. When professors do that throughout the course it's a major advantage ... because you're able to sort of put things in context as you go through a course rather than just struggling with details ... piecemeal as they come along.

> [D]uring the class, he would refer back to the outline, adding material, showing connections and giving us a sense of the forest and the trees.

> It was really helpful when the teacher would recap the previous class's most important points really quickly ..."Okay, this is what I wanted you to get out of the last class." ... Those first five minutes of each class did so much and gave me a better idea of what I should be getting out of the class and how it connected to the big picture.

> [The teacher] gave roadmaps, what she described as the best way to understand the material. She would basically outline on the blackboard what it was that we were going to be doing in the next month and that gave us a very clear picture of what was expected, of what we were going to encounter, and it really summed up the material very well.

When students ask for different teaching methods and a more organized structure, they are not asking for us to lower our expectations or "dumb down" their learning. Instead what comes across is a plea for us to help them learn.

Provide ways for students to be actively involved in class

Students appreciate having opportunities to act like lawyers in class. Repeatedly, students talk about how easy it is for them to tune out when they sit through lectures. Regardless of whether they are engaged in group work, role plays, simulations, or working on other kinds of in-class exercises, students notice how much more they absorb when they are acting like lawyers in class.

> I need to do in order to learn.... I am usually most interested and motivated by how things work in the "real world," and in trying to apply or use theories in a practical way.... I learn quickly if I have the opportunity to engage actively either in or out of the classroom.

> [A]bsent active participation, I am likely to be precluded from offering vital input on a subject, which creates boredom and disinterest. [A] thing that has really worked well for me and for other students is the problem method ... boy, is that helpful to kind of narrow the field down ... trying to figure out what it is you're supposed to glean from this particular subject matter. [R]ole plays do help out a lot because ... it really gets it ingrained in your head because you're actively participating in things.... [W]e can't do skits all the time, but maybe it couldn't hurt every once in a while.

> [S]tudents in all classrooms need some ... way to apply what they've learned, to experience what they've learned, because a lot of students need that in order to learn something well.

We may worry that having students act like lawyers in class will take too much time. We won't be able to cover as much. While such activities probably do limit the amount of material we can expose our students to, our students' greater engagement during the activities will produce deeper understanding and will be far more memorable years later.

Make class preparation assignments reasonable and meaningful

With lots of experience reading legal texts, we are all "expert" legal readers; we know when to speed up and when to read every word closely. Second and third year students are more efficient legal readers than first years, but, faced with new material, even upper level students have to work hard to master material for class. Students want to be engaged in class; giving them shorter assignments helps them do exactly that.

> *[Professors] could probably do better for the students by assigning less reading.... [W]hen you're assigned too many pages to read and people don't finish their reading you're going to lose some students.*
>
> *[W]hen you spend 3 or 4 hours preparing 25 pages of casebook material and the professor does not mention more than 3 of those pages in the entire hour ... it doesn't really encourage you to spend as much time and effort in preparing for the next day's class.*
>
> *[I]t would be far more productive to have small exercises that students can go and prepare for at home and then be engaged with other students, because it's not just reading that we're trying to learn here. We need to be able to talk to people; we need to be able to argue well; we need to be able to stand up on our feet and make presentations.*

Especially if we give long assignments, students appreciate it when we guide them about ways to approach the reading and invite their feedback on assignments.

> *It's helpful when the professor takes the time to include questions about the cases in the syllabus.... I would look for the answers to the questions and then start putting the pieces together.... no matter how hard the material is, you can prepare for class—not just show up. You know what to expect.*
>
> *The best way is to ask.... Is the reading too much or is it going well?.... [I]f you gauge it back to 40 pages ... you can have more discussion and people will pick it up and then you can move on quicker than if you just did the 100 [pages] and everybody's crazy confused and asking fifty-million questions.*

In addition to asking students, consider your own experience when given assignments for conferences or faculty meetings. How helpful is it to read 50 pages of material when the discussion focuses on the first few pages? For more suggestions about making reasonable assignments, consult Chapter 4.

Provide opportunities for students to work with others

Students learn a lot from each other. They learn from verbally analyzing problems together and reading and commenting upon each other's work. They value being part of a community rather than trying to learn difficult material in isolation. They appreciate focusing on learning rather than on grades.

> *[T]his focus on grades ... drives every student off into their own separate world. And I think it's detrimental to the learning, and ultimately I think it makes a ... worse lawyer because what they've cut off are the social skills that this particular person needs to succeed.*
>
> *[L]aw school is much easier when you develop relationships and friendships with people that you know you can count on when you don't understand something.... [L]aw school is tough enough without walking around as a hermit.*
>
> *Working in small groups facilitated discussion not possible in larger groups, and let all of us truly express ourselves without fear of being wrong or sounding dumb.*
>
> *[R]eading the work of others.... made me realize what worked in my classmate's paper that I lacked, which helped me in editing my paper.... I was able to pick up on the different styles of writing, as well as type of vocabularies used.... I learn best by reading and listening to others.*

Cooperative exercises and role playing exercises are very useful.... [A]t some point you're going to end up arguing and even if it's simply mediation ... those are practical models of what you will have to do.

Students appreciate being able to work with their classmates. When structured effectively, even the most introverted, small-group-work-resistant students realize the power of learning with and from their peers.

> **Thinking exercise**: Remember the last time you were at a conference, meeting or event. Consider the break times, as well as what you were doing just before and after. When were you engaged? When did your mind wander?

Be aware of students' concerns about the Socratic method

As with any technique, the Socratic method—engaging in a dialogue with students—can be effective or ineffective, depending on how it is being used. Students who are fans of the Socratic method value having to be prepared because they may be called upon, appreciate the opportunity to practice articulating arguments and responding to questions, and enjoy hearing from a greater range of students. Critics note how intimidating the Socratic method can be, how disruptive it is for those who learn from listening and writing rather than talking, and how it does not engage most of the class.

The Socratic method is incredibly adversarial. And as a result all of us learn to communicate in an adversarial fashion ... I find that a lot of students end up attacking each other.... [W]e forget how to communicate with other people outside of a fashion where we can appreciate and respect other peoples' differences without attacking other people.

[T]he Socratic method is a really good individual learning tool, but unfortunately not everyone gets to participate in that dialogue, and I find myself thinking about, well, maybe I should sit and balance my checkbook, I'm not getting anything from this.

[T]he professors would ask questions and I would sit there and go what in the world are they asking?.... I had no idea what they wanted, and it seemed like they wanted some very specific answers.... I could never figure out what, what is this mysterious process that's going.

[P]rofessors that are good with the Socratic method.... blend in some enthusiasm that keeps you awake, and at the end of each point they clarify, well, that's not correct, or that's a good argument, but there's also this argument.

[T]here is a place for the Socratic method. It's a question of whether it's applied with some humanity and whether you allow the student to maintain some dignity.

Students want to be engaged in class. As the teacher, we are always engaged in class—we are always *doing* something, be it asking questions, writing, talking, listening. To help engage your students, ask not what **you** are doing, but what **they** are doing.

Students want to become good lawyers

The vast majority of our students plan to practice law and want to be good at it. They are eager to learn how our classes relate to their future careers. In their quest to become lawyers, students urge us to be clear about what we expect from them, offer opportunities to practice doing what we will be evaluating them on, provide feedback to help them improve, and allow multiple opportunities for them to show their progress in becoming good lawyers.

Connect what students are learning to the practice of law

Students are eager to hear about how our course connects to practice. It makes the hard work they are doing relate to their future dreams. For many of them, making direct connections to practice helps the law come alive.

> [M]y best experiences in the classroom have been where professors actually gave you concrete examples of what is used in the real world ... actual trial transcripts ... or motions, things that we can put our hands on and say, "Okay, I understand what I'm doing now. I understand what we just spent the last month doing. I can see why we're doing this."
>
> I think it's really unfortunate that we don't spend more time saying, okay ... there is a difference between what you're going to do as a lawyer and what you need to do in law school, let's show you the difference, let's develop the tools, and then let's show you where you can apply each tool in real life.

We can help students by making the connections to practice. We are even more effective when we give students opportunities to actively make those connections themselves.

> I was in a firm with four people; two people would be attorneys, one would be one of our witnesses.... And we actually would really get involved, really figure out what exactly it is that we need to do, that we're going to have to once we get out of this place.... [T]hat class brought back my enthusiasm for wanting to go out and practice.... I want to sit here and practice law, and that's exactly what I was doing.

It's true that there is nothing so practical as a good theory. It is also true that most of our students want to know about how those theories relate to their future way of earning a living. We can help students understand how their studies relate to the practice of law—if we run out of ideas, we can ask them for suggestions or ask them to describe their own, relevant legal experiences.

Be explicit — tell students what you expect

In the best circumstances, disclosing our expectations provides students with a road map of how to become lawyers. What should they do? How should they show us? At the very least, students want to know how they can do well in our courses, as that information helps them focus their studies on the knowledge, skills and values we want them to learn. Because our expectations are usually complex, it helps when we are explicit and put our expectations in writing.

> [W]e're trying to be professional in a very demanding profession. And so I think that the relationship should be very frank and very open ... I need to be given adequate notice of what you expect.
>
> I think that an awful lot of times the professors start teaching a course without really knowing what they want the student to know at the end of the course.
>
> [T]here's just no place in education for professors to try to hide things from you and hope that you're going to find them. I understand that you need to be diligent ... but ... if you're not getting any help in which direction to go ... it's going to be difficult for you to understand what's going on.
>
> [Teachers]should tell us what they want.... [Y]ou find out after you get your test back.... [a]nd that's kind of too late.
>
> [If] a teacher can articulate what they expect of the student ... and then follow through with that through the whole course and through the evaluation, they're a better teacher.

In the way that students beg us to tell them what we want, they manifest their eagerness to do well. The students really do not want to avoid having to learn difficult knowledge, skills, and values. Rather, when you look closely at their pleas for more explicitness in law teaching, you discover that students want to work hard to learn what they need to be learning. Students will work hard so long as they know why and what they are trying to achieve by doing so.

Give students opportunities to practice meeting expectations

Students often talk about the discrepancy between what happens in class and how they earn their grades. They notice that we tell them to "think like a lawyer" by talking through their analysis in class but then expect them to articulate precise analysis **in writing** on an exam. If we are going to use written exams to determine grades, students want practice translating their thinking into words on a page.

> When you're in a final exam you're put into a situation ... where your thinking is nothing that you've practiced.... I kind of realized through outlining that the course has almost nothing to do with the individual cases and it has a lot more to do with synthesizing information on your own outside of the classroom and ... pulling the broader things together.
>
> [The teacher] gave us ... writing assignments, memos ... She also gave us a chance to play different sides of an issue.... I did better in the class because I felt like my learning was checked all the way along.
>
> One of the most effective ways for me to prepare for my examinations last semester was my professor brought in a fact pattern and we sat there in class and we worked through it. And that addresses issue spotting, brings up other sections to the pertinent law or cases.
>
> [T]he classes where I think you take the most away from are where you have application, because I think the exam is where you're finally asked to apply what you have learned.

I felt at the end of that course ... that although it does matter what grade you get ... the grade wasn't as important because I felt that I had learned something in that course.

Students care about their learning and appreciate having the chance to practice using new knowledge and skills. We are no different. Without experience, almost none of us could sit through 28 hours of watching instructional videos on a topic—conducting international arbitrations, for example—and then arbitrate an international dispute in a sophisticated way. We need practice. So do our students.

Give students feedback on their progress

Students want to do well in law school but often become frustrated because they lack sufficient guidance about how to improve. As novices, it is hard for them to see what they are doing well and what they need to change. They want to know, "Am I getting it?" "Should I be trying new learning strategies?" "What else can I do to learn the material and do well?" They want our feedback to help them learn more effectively.

[The teacher] gave us an assignment midway, just five short questions.... It was simply check-check-plus to see how we were doing. And it was perfect because some of us went to see him afterwards and we realized what we were doing wrong. And it was a good method for him to see whether we were getting the material.

[F]eedback is absolutely critical and a lot of professors totally neglect it.... [Y]ou take exams or you write papers and some professors don't put comments on anything. And even if you've done well and there are no comments, it's impossible to learn how to do better or what, I mean, there had to have been shortcomings in your work at some point.

[S]ometimes a paper or test would come back and—especially with some of the papers—there were absolutely no comments. And so you had no idea how you could make it better.

[The teacher] gave us a couple of hypotheticals to turn in. She didn't grade them but she commented upon them and that was very helpful ... because I got to see what a professor was looking for.

Having opportunities to practice and get feedback is amazingly powerful for many students. As one student stated after being shown how to write an exam,

It was incredible. I felt calm. I felt powerful. I felt competent. I felt like yes, you can be a lawyer.

And when students don't do so well, we can still provide them with positive reinforcement about their potential as lawyers.

[O]ne of the things that I think professors can emphasize ... success in law isn't defined only by your grades in law school, that people go on to do wonderful things ... are employed and are happy, even though they weren't in the top 10% of their class.

Even though a particular student doesn't do well in one course in one semester, that student may well develop into a terrific lawyer and leader. Most humans respond better to positive feedback than criticism. We can give them feedback on ways to keep doing what they are doing well, change the things that are ineffective, and build upon their strengths.

Allow students to show their progress in multiple ways

Students repeatedly voice frustration that everything is left to the "do or die final" at the end of the course.

> *[C]lasses where you do some interim small writing assignments, you write up some court visits, maybe you do a small paper or brief, ... prepare skits ... keep a journal ... are also part of the overall grade and that the examination is only a percentage of your grade ... people get to draw on the different skills that they have.... I don't think that that's the way it is in the real world. They don't say you've got three hours to write the brief.*

> *[W]hen you're a lawyer, you're under time pressure but you're not forced to sit in three hours with no books around you and come up with the thing that's going to most help your client.*

> *[T]he best classes that I've had have been ... [where] the professors have them do different types of assignments for a grade.... [T]he more chances ... that you can give students is better, because some students are great orally, some students are great on paper, some students do really well with multiple choice.*

> *There's got to be more than a final exam.*

> *[I]t's very important to have more opportunities to get more points because if your grade is riding on one test ... it may not be the type of test that you need or ... the way that you can best apply yourself.*

Students' perspectives on this issue are consistent with experts' views: evaluating student performance on one graded event is not educationally sound. For more ideas about assessing and evaluating students, refer to Chapter 7.

Parting shots — students' general advice to us

When asked to tell us what we can do specifically to help them learn, law students reiterate many of the themes discussed above. If you ask, and we recommend that you do, your students can offer their own insights about what you can do to improve their learning.

Students' views on pacing and creating a positive environment:

> *[R]epeat things, slow down a little bit ... [you] forget sometimes that we're just learning this stuff for the first time.*

> *[T]here could be more silence in the classroom to let people sort of generate responses.*

> *[R]emember that firstly we're all just people and we're just learning something.... [W]e all need to feel important and to feel recognized.*

Perspectives on us as teachers:

> *[T]o have the honor of being called a teacher-professor, you need to educate yourself about how to be an effective teacher.*

> *[F]eel free to be yourself, to take chances, take risks, and to have fun because ... that's when the learning begins.*

> *[T]ry to integrate some practical applications.*

And perhaps the best advice:
Listen. Listen. That's all.

> **Thinking exercise**: How do you learn about your students?

How to hear *your* students' perspectives.

There are many ways to gather student perspectives during the semester and afterwards. Certainly students' course evaluations are one avenue from which we all can learn. General information from a range of law students is available from the Law School Survey of Student Engagement (LSSSE), which publishes annual reports available at <http://lssse.iub.edu/index.cfm>. In addition, if your school conducted a LSSSE survey, locate and read the results. Having a colleague conduct focus groups with your students is another powerful tool for learning more about what your students think. Because each group of students is different, we encourage you to seek your students' views midway through each course. For more suggestions on how you can gather and include students' perspectives, see Chapter 8.

Checklist for considering the students' perspectives

Illustration 2-1 is a checklist you can use as you consider students' perspectives.

Illustration 2-1: Consider Students' Perspectives

- ❏ **Students want to be treated with respect**
    - ❏ Treat students as colleagues
    - ❏ Include different perspectives in class
    - ❏ Create a positive and welcoming environment
    - ❏ Use students' names
- ❏ **Students want to be engaged in their learning**
    - ❏ Use a variety of teaching methods
    - ❏ Give students an organizational structure
    - ❏ Provide ways for students to be actively involved
    - ❏ Make assignments reasonable
    - ❏ Allow students to work with others
    - ❏ Be aware of problems with the Socratic method
- ❏ **Students want to become good lawyers**
    - ❏ Connect learning to law practice
    - ❏ Be explicit about what you expect
    - ❏ Give students opportunities to practice
    - ❏ Give feedback
    - ❏ Allow students to show progress in multiple ways

Chapter 3

Designing the Course

Introduction

Chapter 3 marks a transition in this book. Whereas Chapters 1 and 2 focused on theory and on understanding law students, this chapter (and all of those that follow) translate years of research on effective teaching into a set of concrete suggestions for planning your courses, for planning class sessions, for selecting among teaching methods, and for assessing students. In short, we move from teaching and learning theory to practice.

Because of this transition, we offer a word about the design for the remaining chapters of this book. Our goal for these chapters is to provide concrete suggestions. At the same time, we worry that, if we were to provide examples of sufficient length to demonstrate how we have applied these principles, this book would be too long to be useful. So, we settled on the compromise of explaining the principles in the text, providing a limited number of examples in the book, and providing more extensive examples in the Appendix.

In this chapter, we offer concrete ideas for designing courses. Most broadly, we see course design as a recursive process, as reflected in Illustration 3-1, in which you: (1) identify the skills, knowledge, and values you want your students to learn ("course goals"); (2) evaluate your students' incoming knowledge, skills, and values ("assess learners"); (3) decide how you will assess (a) whether students have attained the course goals and (b) whether your course design decisions are good ones, and then (c) design appropriate assessments ("plan assessment"); (4) select texts; (5) design the course to help the students achieve the course goals by writing the syllabus ("design the course"); (6) design a course webpage ("design course web")—if you are going to do so; (7) implement the design ("implement design"); (8) evaluate the course design ("evaluate course"); and, finally, (9) using the information you gained from evaluating the course, redesign the course according to the same process.

We have organized the rest of this chapter according to the timeline suggested by Illustration 3-1.

Illustration 3-1: The Recursive Course Design Process

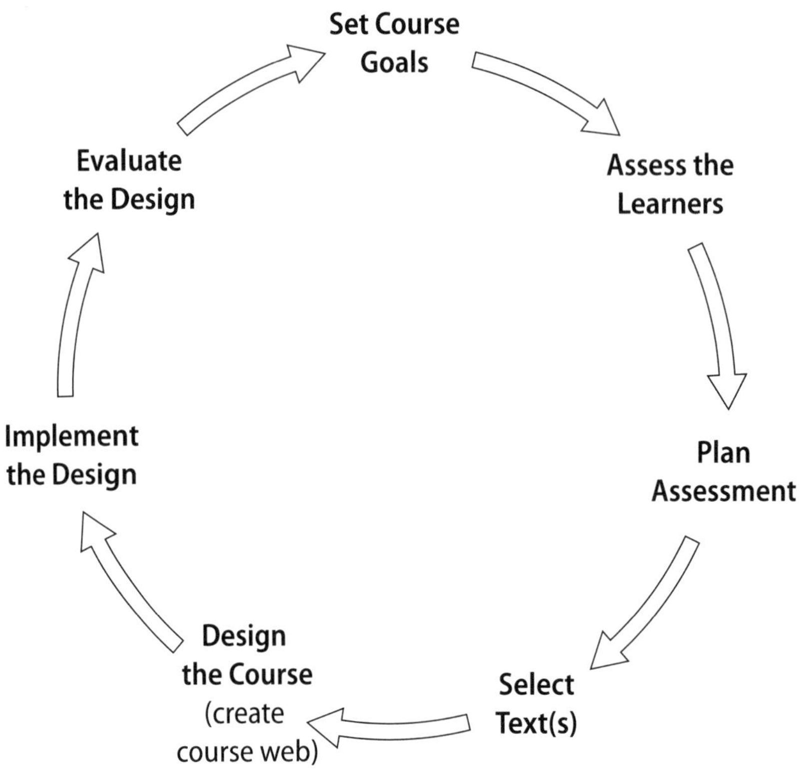

- Set Course Goals
- Assess the Learners
- Plan Assessment
- Select Text(s)
- Design the Course (create course web)
- Implement the Design
- Evaluate the Design

Initiating the design process: setting course goals

A goal is a statement of what students should be able to do by the end of your course. Although experts in education use a wide variety of terms for this concept (instructional goals, instructional objectives, outcomes, learning goals, etc.), they all pretty much mean the same thing. The core idea is articulating what you want your students to get out of your course.

Although few law professors have developed explicit, written statements of their teaching goals, we all teach as if we do have such goals. If you have doubts about whether you teach as if you have explicit teaching goals, try the next Thinking Exercise.

> **Thinking exercise**: Think about a course you just taught. What skills, knowledge and values did you evaluate on your exam(s), paper(s) and other graded assignment(s)? What did you expect your students to do to prepare for class? What did you ask students to do in class?
> *All of these choices are the product of your beliefs as to what students should be learning in your class, i.e., your learning goals.*

While the above thinking exercise is helpful for recognizing the pervasive role of goals in all teaching, it is not the most effective way to settle upon a set of learning goals. It is, in fact, exactly backwards. Goals are most effective when they are the driver, not the passenger, in a teacher's course design progression. Goals influence which topics within the body of law to teach, your expectations for student class preparation, your design of your syllabus and class sessions, and your design of examinations and paper assignments. And, in most courses, your students' likely future use of what they learn in your course should drive your goals.

Consequently, a good place to start in identifying goals is by thinking about what you can do in this field *because* you are an expert. If it has been years since you practiced, you either can try to recall what you did or speak with a practitioner. (We have no doubt you have alumni who would appreciate a phone call or e-mail asking for such information.)

Another way to get at the question is to imagine your students a few years after they have taken your course. What do you hope the students have retained from the course?

We encourage you to be ambitious in describing your course goals—think beyond the limits of your assigned course label (clinic, contracts, legal writing, environmental law) and aspire to produce learning that transcends. We also encourage you to consider course goals that emphasize students' ability to learn and practice in your field, what we call self-regulated learning goals. Finally, consider whether you aspire to help students learn more about themselves or to develop particular values critical to our profession.

Limit yourself to three or four learning goals per course, and focus not on what you know but, rather, what you are able to do. To be useful in course design, goal statements are most effective when they have three qualities:

- They focus on the student—not the teacher,
- They identify high level intellectual activities or important values, not just knowledge, and
- They are concrete and not abstract.

A goal is student focused when it describes what the students will be able to do or what value(s) they will adopt as their own and not what the teacher will do or say in the class.

A goal addresses high-level intellectual activities when it focuses on having students apply learning to new texts and problems. All courses involve a mix of higher-level and lower-level thinking skills. In general, however, the higher-level skills require students to develop the lower-level skills. In the law school context, higher-level skills include: drafting law-related documents, analyzing and solving legal problems, evaluating cases, conducting client and witness interviews, etc. These higher-level skills implicate lower level skills such as knowing and being able to explain the applicable law, being able to find a case or statute on point in a particular state, and generating policy justifications for the current state of the law or for changing the law.

A goal is concrete if you can measure its attainment. New goal writers tend to write goals that are so abstract that they provide little guidance in designing the course or assessing whether the students have attained those goals. Avoid goals that entail grasping ideas, e.g., "appreciating legal indeterminacy" or "understanding the complexity in legal decision-making." Neither phrase provides much useful guidance for designing a course. Instead, focus on how your students would show their appreciation and understanding, such as developing an original legal argument that is convincing yet runs counter to established doctrine or generating a statutory analysis that emphasizes the indeterminacy of a proposed statute to the types of problems that may arise.

Illustration 3-2: An Excerpted, Example Set of Course Goals for a Remedies Course

> By the end of this course, given a legally-cognizable dispute, you will be able to
> - Accurately identify the remedial options potentially available to the parties to that dispute.
> - Anticipate and articulate the arguments lawyers representing all of the parties to the dispute would make in trying to secure and defend against the potentially-available remedial options.
> - Correctly evaluate the likelihood that each of the parties would succeed in obtaining each of the remedial options potentially available to them
> - Effectively explain to a client the remedial alternatives potentially available, the arguments lawyers representing all of the parties to the dispute would make in trying to secure and defend against those remedies, and the likelihood that the parties would succeed in obtaining each of the remedial options potentially available to them.

Take a look at the example sets of course goals in Illustration 3-2, and, if you have time, the course goals we have provided in Appendix 3-1. Why do these sets of objectives satisfy the above three criteria?

Once you have established your overarching course goals, you need to identify the subsidiary skills, knowledge, and values students need to achieve your course goals. In other words, what skills, knowledge and values would an expert need to perform each of the skills? For example, to analyze problems in a doctrinal field, a practitioner would need either to know the relevant law or, at least, know enough of the law that he readily can recognize the doctrinal areas implicated by a problem and can find the law implicated by that problem. Likewise, a practitioner would need to be able to perform skills such as issue-spotting, evaluating evidence, distinguishing relevant and irrelevant facts, reading statutes and cases, applying rules to facts, applying and distinguishing cases.

Educators label the process of identifying subsidiary skills, knowledge, and values *conducting a task analysis*. A task analysis will allow you to generate a fairly long list of subsidiary goals, often called "learning objectives" or, more simply, "objectives." Together with the course goals, the learning objectives provide a tool you will find useful as you struggle to make many of the decisions with which we law professors struggle: doctrinal coverage, student expectations and assignments, how to assess your students' learning, and the use of class time. In other words, your course should address, at a minimum, those things necessary to allow students to perform the tasks envisioned by your course goals.

Certainly, it is possible to do a task analysis on your own, but the ideal way to conduct a task analysis is to design a problem you would expect your students to solve by the end of your course and then ask two experts to speak aloud their thinking process as they analyze and resolve it. As they work on the problem, ask them how and why they made their various decisions. To elicit the information you need, use questions such as: Why did you immediately reject _____ as a possibility? How did you know you needed to do _____?

Once you have completed your task analysis, you are ready to write your learning objectives. Generally, learning objectives should conform to the criteria suggested above for course goals, but, of course, you should not limit yourself to only stating high-level intellectual skills. In fact, the opposite is true: strive to include objectives across the full spectrum of intellectual skills. To assist you in that task, the comparison chart in Illus-

Illustration 3-3: Types of learning

Intellectual Task	Description in the Law School Context	Example
Problem-Solving Learning	Given a legal problem, the student identifies the issues, applies the doctrine, cases and policy to the facts employing the kinds of arguments lawyers make, and predicts how a court might resolve those issues	The student interviews a witness to an alleged crime asking questions that reflect an understanding of the crimes implicated, the possible application of doctrine to the facts, and the kinds of arguments he would need to make
Cognitive Strategy Learning	The student adopts effective strategies for learning an aspect of doctrine the student has not previously encountered	Given a problem raising an issue of tort law the student has not yet learned (e.g., the intrusion upon seclusion form of invasion of privacy), the student effectively can teach herself the applicable law
Attitude Learning	The student adopts as his own a desired value, goal or ethic	The student plans to devote 5% of her future practice time to pro bono work
Principle Learning	The student applies individual rules and can apply and distinguish cases pertinent to a previously unseen problem	Given a potential lawsuit, the student can identify all jurisdictions that successfully could assert personal jurisdiction over the defendant
Procedure Learning	The student can follow all the steps involved in performing a lawyering skill	Given a problem raising a discrete legal issue, the student can follow the process of finding if there is a case or statute on point
Concept Learning	Given a legal problem, the student identifies the implicated legal issues	Given a contract, the student identifies contract language that a could create an express condition
Declarative Knowledge Learning	The student accurately articulates a rule of law, case holding or public policy	Given a problem about an issue of adverse possession, the student can state the elements of adverse possession

tration 3-3 identifies one commonly used set of classifications of skills and provides examples from law school learning.

Note that, in Illustration 3-3, the skills generally are sequenced from the highest intellectual tasks to the lowest level intellectual tasks.

As noted above, higher level skills implicate lower level skills. Thus, the highest level intellectual task, problem solving, requires students to know the law (declarative knowledge), identify issues (concept learning), apply and distinguish authority (principle learning), perform all these skills in writing (procedural learning) using IRAC or some other tool for communicating legal reasoning, and possess both the skills needed to learn all of these skills (cognitive strategy learning) and value learning it (attitude learning). We believe most law professors have intuited this hierarchy. If you ever have told a student that you do not want him to memorize the law but, instead, know how and when to apply it, you are suggesting this hierarchy. You are communicating that declarative knowledge is not enough; students must acquire principle and procedural learning so they can spot issues and apply the doctrine.

You may find it helpful, as you develop your learning objectives, to refer back to this chart. An additional set of learning objectives is included in Appendix 3-2.

One additional point about goals and objectives is worth noting: all of us expect our students to come to law school with some of the skills and knowledge they need to meet the course goals. (Of course, those of us who teach upper division courses also expect our students to have learned certain things in their prior law school courses.) Judging from the many times we have heard colleagues complain about what their students don't know or aren't yet able to do well, we suspect many of us have, on occasion, overestimated our students' entering skills, knowledge and values.

For this reason, in addition to establishing learning objectives, you also need to determine what your students *bring* to their engagement in your course.

Know your students: assessing the learners

While many of us have made the mistake of assuming, without any basis in actual assessment, what our students know and are able to do, the most common error committed by law professors is assuming their students are like them. In fact, recent studies suggest law professors are more like each other and much less like their students in terms of many of the characteristics that might influence how you should design your courses.

Those differences include the skills, knowledge, and values with which the students' enter law school. In this sense, law professors are, at most, similar to their strongest students and quite different from a large percentage of the rest of the student body. Law professors typically were near the top of their law school classes and attended more exclusive law schools than those at which they teach (or, at least, attended law schools as exclusive as the law schools at which they teach). It's pretty much mathematically impossible that a significant number of your students are your equals in terms of entrance credentials, law school results, learning skills, time and workload management skills, writing skills, and knowledge of relevant concepts.

This difference between us law professors and our students is exacerbated by the fact that our own law school experiences are several years in the past (and may even be repressed for those of us who experienced law school as traumatic). As a result, some of us may inaccurately recall the knowledge and skill we possessed when we went to law school. We either may overestimate what we knew and what we think our students *should* know or be frustrated when our students do not live up to a somewhat distorted recollection of our past selves.

> **Thinking exercise**: Can you actually recall what you wrote in response to any of your law school exams? How deeply did you analyze the legal issues? How many original, creative arguments did you generate? How well did you integrate legal theory?

Law professors also often have different learning style preferences than their students. Many law professors enjoy learning on their own, whereas many law students are more extroverted than their professors, preferring to learn through collaboration with others. Similarly, while law professors tend to be comfortable learning from texts and by listening to lectures, many law students prefer visually-focused teaching and learning experiences or prefer learning experiences which are situated in authentic law practice contexts. More significantly, law students vary among themselves in their learning preferences; assuming that we should teach the way we liked to learn as law students is just wishful thinking.

In a perfect world, you would conduct your own studies and discover your students' learning style preferences and whether they prefer working alone or in small groups. In fact, there are free, online versions of learning style assessments available on the web, such as http://www.chaminade.org/inspire/learnstl.htm, http://www.vark-learn.com/english/index.asp, http://www4.ncsu.edu/unity/lockers/users/f/felder/public/ILSpage.html, and http://www.humanmetrics.com/cgi-win/JTypes2.asp. None takes much time, and, by having your students self-report their results, you may learn something useful about them.

Assessing your students' entering knowledge may be more challenging and labor-intensive, but there are some shortcuts you could try. For example, you could develop a short survey and have students take the survey on the first day of class or create a multiple-choice, pre- and post-test of essential knowledge to discover what students know when they start your course and what they know by the end.

If you choose not to assess your learners, your students will benefit if you work from assumptions that (1) your students may not know everything you wish they knew and therefore will need instruction addressing skills and knowledge you think they already should possess, and (2) your students not only probably prefer to learn in different ways than you do but also vary greatly among themselves in terms of how they prefer to learn.

Determining who your students are, what they know, and how they prefer to learn is one form of assessment. The next step in your course design process will be to focus on other forms of assessment, including, among other things, how you will evaluate your students and how you will evaluate your course design.

Plan assessment: how will you know whether your students are learning?

Introduction

Please note that the choice to make assessment the next topic (*after* articulating course goals and objectives and conducting a learner assessment and *before* you design the course) is an intentional one. Thinking about assessment, even before you start designing your course, may seem counter-intuitive to you (and it is certainly counter to common law school teaching practice). You may even worry that, if you were to design assessment instruments before you designed your course, you could be accused of "teaching to the test" or of some equally anti-intellectual crime. Educational experts, however, recognize that designing assessment right after you have articulated your objectives and before you design your course ensures that your assessment instruments are congruent with your goals. Congruence among a teacher's goals, assessment, and course design is essential to designing and teaching an effective course.

In fact, the process of designing the assessment should and often does influence your course goals and objectives. As you draft your assessment instruments—exams, law practice exercises, multiple choice questions, etc.—you may discover additional subsidiary goals and, in some instances, even reveal an additional course goal. You are even more likely to revise how you articulate your goals.

The process also will increase the likelihood that you include assessment items aimed at all thinking levels (from problem-solving to application to issue spotting to understanding). This variety of assessment items will, in turn, benefit both your students and you. It will assist your students in identifying at what level(s) they are struggling, and it will help you identify at what level(s) you need to improve the design of your course.

Even more significantly, designing your assessment instruments and revising your goals will (and should) influence how you design your course. Your assessment instruments should focus on assessing student learning of the skills you regard as most important, and you should be designing your course so that you and your students devote the greatest amount of time and effort to developing those skills.

By starting early, you also may create more and higher-quality instruments and will have more opportunities to vet your instruments with colleagues (all three of us have had the experience of not discovering an error in a question until we read our students' responses to it—that sinking "uh-oh—my exam isn't a very good one" feeling is much worse if it happens at that late stage).

In fact, in an ideal world, you would write many more assessment items than you will need for any given offering of your course. By designing multiple sets of assessment instruments, you will gain greater insight into your objectives, increase the likelihood that your assessments are consistent over time, and generally feel less end-of-the-semester stress.

One final word about terminology to clarify our message. We have chosen to use the term "assessment instruments" and not "tests" or "tests and assignments" to communicate that we envision your assessment can and (we believe) should expand beyond traditional pen-and-paper, timed, in-the-classroom tests. We are using the term "assessment instrument" to broadly refer to any effort to determine the degree to which students are learning, and we envision you using your assessment results in at least three, very different ways.

The three uses of student assessment

This section discusses three uses of student assessment. The first use of assessment involves evaluating student performances on an aggregate level for the purpose of evaluating the effectiveness of your course. Your goal, in conducting this form of assessment, is to identify whether your students, on the whole, are learning what you want them to be learning. Generally speaking, educational experts have adopted Dr. Benjamin Bloom's 80-80 mastery learning standard as the hallmark of success: if 80% of your students have learned 80% of the skills, knowledge and values you have stated as your learning objectives, your course design is working. Chapter 7 will provide a myriad of suggestions for conducting this type of assessment.

It is not enough, in the context of this particular use of assessment, simply to assume, based on your perception, that 80% of your students are learning 80% of what you want them to learn. This use of assessment counsels that you design assessment instruments that will allow you to know, with some certainty, whether you are meeting the standard.

The second and third uses of student assessment are addressed in Chapters 5 and 7 and therefore only are touched on here. The second use of assessment is to help students not only learn more and learn better in your class but also learn to take control over their learning process, to self-regulate their learning.

The third and final use of assessment is the one we regard as least significant in terms of its potential for improving the teaching and learning environment in your courses—evaluating student performances for the purpose of assigning grades. Before you started reading this book, you may have thought of assessment as being solely focused on evaluating students for the purpose of assigning grades. Because our goal is to help you become a more effective teacher, we are interested in the two other uses of assessment.

Having decided what you want your students to learn, determined who your students are, and how you will determine whether your students are learning, you are now in a position to select a textbook. While it is possible (and, perhaps in an ideal world, may be better) to design your course and then select a textbook that will help you accomplish your design, we have found it helpful to select a textbook first. If you would feel more comfortable designing the course first, we encourage you to do so. There is no correct order with respect to these two tasks.

Finding the book of your dreams: sifting the morass to find the right textbooks for you

While this discussion suggests some broad principles of textbook selection and provides a checklist you can use as you compare textbooks, we are not inclined to recommend particular texts or a particular textbook series. Because we know what we are trying to accomplish in our classes, we have a very good idea as to what we need in a textbook, but we have no desire to impose our course goals on you.

Broad principles of textbook selection

Assume that no textbook will meet all of your needs such that you can have a turnkey course design process and teaching experience. We certainly never have had that experience, and, together, we have used dozens of textbooks. In our experience, each book you use will have strengths and weaknesses, and each will include cases or materials you love and omit cases and materials you wish were included. We always end up creating and providing our students with supplemental materials. Thus, as you consider your choices, recognize any book will not be the ideal for achieving your course goals; what you need is a book that you readily and easily can supplement.

Many law (and other higher education) teachers will suggest that you survey others who teach your subject or ask a colleague. We endorse that advice (mostly for political reasons), but we do not endorse the idea of allowing those suggestions to make the decision for you. The fact that a book has been adopted by a colleague or by many law teachers says little about its efficacy as a tool for helping students accomplish the course goals for which those professors adopted that text and even less about the book's efficacy for helping your students attain your course goals.

The core principle in selecting a textbook, therefore, is finding the book that best furthers as many of your course goals as possible without undermining any of your other course goals. A good textbook for you is one that makes it easier for you to engage your students in learning experiences that will help them develop the skills, knowledge and values you hope to teach them. If, for example, one of your goals involves students developing the ability to use the indeterminacy of doctrine and policy as a mechanism for developing creative and original legal arguments, your ideal textbook might pair cases that reach opposite results for conflicting reasons and would include problems that allow students to use the cases to build arguments and other ideas for analyzing and resolving those problems.

Some points of textbook comparison we regard as significant

This short discussion is intended to provide you with tools for comparing your textbook alternatives. We start with a description of our ideal textbooks, and, then, to assist you in selecting from among the less-than-ideal choice available, we provide a casebook evaluation tool (Illustration 3-4) that you can use when you are comparing textbooks.

In general terms, an ideal textbook would

- Be congruent with all of your course goals and learning objectives;
- Adopt cases that engage students, address significant issues, and are not unduly confusing;
- Include necessary statutory material and the resources students need to learn to read and interpret those materials;

Illustration 3-4: Textbook Evaluation Tool

Author(s) Title Publisher	Congruence with Your Objectives	Case Selection and Sequencing	Quality and Quantity of Problems	Quality and Quantity of Questions	Teacher's Manual: Assessment Help	Teacher's Manual: Teaching Help
Text #1:						
Text #2:						
Text #3:						
Text #4:						
Text #5						

- Have both large-scale law practice problems that require students to combine concepts and smaller-scale hypotheticals that allow students to practice applying the concepts as they are learning them;
- Introduce topics with overviews and a problem the students can solve once they have learned the topic;
- Sequence concepts so that students don't start with the most difficult concepts;
- Include thinking questions at all thinking levels (from problem-solving to application to issue spotting to understanding) so that students acquire all the skills, knowledge and values in your learning objectives;
- Include activities that engage students in adopting and reflecting on their adoption of cognitive strategies;
- Engage a wide variety of types of learners and not just the read-write learners;
- Provide a teacher's manual that facilitates multiple means of assessment, including assessment of the course, assessment for the benefit of student learning, and assessment for evaluation purposes; and
- Provide a teacher's manual that suggests varied methods of instruction.

Converting goals to results: designing the course to increase the likelihood students will learn what you want them to learn

Introduction

This discussion focuses broadly on what we see as the guiding principles for course design. The chapter following this one, Chapter 4, focuses on the design of individual class sessions. The current discussion focuses on designing individual learning units (e.g., personal jurisdiction, negligence, the parol evidence rule) and synthesizing those individual units into a comprehensive course design. The succeeding sections address how to effectively communicate your design in a syllabus and how to create an effective course webpage.

As you consider these suggestions in the light of your own course planning efforts, be sure to have your list of learning objectives and assessments by your side. As the discussion below reflects, the learning objectives and assessments will guide your course design decisions. Be sure you also have a sense of the other courses your students are likely to be taking.

Designing learning units and synthesizing those units in an overall course design

To design your course at the level of the instructional unit and then synthesize those instructional units into a cohesive course, you need to start by dividing the subject area into at least five and as many as eight or nine sub-categories, which we, in this book, are calling "learning units." For doctrinal courses, nearly all of us make the division into learning units based solely on doctrinal categories. For example, in contracts, your learning units might be: formation, defenses, remedies, interpretation and the parol evidence rule, conditions and performance, and third party contract rights (third party beneficiaries, assignment and delegation).

We cannot encourage you enough to avoid obsessing over coverage. While we all believe that coverage is not irrelevant, we are convinced that law professors often sacrifice effectiveness on the altar of coverage. Look over your list of teaching units. Try cutting all or a part of one or more units or consider giving students a choice of topics from which they can select (see the discussion of syllabus construction below).

While we encourage you to develop such a list of doctrinal categories, we discourage you from limiting your sub-category list to doctrine. If your course goals include developing your students' ability to engage in problem-solving in your field (for example, if you, like most law professors, expect your students to be able to analyze a problem in your field that implicates multiple sub-topics in that field), you need to reserve instructional time for problem-solving instruction.

New learners in a field need learning experiences that allow them to practice applying each of the concepts and principles in isolation (more on this point in the section that immediately follows this introduction and in Chapter 4), *and* they need instruction in combing those concepts and principles and procedures to analyze complex problems that implicate multiple doctrinal areas. It is tempting, in an effort to save time or to maximize the number of doctrinal areas you cover, to consider jettisoning either instruction focused on applying some of the concepts in a course or problem-solving instruction. Both choices reflect a misunderstanding of what it means to be a novice law student.

Novices in a field experience each application of each concept as its own unique skill. When your students tell you that your course requires a vastly different form of analysis than one or more of your colleagues' courses (even though you know the differences are relatively minor), your students are communicating their struggle to transfer what they have learned in your class to what they are learning in your colleagues' classes and vice-versa. In fact, they struggle with transfer even within a single course. The fact that your students have learned to apply the law governing the intent requirement for intentional torts, for example, does not ensure they will know how to apply the actual malice standard to an alleged defamation of a public figure.

The problem-solving instruction is equally crucial. All three of us have had law teaching colleagues complain about the inability of their students to see and understand the big picture. The essay answers of such students read as if the exam consisted of a series of one element mini-hypos, and the paragraphs in such students' essays are linked only by facile transitions such as "The first issue ..." "The next issue" etc. The students fail to demonstrate an understanding of the context in which each issue arises and the stakes of each issue, leaving the reader no sense that the student has been asked to analyze a single, complete problem.

Instruction specifically focused on building students' legal problem-solving skills *is* possible. Providing students with readings and other materials specifically directed to the problem-solving tasks in which they will be engaging (e.g., readings on conducting client interviews, analyzing law school hypotheticals, drafting pleadings, briefs, and contracts, etc.) gives them some guidance. Examples of how an expert would perform the skill, particularly in the form of a cognitive think-aloud (see Chapter 6), can be of enormous help, especially for students who prefer to learn through illustration. Creating multiple opportunities for practice and feedback in solving problems is crucial. While we commend the practice, a single session, final exam "review" is insufficient, even if the professor engages a discussion of the analysis of a problem or two. During their initial practice efforts, students need significant hints and cues. To maximize their skill development, you may need to point them in the right direction by, for example, suggesting the number of issues they should be identifying, by asking open-ended questions that help them develop difficult counter-arguments, and by suggesting combinations of analogous cases they have read. As your students become more comfortable with the problem-solving process, however, you can gradually withdraw such support, a teaching tactic colorfully referred to as "fading the cue."

While we have reserved Chapters 4 and 6 for a more full discussion of these techniques, we have introduced these ideas here and suggested some instructional strategies to emphasize the need to treat problem-solving instruction as its own sub-category in your course planning efforts.

Designing each learning unit. This discussion will address some basic ideas about designing learning units. Chapters 4 and 6, as noted above, focus on the design of daily class sessions and, more particularly, on the wide range of teaching techniques from which you may choose. In this section, we focus on more general principles for organizing your students' work in your courses. This section discusses the relationship between in-class learning activities and students' out-of-class preparation, the kinds of class preparation activities you should be creating, and the types of learning activities for which your presence, as a live teacher, is essential.

We all have a basic sense that students' out-of-class work should consist of reviewing what they learned in the previous class session (and synthesizing that new learning with what they learned in prior class sessions) and preparing for the next class session. Most of us, however, only explicitly develop assignments relating to preparing for subsequent class sessions. Moreover, most such requirements focus exclusively on textbook reading tasks.

In terms of class preparation assignments, the research strongly suggests that students learn more and learn it better when they read cases for the purpose of solving a problem. Even more generally, there is reason to believe that students are more likely to give skills reading assignments the required attention if those assignments are situated in a simulated law practice problem. Consider how a practicing lawyer would use the principles and skills you seek to teach in each of your learning units and introduce each topic with an appropriate problem the can students solve by the time they complete the unit. Your students will engage themselves in the reading because they will be looking for ideas they can use to solve the law practice problem.

The research also suggests law students learn more from cases when they possess relevant prior knowledge *before* they begin reading. Consider providing or assigning introductions (from secondary sources, for example) to each of your learning units. These introductions will provide students with a schema for organizing what they learn from the assigned cases. If you do so, you will not only enhance your students' ability to remember the concepts but also facilitate their development of issue spotting skills within the domain (concept learning).

Moreover, students learn more when they engage in deep processing of the materials. By expanding your conception of the term "assignments" and therefore explicitly assigning tasks in addition to reading a list of assigned cases and statutes, you can engage your students in a wide spectrum of intellectually-challenging processing activities, including:

- developing a theory that explains the need for the doctrine;
- synthesizing the reading assignments with past assignments in this and other courses by creating a graphic organizers or flowchart or by analyzing a multi-subject problem;
- comparing a case or series of cases to an existing or proposed statute;
- developing examples and non-examples of a concept addressed in their readings;
- analyzing hypotheticals that require the students to apply the new concepts they are learning;
- generating hypothetical problems about which reasonable lawyers would disagree;
- drafting a pleading or contract clause designed to address the problem; or
- drafting a proposed statute to address a problem raised by a line of cases.

Consequently, merely assigning a list of cases (or a range of page numbers from a casebook) is aiming too low. Illustration 3-5 suggests the relationships between these types of assignments and the higher level intellectual goals discussed in the section on course goals and learning objectives. It also provides examples of each of the types of processing assignments and explains the relationship between the assignment and the objective. Please note: because each of the assignments engages students in using a cognitive strategy to process what they are learning, you should also consider each of the activities as directed at cognitive strategy learning. You can make such an exercise even more explicitly a cognitive strategy exercise by also asking students to compare the usefulness of engaging in one activity to the usefulness of other assigned activities and reflecting on why in light of what they know about their learning processes and preferences.

> **Thinking exercise**: As you look over Illustration 3-5, try to imagine what a similar assignment in one of your courses might look like.

To maximize your students' learning experience, consider creating learning experiences that engage students in a wide variety of the activities described and exemplified in Illustration 3-5. This approach will help you better address the variety of learning styles represented by your student population and the variety will serve as a mechanism for retaining your students' attention.

If you choose to have your students engage in any class preparation activities, whether those assignments include activities similar to those described in Illustration 3-5 or more traditional class preparation activities, such as just reading cases and statutes, your classroom activities should be linked to and dependent on these preparation efforts. Thus, if your students prepare for class by drafting a proposed statute, their classroom experience should engage them in discussing and evaluating such solutions in light of the principles they learned by reading other assigned materials.

Thinking through the kinds of activities in which you want your students to engage is crucial because you want to be sure that you maximize your classroom time with students.

(Warning: If you are prone to excessive ego, please take the comments in this and the following paragraph with a grain of salt.) Educational experts frequently talk in terms of

Illustration 3-5: Deep Processing Activities and Higher Level Intellectual Learning Objectives

Learning Activity	Example	Type of Learning Objective
Required theory development	Be prepared to explain the policy trade-offs implicit in granting or denying relief for unilateral mistake.	Principle learning (because students are constructing an understanding as to the whys underlying the rules which will help them be able to apply the rules)
Synthesizing new cases with prior cases and other courses by creating a graphic organizer	Create a mind map depicting how negligence per se fits within the larger body of negligence doctrine.	Concept learning (because students are developing an understanding of how concepts fit together, which will help them be able to spot issues)
Comparing cases and statutes	Evaluate whether a proposed criminal code section solves the problem addressed in the assigned case.	Principle learning (because students are applying the proposed rule to the problem)
Developing examples and non-examples	Generate two original examples of common law burglaries and two non-examples (the non-examples should have facts identical to the examples in all non-critical respects).	Principle learning (because students must understand how to apply the principle to be able to generate examples and non-examples)
Analyzing practice hypos	Prepare a written analysis of the following adverse possession hypos.	Principle learning (because the students are practicing applying the principle but not in the context of analyzing any related issues)
Generating debatable hypotheticals	Create a hypothetical for which the application of intentional infliction of emotional distress doctrine would be unclear.	Principle learning (because students must really understand the application of the principle to generate a debatable hypo)
Drafting pleadings or contract terms	Create a contract clause that unquestionably making getting a home loan an express condition of purchasing a home.	Problem solving (because the student is engaged in using what she has learned to solve a practice-oriented problem)
Drafting a proposed statute to resolve a doctrinal problem	Revise section _____ of the _____ code to eliminate the defendant's argument in the _____ case.	Problem solving (because the student is engaged in using what she has learned to solve a practice-oriented problem)

selecting the best medium for delivering a particular aspect of students' learning. Available instructional media include: texts, live teachers, computer programs—such as CALI exercises—and websites, videotapes and podcasts, and small group experiences. Live teachers are, by far, the most expensive medium of instruction. In comparison to computer programs and websites, live teachers are less able to individualize instruction for every student in a single moment. They also are generally less reliable in terms of how they present information and teach skills. However, live teachers, in comparison to all alternative media of instruction, are uniquely flexible and adaptable and uniquely possess empathy. Live teachers can be the best instructional medium for inspiring learners and possess the unique ability to teach by functioning as role models.

Consequently, you need to be making conscious decisions about what aspects of your teaching require your physical presence and what aspects can be moved to another instructional medium. You should consider, for example, whether you can present instruction focused on declarative knowledge by videotape or podcast. For example, if you were to decide your students need to know things about the construction contracting process to understanding some of the major contracts cases or information about banking for a payment systems course, you could save classroom time by presenting this instruction via a podcast (even with PowerPoint slides) and offering it to students on your course webpage. This approach has the extra benefit of respecting the fact that some of your students will know this knowledge based on their life experiences and past jobs.

You may also consider whether the time you spend on announcements, on communicating assignments and syllabus adjustments, and on remediating student confusion is an optimal use of your extremely limited time with students. Announcements, assignments and syllabus revisions easily can be delivered via e-mail or using the announcements function on your course webpage. You can use an FAQ (frequently-asked questions) page of your course webpage and e-mail messages to address common areas of student confusion you have identified based on questions you have received from students, your review of student responses to your use of Classroom Assessment Techniques (See Chapter 7 for information about this technique), or the common errors students make in response to practice exercises, quizzes, tests and midterms.

Finally, you may be able to move some assessment activities outside the classroom. Consider asking students to take quizzes online or at home and to submit classroom assessment responses by e-mail.

> **Thinking exercise**: What aspects of a course you currently teach require your live presence? What aspects of your teaching can you move outside the classroom? How will you deliver such outside-the-classroom instruction?

Synthesizing the learning units in a course design. Having decided how you will structure each individual learning unit, you are ready to consider how you will combine the units to create a course design. There are a number of considerations that warrant attention as you begin this synthesis process, each of which we explain below.

First, consider how best to sequence your learning units and, within each learning unit, consider how best to sequence students' progress through that unit. It may be tempting to adopt the sequence used by the author of the casebook you have selected. Don't assume the author of your casebook knows best. Students prosper most when their learning experiences are challenging but not overwhelming. In particular, strive for a progression from relatively easier learning units to relatively harder learning units and, within each unit, from easier topics to more challenging topics. By designing your course with a goal of getting your students to experience success right from the beginning, you increase the likelihood students will have the self-efficacy they need to persist when they encounter the more difficult concepts.

We are not suggesting that you alter some of the learning units in your course to make them appear easier than they are. In fact, even students' first learning unit in your course should be challenging. We are suggesting you account for the fact that novices are encouraged by early successes and can be discouraged by early failures and then design your course with this idea in mind. For example, if you teach civil procedure as a first semester course, it is worth considering whether you should start with personal jurisdiction and, within personal jurisdiction, it is worth considering whether to start with a case as challenging as *Pennoyer v. Neff*, 95 U.S. 714 (1877).

It is equally important to gradually increase the difficulty of the intellectual challenge in your course. Give students a sense of progression and growth. If your students perceive the material as too easy or repetitive, they are likely to disengage. For example, if you are teaching statutory construction skills, the statutes with which your students work at the end of the semester should be the most challenging statutes they must analyze, and, at least by the end of the semester, they should be interpreting the statutes on their own and for a purpose they previously have not encountered.

Sequencing also is a matter of prioritizing. Many law professors ignore the issue of prioritizing and teach their courses as if the most important topics are the ones with which their courses start and the least important are those with which they end their courses. For generations, law students (and, for that matter, other higher education students) have complained about the end-of-the-semester rush. You know the teaching tactic to which we are referring: the professor abandons all semblance of active learning or even vicarious learning (via the law school Socratic-style teaching method), uses lecture format all the time, and moves through the materials like a tank going through wet paper. On the one hand, the adoption of this teaching method suggests the materials are relatively unimportant; on the other hand, the desperate nature of this choice suggests the students are receiving essential instruction without which they cannot survive as lawyers.

Second, consider the burden you are imposing on the students, their competing obligations in other courses, and the importance of school-life balance for your students.

Third, make sure you consciously sequence your course for variety. As we explained in Chapter 1, variety allows us to retain our students' attention, and their attention is a foundational prerequisite to their learning. The law practice problems should engage students in the wide spectrum of activities in which lawyers engage, including arguing, evaluating, reading, drafting, re-writing, negotiating, communicating with others (clients, colleagues, other lawyers, judges), interviewing, planning and presenting. Your class participation assignments also should have variety in terms of both the intellectual skills the assignments implicate and in terms of the type of activity. Not only should students' experiences within any given class session vary (see Chapter 4), but, also, their experiences between classes should have variety.

Finally, carefully plan how you will begin and end your course. At the beginning of a course, students are most eager to learn your expectations (see "Writing your syllabus" below). They also are hoping you will provide a few other things: (1) context—how what they learn in your course fits in with what they already have learned and what they will learn in other courses and the relationship between the concepts they are studying and their future practice of law; (2) inspiration—what is exciting about your course; and (3) reassurance—you know what you are doing and are trustworthy. You can provide context by showing them the kinds of problems they will be able to solve by the end of your course and helping them to identify how they will use what they have learned in your course in practice. For example, in Mike's contracts class, he gives students a contract on the first day of class and explains his goal that the students develop the ability to review such a contract, recognize and understand the implications of the various types of contract clauses the students have studied (e.g., liquidated damages clauses, express and constructive conditions, merger clauses, time is of the essence clauses, force majeure clauses), and identify potential ambiguities.

You can share what is exciting about your course by introducing students to the big questions and big problems in your field. For example, in a torts class, you can start the course with a hypothetical involving a person who became distraught after hearing a nasty insult and use the discussion of whether to grant relief as a springboard for introducing the goals and policy trade-offs in the torts field. In a civil procedure class, you might start with a professionalism problem raising the conflicts among what you legally can do, a client's professed strategic goals, the high cost of litigation especially for non-corporate actors, and the lawyer's role as an officer of the court.

You can convince students you know what you are doing by your level of preparation, by your organization of the course, by your explanation of the relationship between your course goals and your syllabus, and by the overall clarity of your syllabus. By adopting recurring practices, such as having a rolling outline on a whiteboard or chalkboard, you can communicate the overarching structure of the course and give students a constant sense of where in the course they are, where they are headed, and your plans for making sure they get from where they are to where they need to be.

A well-designed course ending provides students with opportunities to recall and reflect on how much they have learned, guides students to consider how they will use what they have learned in the future, and solicits ideas for improving the course in the future. It is particularly important that you save time, at least at the end of your course and, ideally, at additional junctures throughout, to focus on your problem-solving learning unit. As the semester progresses and you do not go through the material as rapidly as you had hoped, you will be tempted to jettison this part of your course in favor of covering additional substance. That choice would be a mistake. At best, your students will retain the additional material just long enough to excel (or pass) your exam; their efforts at building their legal problem-solving skills are likely to stay with them and serve them for years.

Writing your syllabus

Introduction

Your syllabus can be no more than just a list of assignments. But it also can be culture-making. In many instances, our first interaction with our students occurs via the course syllabus. These pages have the potential to engage students, to inspire their confidence and interest in you and your subject, to communicate your investment in their success, to display your professionalism as a teacher, to demonstrate your skill in planning the course, and to establish high expectations in terms of the effort you want them to put into your course and their likelihood of succeeding in learning what you want them to learn. Your syllabus also can leave students cold or, worse yet, discouraged, disinterested, disengaged, anxious, confused, and hostile. In other words, your syllabus can and likely will influence whether your new students anticipate that your class will be a healthy and productive learning environment.

Syllabus construction is mostly a matter of science and careful decision-making, but it is not completely artless. It is a matter of science because there are certain topics you should address in your syllabus, and there are some best practices for addressing those topics. At the same time, your syllabus communicates a lot about you: based on your syllabus, your students will draw inferences about who you are and how you will teach. They will look for clues as to whether you are, among other things, professional, flexible, creative, open-minded, demanding, passionate, organized, funny, caring, and accessible. Or not.

We have divided this discussion into two sections. The first section explores the topics you should address in your syllabus and articulates our views on trade-offs in establishing course policies. We do not provide "model policies" because we see the proper resolution of the trade-offs as indeterminate. The second section focuses on what we see as the more important goals of syllabus construction: communicating a tone of excitement, engagement, and passion; conveying high expectations; establishing your view of student learning; and giving students a role in structuring their own learning process.

What topics should be addressed in your syllabus?

Your syllabus serves as a contract between you and the students. It defines your relationship, establishes your respective rights, and creates your respective responsibilities. As with any contract, problems arise if the obligations it describes are expressed ambiguously or if either party asserts rules or expectations not articulated in the writing. Consequently, make sure you have a colleague read your syllabus before you distribute it to students.

Syllabi should provide the basic information students need and should address all the issues that reasonably might arise in the class, including:

- the name of and contact information for the professor, and policies about office hours, appointments and e-mails;
- the name of the course, the required texts, and a description of the course;
- attendance and timely arrival for class;
- course goals, statement of teaching philosophy, and teaching methods;
- expectations for class preparation and other classroom conduct;
- schedule of class meetings, readings, projects, and other assignments;
- grading, late assignments, and failures to complete assigned projects; and
- plagiarism and/or any other forms of academic misconduct that may arise in your class.

If you have a course webpage, your syllabus should provide information about accessing it and your policies for using it. Finally, an increasingly large number of law professors choose to address laptop use in the classroom in their syllabi; a few ban the use of laptops, a choice the three of us never have made.

(Some institutions mandate the inclusion of certain additional information in syllabi, such as the institution's mission statement, information about disability accommodations, general information about academic misconduct, and other such matters. Check with your institution.)

It is useful, at the outset, to consider the degree to which you wish to give yourself leeway to modify policies stated in your syllabus. For example, you may decide to devote an extra class session to a topic because the students are struggling, or you may choose to modify the form or content of your final examination. If you wish to retain the ability to modify your course policies, be sure your syllabus communicates that you can do so. You either can have a general caveat explaining that the syllabus is subject to change or specifically address areas where change is a genuine possibility. For example, if you wish to retain the right to modify your final exam, you can say, "The format of the final exam is subject to change."

Another good starting question involves assessing the degree to which you adopt strict rules and retain the discretion to modify their application to extraordinary circumstances or adopt less onerous rules to set a positive tone. The former approach, which many have likened to defensive driving, protects you against later challenge by outlier students who are unprofessional or disrespectful. It allows you to resort to objective principles and helps you avoid claims of bias. The latter approach communicates confidence in your ability to manage the class and to address outlier problems by directly confronting such students about their behavior.

A few other, relatively minor points are worth considering. First, if you were to adopt all of the suggestions below, your syllabus would be quite long and daunting. You make an important trade-off if you choose completeness. Some students may be less likely to read significant portions of a very long syllabus; others may draw the inference that you must be a particularly officious professor. Second, there are some things you can do to offset these effects. Some experts recommend splitting off the assignments from the rest of syllabus (the "Course Policies"). Others try to create an incentive for students to study their syllabi by including a few questions regarding course policies on students' first quiz and disclosing (in advance) their plans to do so.

The remainder of this discussion addresses our suggestions for each of the topics listed above. In Appendix 3-3, we have included several exemplar syllabi that reflect our own efforts to implement these principles.

The name of and contact information for the professor, and policies about office hours, appointments and e-mails. Generally, the contact information includes the professor's name, office hours, office location, telephone number and e-mail address. While some law professors may not be frequent users of e-mail, the current student population regards e-mail contact as essential. Many law professors choose to include a statement about the frequency with which the professor will check e-mail and respond to student messages.

This section of the syllabus also should identify the instructor's preferred method of contact—telephone, email, carrier pigeon, or telepathy—should communicate office hours (if the professor holds office hours), and should explain what students need to do if they wish to make an appointment with the professor.

The name of the course, the required texts and a description of the course. Including the name of the course, the titles and required editions of texts is valued by students and quite common. It is also common to include a description of the course. Most professors lift the description right from their law school's catalog. We suggest you instead try to capture what you find exciting about the course. Consider describing how the course relates to students' future law practice and to their current lives. This approach is more likely to bring the course to life for students whereas a lifted catalog description adds no real value.

Course goals, statement of your teaching philosophy and teaching and learning methods. Although students consider a section on course goals an important syllabus component, professors tend to underestimate the value of this information. The course goals section allows students to self-evaluate their progress in your course. Moreover, your choice to make those goals explicit communicates that students have an important role in meeting those goals. In fact, you may want to explicitly communicate your belief that attaining the course goals is a collaborative student-teacher venture.

The description of your teaching philosophy and the teaching and learning methods, along with your assignments, lets students know how they will achieve the course goals. We think it's helpful to use the label "learning philosophy" or, at least, "teaching and learning philosophy," and to emphasize that you regard teaching methods as effective only if they produce learning. We also like to emphasize the central role of active learning.

The link among the goals, the assignments (see below), your teaching and learning philosophy, and your teaching methods should be transparent, allowing students to recognize the connection between what you are asking of your students and what the students should be learning. This link gives students a sense that you know what you are doing, believe in yourself, and believe in them.

Attendance and timely arrival for class. We think it's valuable that you address both issues in your syllabus, but we have no opinion as to a right set of policies. We have found that inspiring students to want to be on time for class and to attend class is the most effective way to achieve both goals. Chapters 4, 5, and 6 describe our ideas about engaging students. That said, stating policies that limit absenteeism and tardiness will minimize your time on these issues and make it simpler to deal with students who refuse to attend your class or to show up on time. Finally, it is worth noting that the conventional wisdom is that the ABA Standards for the Approval of Law Schools implicitly prescribe a requirement that students attend 80% of your class time.

Expectations for class preparation and other classroom conduct. As a preliminary matter, we find it useful to communicate expectations of ourselves as well as expectations for our students. This approach combats the top-down, excessively and obsessively hierarchical law professor-law student dynamic and communicates your commitment to doing right by your students.

It also is helpful to frame your class preparation expectations in terms that make explicit your sense that care and preparation are crucial aspects of what professionals do. We also find it useful to address what students should do if, for some reason, they are unable to be prepared for class and to analogize the students' obligation in such circumstances to what lawyers do when their workloads or personal lives prevent them from completing a law practice task on time.

Finally, even though most law schools' honor codes include statements about non-discrimination and many address issues of tolerance and respect, you may find it useful not only to communicate those policies but also to directly address respect for others' ideas and differences, not only differences in terms of culture, life experiences, race and ethnicity but differences in terms of learning styles. Some students, particularly extroverts, learn best by wholly engaging themselves in the class discussions; at some law schools, such students are quickly labeled "gunners" and are thereby discouraged from learning according to their preferred method.

Schedule of assignments. For many students, the schedule of class assignments is the only section they carefully read. Students want specific details about when and how the professor expects them to fulfill their scholastic duties. Your schedule should include all assignments and projects, the dates they are due, and the dates of any exams. Organize these elements by topic rather than by chapter or page numbers. In other words, slot reading assignments addressing promissory estoppel under a heading labeled "promissory estoppel." Doing so helps reinforce the connection between the assignment and the course goals and provides useful context for students' efforts to understand the cases, statutes, and other course materials.

A clear course road map provides each student an opportunity to form a "plan of attack" that compliments his or her learning style. Your assignments, as explained above, should include a wide variety of learning experiences. Accordingly, it is unlikely that any student will appreciate an effort to address his learning style in every assignment. If you clearly identity the events and assignments in your syllabus, however, students have the opportunity to plan additional activities that relate the course materials to their individual learning styles. For example, if you were to choose to assign students to a cooperative learning exercise in which they will be teaching each other the concepts, your read-write learners can do some extra reading to prepare themselves and your visual learners can develop graphic organizers or visual metaphors of the concepts.

Of course, students only can adapt their learning preferences to your teaching schedule if your schedule is reliable. At the same time, both students and professors prefer the professor to retain some discretion to modify the assignments after the semester begins. An easy way to retain this flexibility is by including a disclaimer at the beginning of this section of your syllabus that states "To maximize student learning in this class, I may need to adjust the assignments. I promise to give you at least one week's notice before implementing any such change." Requiring one week notice prior to a change respects students' need to manage their coursework and maintains students' overall sense that your schedule is reliable yet allows you the flexibility to adapt your course on the fly and in response to your students' needs. Another approach is to give out assignments for three-to-four weeks at a time. This gives you greater flexibility in tailoring teaching and learning to students' needs.

Grading system. For many law students, the grading section of the syllabus is the most important section of the syllabus. The combination of their past educational successes and the mythology (and fact) of law school grading practices leaves students very concerned about how they will be graded. Students want to know what weight will be placed on the various graded activities in the course and whether other factors such as class participation and course webpage contributions will be factored into their grades. It is particularly useful to provide students with guidance about the standards by which you will be evaluating their work. Such grading rubrics (see Chapter 7 for additional information) help eliminate confusion and concerns over the accuracy or fairness of grading. If your students will be handing in work, make sure you also communicate policies addressing what happens if students hand in assignments late or not at all.

Tone, high expectations, communicating your attitude about student learning, giving students a role in constructing your syllabus

None of the above suggestions, as important as each is, trumps the suggestions in this section. In fact, if you successfully implement the recommendations discussed below, your students will be very likely to forgive any errors you make in omitting information they want or in being overly inclusive and creating a tome of a syllabus.

Before you start writing any of the above sections, think carefully about the overarching messages you wish to communicate to your students. Whether you want them to do so or not, students will draw inferences about who you are, what you value, what you think of your students, and how you will teach based solely on what you say in your syllabus and the tone with which you say it. Thus, you need to carefully consider what message(s) you wish to communicate in your syllabus.

> **Thinking exercise**: What do you want your students to know about you and your course from reading your syllabus?

At the most general level, your tone sends messages about who you are and how you will teach the class. Note, for example, our suggested language for communicating the possibility of changes to the schedule of assignments, "To maximize student learning in this class, I may need to adjust the assignments. I promise to give you at least one week's notice before implementing any such change." This language communicates that the professor treats student learning as the highest ethic in the class, sees himself as part of a community to which he owes obligations, and has respect for the impact of his decisions on his students. You also may find it helpful to express humility and to include some self-deprecating humor in your syllabus. Many law students experience law professors as arrogant. You can disabuse this assumption with statement such as, "Any typos or other errors in this syllabus are the sole fault of your professor and are excused, if at all, by the brain cell losses that have accompanied your professor's aging process." Similarly, when you are explaining you class preparation requirements, you can explain, "I do not treat incorrect responses to my questions or problems as irrefutable evidence of a lack of preparation. Smart, effective, well-prepared lawyers err, and I certainly will make errors in teaching this class."

The research on teacher expectations suggests the most effective teachers demand a lot of their students, communicate confidence in their ability to teach and confidence in their students' ability to learn. Thus, your section on teaching methods might communicate your knowledge of the various teaching techniques you plan to deploy and explain that you are doing so to meet the learning needs of a wide variety of types of learners. Likewise, consider writing your section on course goals as if you have no doubt the students will learn; for example, you can express pleasure about all they will learn in your class. Finally, your schedule of assignments can manifest confidence by making explicit the relationship between the assignments, the classroom activities and the course goals; referring to the goals in short hand next to class sessions in which the students will be introduced to the skills, practice the skills or demonstrate mastery sends the right message. Explicit references to your sequencing choices also can help communicate your confidence in yourself and the students.

Studies of effective teachers also suggest that teacher enthusiasm plays an important role in student learning. Your syllabus should capture your enthusiasm for your subject. Your enthusiasm is probably best communicated by how you describe the course. Consider showing that enthusiasm by expressing excitement about the area of law, about the importance of the policy questions the class will be unpacking, about how the students will use what they are learning in your class, or about the cases they will be reading.

Your explanation about your teaching philosophy can offer particular insights into how you will teach your class. Be explicit about why you do what you do. If you place great emphasis on authentic, law practice problems, explain that you believe students learn better and retain their learning more when their professors ask them to use what they have learned to solve the kinds of problems lawyers in the field must be able to solve. If it's important to you that your students become independent, self-directed learners (what we have called "self-regulated learners" in this book), let your students know that you have created opportunities for the students to learn more about their own learning processes and to learn to manage their learning.

Because law students are adult learners (for the most part), one of the best things you can do to enhance their learning experience is to share your power to establish course policies. By ceding some power to students, you convey important messages about your sense of the students' competence, autonomy, and abilities. You also show that you have faith in and respect for them and that you have confidence in your own ability to synthesize their needs and the course goals.

With first-semester students, who know very little about the law school learning process, this effort at sharing may be no more than just letting them know why you have designed the course the way you have designed it. For example, if you choose to adopt the recommendations of this book, you will quickly discover that many of your colleagues may choose not to provide multiple assessments and other opportunities for practice and feedback. Your syllabus can explain that you have done so because you are passionate about and committed to their development as lawyers and concerned about making your grading as fair and accurate as possible. Similarly, if you choose to supplement traditional law school Socratic-style teaching with other teaching methods, explain that you are doing so to meet the widest possible variety of student learning style preferences and because you believe active learning experiences produce deeper learning than passive (lecture) or vicarious (law school semi-Socratic) teaching methods.

In later semesters, consider ways you can engage your students in making decisions about course policies and assignments. The easiest facet of your syllabus for sharing control is course coverage. Most law professors find it difficult if not impossible to cover all possible topics within a subject area. We three, in fact, focus on deep learning of the topics we do cover rather than coverage of all topics within the subjects we teach. If you are inclined to do so, select those topics you regard as essential and then let your students select from among the remaining topics. All three of us also have found it easy to allow students to articulate their expectations of us and to suggest teaching methods they would like us to include in our repertoire. Because we hold variety as an ethic in our teaching and therefore use a wide variety of teaching methods and have very high expectations for ourselves, the students have yet to suggest expectations or methods we were not already planning to use.

You can also ask students to develop or contribute to your list of student expectations and for input into your grading scheme. Because we also greatly value multiple assessments and criterion-referenced grading (see Chapter 7), we do not leave the grading scheme entirely to the students but instead communicate that the scheme must incorporate those principles because we see them as essential.

If you are inclined to try allowing students input into your syllabus construction process, we suggest you start small. For some of us, the uncertainty of jumping off the syllabus design bridge proves too uncomfortable, and they regret ceding so much control. Mike has a colleague who greatly regrets adopting this particular set of recommendations. For others, of course, all that open space is thrilling.

Course web page design

All three of us use course web pages. While Mike is an unabashed course webpage enthusiast, Gerry has taken only baby steps in this area. Sophie is somewhere in the middle but favors the use of well-designed course webpages in law teaching. We all agree, however, that neither the medium (the particular platform — Blackboard, TWEN, your law school's own, designated platform) nor the mere existence of a course webpage is the message. A webpage is useful or useless to students based on the quality of its content.

At the simplest level, course webpages provide a mechanism for easy and environmentally-conscious transmittal of information. Most simply, the ability to easily contact an entire class of students (by e-mail) improves communication.

Course webpages, however, also provide a mechanism for transmitting student learning tools. For example, a course webpage is a good tool for communicating lesson-by-lesson learning objectives, answers to frequently-asked questions, and studying suggestions. All of these tools have the potential to benefit some students (and to be ignored by others). Many will look at them only when they are struggling in your course.

Similarly, studies of student classroom note-taking reveal that even the best students record less than 90% of what their instructors believe is important and many students record as little as 9%. When instructors provide scaffolding in the form of skeletal note-taking outlines, however, student note-taking greatly improves. In fact, studies show students provided with skeletal note-taking outlines learn more and better than students who receive no such guidance from their professors and better than students who are given their instructors' lecture notes. If you do provide note-taking outlines, make sure to provide space for notes relating to both skills and doctrinal coverage; otherwise, your students will get the idea that what they really are supposed to be learning is only doctrine.

Both because experts in all fields — including legal experts — possess more and better-organized knowledge than their novice peers, and to address students' varying learning styles, uploading partially-completed outlines and graphic organizers, including mindmaps, hierarchy charts and flowcharts, to your course webpage also can benefit your students. Requiring, encouraging, or even rewarding students who develop and post their own outlines and graphic organizers is even better. These tools help students develop their schemata for retaining their new learning and help students attempt and evaluate these powerful cognitive organizational strategies.

You also can use your course webpage to facilitate your efforts to implement the cooperative learning ideas addressed in Chapter 6 of this book. For example, you can create separate discussion boards for each of the groups you have created for your class. These discussion boards can make it easier for your students to collaborate, particularly those who commute to your law school or who work.

The testing functions available on most course webpages are particularly powerful learning tools. Many, if not most, law professors provide students with few opportunities to practice the skills they are expected to display on their examinations or to obtain corrective feedback on their practice efforts. In fact, for many law students, the only concrete feedback they get comes at a time when they cannot learn from it, when they get their final examination grades. Efforts to solve this problem, however, are often burdensome on instructors; many law professors regard the task of evaluating and commenting on 120 students' practice examinations even twice over the course of a semester as prohibitively burdensome. Course webpages provide possible solutions.

While multiple choice and short answer practice questions may not address the high level intellectual skills implicated on many law school examinations, such questions do provide students with useful signposts along the way and can supplement your efforts to evaluate your students for the purpose of assigning grades. Weekly 10–15 question multiple choice quizzes usefully can supplement the traditional teaching and learning process. In fact, well-drafted multiple choice questions can test not only knowledge but also a wider range of legal analysis skills, including issue spotting skills, argument evaluation skills, statutory construction skills, legal reasoning skills, and case reading and case evaluation skills.

The testing software's feedback function also allows you to direct students' efforts at re-learning the material if they answer a question incorrectly. You can suggest cases the students may want to re-read, additional cases exploring the issues, and excerpts from law review articles and supplemental texts.

Most importantly, student results on such quizzes can serve as a tool for you to evaluate the effectiveness of your teaching and course design. You can discover what students have learned and have not learned and, as a result, develop learning experiences aimed at remediating unanticipated gaps in your students' understanding.

Course webpages also can allow you to offer students opportunities to write practice exams without dramatically overburdening yourself. In addition to the cooperative learning group practice exam experience described below, you can ask small groups of students to post their analyses of hypos and ask other peers to comment on the essays. You can chime in if the students' peer commenting is insufficient. This approach benefits the authors of the answers, the commenting students, and the rest of the class. The authors get the benefit practice and feedback, and the rest of the class, especially those that try to answer the hypos themselves, get vicarious feedback. But the peer commentators, who need to understand the problem well enough to provide productive feedback, often develop even the deepest understandings, and, by being forced to identify flaws in a peer's paper, they become better able to see similar errors in their own work.

Perhaps the most powerful tools made available by course webpages are the discussion boards. Discussion boards allow students freely to ask questions, provide help, explore ideas, and discuss their learning experiences with each other, subject to faculty monitoring. In other words, a discussion board can serve as a significant supplement to students' classroom learning experiences. In this way, you can move instruction outside the classroom and, thereby, free up classroom time for activities for which your physical presence is essential. Such discussions also allow you to identify those students who are able to generate wonderful and useful insights in writing but for whom the large classroom experience is anathema. In fact, some experts hypothesize that students who are members of traditionally-disenfranchised groups may be especially well-represented among those who shine on a course webpage. Mike's experience using course webpages with a very diverse law student population is entirely consistent with this research.

Finally, course webpages also provide a mechanism for providing students with links to helpful learning resources, such as links to CALI exercises, to law school learning resources such as Professor Barbara Glesner Fines' "Teaching and Learning Law" website (at http://www.law.umkc.edu/faculty/profiles/glesnerfines/bgf-edu.htm) and to helpful cases and law review articles.

Evaluate the design and plan for the future

Having designed the course, created a syllabus and set up a course webpage, the next logical step, of course, would be to implement, i.e., teach, the course. If you have adopted the recommendations of this book, your course design has embedded multiple assessments throughout so that, during the semester, you are gathering data about how well your students are learning and, where possible, making what we could call online adjustments in the design of your course.

Ideally, the goal in course evaluation and redesign is to be systematic, reflective and continuous. Your approach is systematic to the extent that the information you strive to develop from your efforts at assessing your students' learning covers the breadth and depth of skills, knowledge and values you teach and evaluates student learning up and down the hierarchy of learning objectives. No one in legal education has managed to be perfectly systematic. Strive for the best approximation and use all of the information available to you. After you have finished reviewing your students' exams for the purpose of assigning grades, look at them for the purpose of identifying patterns of error. Consider adding just 2–3 multiple choice questions each class and keep track of your students' aggregate results. In one paragraph, summarize the results of each Classroom Assessment Technique you have administered (see Chapter 7).

Your evaluation process is reflective if you devote time and effort to reflecting (in a teaching journal of some sort) on each class session after it ends and reflect on the results of your efforts at assessment. Even five minutes of writing can serve as a crucial resource when you go back and consider how you can improve your course.

Finally, the word "continuous" conveys the idea that your efforts should continue throughout the semester and with respect to each offering of your course. The idea is analogous to the continuous improvement model in business planning or the self-regulated learning cycle described in Chapter 1. In both contexts, data is used to inform future planning and each implementation is treated as an opportunity to improve.

Checklist for course design process

Illustration 3-6 is a checklist you can use as you work through the course design process.

Illustration 3-6: Course Design Checklist

- ❑ **Determine what you want students to know, value, and be able to do**
- ❑ **Figure out who your students are**
- ❑ **Decide how you will assess students and draft assessments**
- ❑ **Choose texts**
- ❑ **Design each part of the course**
- ❑ **Design the course as a whole**
- ❑ **Create a syllabus that**
    - ❑ Provides the basic information students need and addresses all the issues that reasonably might arise in the class;
    - ❑ Engages students;
    - ❑ Communicates high expectations;
    - ❑ Includes challenging and appropriate reading and problem-solving assignments;
    - ❑ Paces the course carefully to make sure the course has an engaging opening and an effective closing and avoids the end-of-semester rush; and
    - ❑ Devotes instructional time to problem-solving instruction and experiences.
- ❑ **Create a course webpage (if you have decided to have one)**
- ❑ **Implement your design**
- ❑ **Evaluate your design**

Chapter 4

Designing Each Class Session

Planning an individual class session is pretty straightforward for many law teachers. They decide how many pages in the casebook they will try to "cover" in the next class session. The cases and problems in the text, along with a statutory supplement perhaps, make up the primary material for the class. The class will begin with a brief lecture to remind students where they are in the course. The rest of the class will consist of modified Socratic dialog and large group discussion on the assigned cases and problems. The teacher may decide to provide visual aids by writing on the whiteboard or projecting slides. The class will conclude with final comments from the teacher about the material covered that day and a reminder of the assignment for the next class.

We believe that law school class sessions can lead to more significant student learning, and teacher satisfaction too, through a more intentional approach to class design. We recommend a five step class design process, reflected in Illustration 4-1. The remainder of this chapter will explore each element in detail. However, a few preliminary comments may be helpful.

We recognize that our five step process to class design is more elaborate than the class planning most law teachers currently do. But we intend our process to be useful, not intimidating or overwhelming. Many law teachers implicitly engage in some or all of the elements of our process. This chapter can help those teachers be a bit more explicit in their planning. In addition, our proposed process is not an all-or-nothing deal. Even if the entire five-step process is not for you, we believe that you can improve your teaching and your students' learning by expanding your class design efforts in any of the elements described below.

Context → Class Objectives → Instructional Activities → Feedback → Materials

Context

Although each class session can be a singular event for design purposes, it does not take place in isolation. Instead, each class occurs in a larger context, which includes important background aspects of the course, the students, and the teacher.

Course context

The nature of the course affects class design. Is the course required or elective? Law schools may mandate that certain concepts or skills be taught in required courses to prepare students for subsequent courses, the bar exam, or practice. For example, a law school may expect that a legal research and writing course include instruction on legal research over the Internet; if so, the teacher may design a class, or series of classes, to help students become proficient in that area. Elective courses may provide faculty members with more options in choosing learning objectives, appropriate instructional activities, and accompanying materials.

Time and scheduling matter in class planning as well. Is the class in the day or evening? How many times does it meet each week? How long is the class? The number of learning objectives, the types of instructional activities, and the nature of the material may differ substantially in a class that meets during the day for 50 minutes, three times per week compared to an evening class that takes place for three hours once per week.

The classroom for the course plays a role in class planning. Does the room configuration and seating lend itself to particular methods? For example, small group discussions are easier in flat classrooms with movable chairs. The room affects the choice of visual aid materials. Does the room contain a computer? Whiteboard? Document projector? It may be necessary to move to a different room to accomplish particular goals and activities for a class session. For example, an oral argument exercise may be more effective in the moot courtroom.

Where the class fits in the life of the course has a significant influence on class design. Will the class be toward the beginning, middle, or end of the course? At the beginning or end of a unit? Will the class introduce new concepts or skills? Or will the class be designed to reinforce earlier learning or deepen analysis? What instructional activities did you use in the prior couple classes? Is it time for a bit of variety in methods for the next class?

Student context

The needs and motivation of our students change as they progress through law school. For example, many first-semester, first-year students are interested in their courses and eager to learn, but most lack basic legal analysis skills and are uncertain about what they should be learning. Those characteristics of first-year students may lead us design a class session with an objective that focuses explicitly on analytical skills (such as an element of case or statutory analysis), an exercise to practice the skill, and feedback to students on their progress in learning the skill. On the other hand, second-semester, third-year law students may display less interest in their courses but are eager to graduate, pass the bar exam, and begin their careers. Those attributes could lead us to design a class with an objective dealing with content and skills that are directly relevant to law practice (preparing a valid will, for example), a drafting exercise, and feedback designed to refine the skill.

Our students' prior learning and real-life experience can affect our design decisions. Have all of the students encountered a concept or skill in a prerequisite course? If so, we may decide to briefly refresh that learning and then move to more sophisticated aspects of the content or skill. Or, if some students are encountering the content for the first time, we may decide to incorporate background reading or a CALI exercise to bring them up to speed. If we know that some students have real world experience with the content of an upcoming class, we can decide whether and how to incorporate that experience in the class. For example, in a class session dealing with service of process, we may choose to devote five minutes of class to student stories about serving papers.

We know that our students have a range of preferred learning styles. Some prefer to learn through reading and individual reflection, others through discussion, hands-on experience, or collaboration with a small group of peers. Consequently, as we design class sessions, we can maximize student learning by incorporating a variety of methods. Even in a 50 minute class session, student engagement and attention will benefit from using more than one learning activity.

As we plan our class sessions, we should be cognizant of other academic and life challenges our students are facing. If our students have a major assignment or exam immediately before our class, we can build a session with that reality in mind. For example, introducing complex new material through lecture or Socratic questioning may not be effective that day while a problem set that reinforces and deepens prior learning may succeed. Likewise, if we know that an individual student is struggling with a significant life event, we may decide not to call on that student for that day.

A final student context factor is the number of students enrolled in the course. We believe strongly that a variety of active learning methods and feedback are essential elements of successful class sessions regardless of the size of the class. Nevertheless, enrollment affects the types of objectives, instructional activities, material, and feedback that we select for a class. For example, in a small class, individual drafting assignments including individual feedback from the teacher is preferable, while in a large class the same assignment may be completed by small groups of students.

Teacher context

The third context element is our own professional and personal situation. We all have strengths and weaknesses as teachers. We are more comfortable with some methods than others. Our level of understanding of content and competence with skills varies. And at different times during the course we are overwhelmed with challenges in other aspects of our professional and personal lives. In class design, we should build on our strengths and address our weaknesses. Classes that address content and skills with which we are comfortable may be appropriate for us to experiment with new learning and feedback activities. On the other hand, on days when we are on shakier ground or are struggling with other matters, we may choose to stick with the tried and true.

The course, students, and teacher are all important elements of the context in which we design classes. However, analyzing the context should consume very little of the teacher's planning time. All we need to do is spend a few minutes thinking about the context as we move along the rest of the class design process.

Class objectives

In Chapter 3, we showed how course goals and learning objectives should drive course design. Similarly, objectives are the foundation on which each class should be built. The objectives for each class, which we creatively call "class objectives," share the three basic characteristics of course goals and learning objectives:

- Learner, rather than teacher, centered;
- Encompassing a broad range of professional knowledge, skills, and values; and
- Clear and concrete.

We discuss each of those characteristics below, after we address the question, "How many objectives are appropriate for a single class session?" The answer is, of course, "It depends." On what? All of the context issues we discussed above. But in general, we favor depth over breadth, significant learning versus coverage. Consequently, one to three class objectives are generally appropriate for a one-hour class session.

Learner centered

Articulating learner-centered goals represents a subtle, but fundamental, shift for many faculty members. For some teachers the objective for the class is to get through 20 pages of material, or to cover three cases, or to discuss four problems. Other teachers may say that their objective is to present an analytical framework for an aspect of the course or to demonstrate a skill, such as interviewing. All those objectives are teacher centered—they describe what the teacher hopes to accomplish in class.

Learner-centered objectives focus on what students will learn, rather than what will be covered or what the teacher will do in class. To shift the focus to student learning, we begin class objectives with the phrase "As a result of this class, students will be able to". Then, we complete each objective with the knowledge, skills, or values that students should learn in the class session. For example, "As a result of this class, students will be able to define the concept of 'specific jurisdiction' and each element of the applicable 'minimum contacts' analysis." Or, "After this class, students will use six components of statutory interpretation to analyze problems involving statutes and regulations."

Professional knowledge, skills, and values

Success as a legal professional rests on a set of knowledge, skills, and values. Consequently, our course goals and class objectives should focus on students learning and practicing knowledge, skills, and values related to the course. We cannot effectively teach in the three years of law school everything a lawyer needs to thrive in the profession. We must make choices. So as we design a class session, we should choose to focus on the critical knowledge, skills, or values for that day. The process of articulating class objectives helps discipline us to make those choices intentionally.

For most law school courses, knowledge includes legal doctrine, policy, and theory. An individual class session will focus on a small subset of the relevant knowledge for the course; for example, the analytical framework for the Seventh Amendment right to a jury trial and the role that civil juries play in a democracy.

Most law teachers strive to teach thinking skills in their courses, such as case analysis, statutory analysis, problem solving, or critical thinking. Each thinking skill is made up of components. For example, it is possible to see statutory analysis as a process that requires lawyers to consider six elements — (1) language of the applicable statute, (2) purpose of the statute, (3) overall statutory scheme, (4) legislative history, (5) regulations interpreting the statute, and (6) cases interpreting the statute. A simple objective for a statutory analysis class in the context of environmental law would be "As a result of this class, students will be able to identify six elements of statutory analysis the Supreme Court employed in *TVA v. Hill*."

Thinking skills are hierarchical. In the 1950s, Dr. Benjamin Bloom developed a taxonomy of educational objectives, which was revised in 2001 to improve its pedagogical accuracy. Illustration 4-2 summarizes the revised taxonomy and applies it to legal education.

The important point here is not to fit our objectives into boxes but to recognize that thinking skills applicable to law school and law practice vary in sophistication. Not every class session will include objectives at all levels of thinking. Students need to understand concepts before they can apply or evaluate them. Over the span of a course, however, we should include objectives in some class sessions that reach the most complex levels of thinking.

In most courses, relevant skills should go beyond thinking skills to include other skills lawyers need to succeed in practice. For example, the MacCrate Report lists ten "Fundamental Lawyering Skills": problem solving, legal analysis and reasoning, legal research, fact investigations, oral and written communication, counseling, negotiation, litigation

Illustration 4-2. Levels of Thinking Skills

Level of thinking	Taxonomy for teaching and learning	Law school application
Higher level	6. **Create** - reorganize elements or ideas to create a new pattern or structure	Students make arguments for the extension or reversal of existing law
	5. **Evaluate** - judge based on a set of criteria	Students use the IRAC method to respond to an essay question; students evaluate the relative strengths of different causes of action
	4. **Analyze** - break ideas into component parts to understand organizational scheme	Students outline the law and policy of perfecting security interests
	3. **Apply** - use new learning to solve problems or complete tasks	Students use electronic research to find authority relevant to a hypothetical
	2. **Understand** - explain concepts in own words	Students are able to define proximate cause or give examples of illusory promises
Lower level	1. **Remember** - retrieve knowledge from long-term memory	Students can identify the elements of negligence or the defenses to first-degree murder.

and alternative dispute resolution, organization and management of legal work, and recognizing and resolving ethical dilemmas.

A sophisticated class objective in a civil procedure course could be "As a result of this class, students will be able to create a cost effective fact investigation plan for a hypothetical lawsuit using the formal discovery devices under the Federal Rules of Civil Procedure and informal investigation methods."

Professional attributes and values are perhaps the most overlooked aspect of traditional legal education. Yet lawyers consistently identify a number of aspects of professionalism as important to success in law practice, including honesty, integrity, reliability, responsibility, judgment, diligence, tolerance, self-motivation, empathy, and respect for clients, lawyers, judges, and staff. We should look for opportunities to include values in our class objectives. For example, a trial advocacy course could include an objective that "Students will be able to give five examples of respectful and disrespectful behavior toward opposing counsel in civil litigation."

> **Thinking exercise**: In the context of a course that you teach, identify one item that would be appropriate to address in a class session or sessions for each of the following categories:
> - Legal doctrine
> - Legal theory
> - Low-level thinking skill
> - High-level thinking skill
> - Lawyering skill other than legal analysis or problem solving
> - Professional value.

Clear and concrete

The key to clear and concrete class objectives is to focus on observable student behavior. We can't observe students "understanding" a concept or "appreciating" a value. We can observe students' ability to set out the analytical framework for an area of law, students' identification of legal issues in a fact pattern, or students' demonstration of respect for other students in the classroom. To help you generate concrete objectives, Illustration 4-3 contains a list of action verbs applicable to various levels of thinking according to Bloom's original taxonomy of educational objectives.

There is nothing magic about this list of verbs. Other verbs may more accurately capture the type of student learning that you seek. And many of the verbs could fit in more than one category. Although we believe deeply in the importance of articulating class objectives, we are not dogmatic about their precise form. The critical point is that for each class we ask ourselves "What are the few 'essentials' in terms of knowledge, skills, or values that the students should have when they leave this class session?" The answers to that question are the heart of our class objectives. And those answers should drive our design of instructional activities, feedback, and materials.

Illustration 4-3. Action Verbs for Concrete Class Objectives

Knowledge	Comprehension	Application	Analysis	Synthesis	Evaluation
count	associate	apply	analyze	categorize	appraise
define	convert	classify	arrange	combine	assess
describe	defend	complete	break down	compile	compare
identify	discuss	compute	combine	compose	conclude
label	distinguish	demonstrate	design	create	contrast
list	estimate	discover	detect	derive	criticize
outline	explain	divide	develop	generate	critique
read	extend	examine	differentiate	group	determine
recall	extrapolate	interpret	discriminate	integrate	grade
recognize	generalize	modify	illustrate	order	interpret
record	give examples	operate	relate	outline	judge
reproduce	infer	prepare	select	plan	justify
select	paraphrase	produce	separate	propose	measure
state	summarize	solve	use	revise	rank

Instructional activities

We chose to label this aspect of class design "instructional activities" rather than "teaching methods" or "learning activities" because effective class planning requires attention to both what we will do during the class and what our students will do. For design purposes, we divide the class into three parts: (1) opening—the first one to five minutes; (2) body—the bulk of the class period; and (3) closing—the final one to five minutes.

Opening

The first few minutes of a class can be the most valuable. Our opening can grab attention, motivate, communicate objectives, and build a bridge to previous learning. We may not attempt to accomplish all those items in the first few minutes, but each is worthy of our consideration in class planning.

> **Thinking exercise**: Reflect on the last several class sessions you have taught. What happened in the first few minutes of those classes? Keep track of what happens in the first few minutes of the next several classes you teach. How can you maximize the effectiveness of your openings?

Students won't learn much in the classroom if they are not paying attention to what happens there. We can plan to gain students' attention in many different ways—a projected image relevant to the subject for that day, a mental challenge represented by an overarching question for the lesson, a news story, a personal anecdote, or by celebrating student success, such as excellent performance in a trial or competition.

Once we have students' attention, we should provide motivation for them to maintain their focus throughout the class. We can motivate students by communicating our own passion for the class, that we are excited to be in the classroom with them exploring interesting ideas. Show students how the concepts or skills for the class will be relevant and valuable to them in the future — in their personal lives, on the bar exam, or in practice.

Share class objectives with the students. The process of articulating class objectives helps us focus our teaching. Likewise, objectives focus student learning. When students know what content, skills, and values matter for that day's class, they can devote their effort to learning the essentials, rather than tangential matters. We can inform students of the class objectives orally, on the board, in a handout, or on a slide.

Plan the transition from previous classes. We should put the day's class in the larger context of the course. Many students have difficulty seeing the big picture. A chart or diagram can help students fit the lesson into the broader context. Further, we should prompt student recall of relevant prior learning — the concepts, skills, and values learned earlier in the course that apply to the class at hand.

Body

The primary design decision for the body of the class is the selection of teaching and learning methods, including grouping strategies. For example, we could plan a class session to include small group problem solving, followed by Socratic questioning of individual students, culminating in a large group discussion. Our selection of teaching and learning methods should be guided by one overarching principle — choose methods to maximize student learning of class objectives.

Teaching and learning methods do not have inherent value, or lack thereof. Socratic dialogue, lecture, or simulations are not "good" or "bad" methods. They are tools to facilitate student learning. The appropriateness of methods varies according to class objectives. For example, if our objective is that students will accurately articulate the elements of a doctrine, we may choose to lecture or conduct a Socratic dialogue with a case that explores the elements. If our goal is for students to develop interviewing skills, we may do a demonstration followed by students interviewing one another in pairs.

Two subsidiary considerations are relevant to our choice of teaching and learning methods — learning styles and depth of learning. Over a dozen models of learning styles exist and two have been applied often to legal education — Kolb's cycle of learning modes and the Myers-Briggs temperament typology. We have chosen to summarize and apply Fleming and Mills' sensory-based learning style model because of its simplicity and relevance. This model identifies four learning style preferences but presumes that most students (and their teachers) rely on more than one style. Illustration 4-4 identifies the four styles and examples of teaching learning methods that are most comfortable for each style.

Does the learning styles literature suggest we must plan methods for each class session to address each learning style? No. Instead, it means that, because we know our students prefer to learn in various ways, we should plan to use more than one method for each class session and should incorporate many methods over the life of the course. In fact, there is evidence that all students benefit from the mental effort necessary to learn in ways with which they are less comfortable; perhaps, the mental energy needed to go against type produces a stronger mental trace. In any event, there is great value in variety.

Illustration 4-4. Sensory Based Learning Styles

Learning Style	Teaching/Learning Methods
Digital • Learn via reading and writing • Logical, deductive reasoning • Abstract thinkers • Find patterns and organization	• Read to prepare for class • Brief cases • Write responses to problems • Outline course • Lecture—listen and take notes
Auditory • Learn via hearing and speaking • Process and store information chronologically • Memory aided by mnemonic devices	• Socratic dialogue • Large group discussion • Small group problem solving • Debate • Listen to stories, cases, hypotheticals
Visual • Learn via sight • Organize concepts through spatial relationships • Store ideas graphically	• Visual tools of all types—whiteboard, pictures, videos, handouts, slides • Diagrams, flow charts, graphs, concept maps
Kinesthetic • Learn by doing • Store knowledge as experience • Attend to physical and emotional manifestation of concepts	• Simulations and role plays • Authentic law practice experiences, including service learning, clinical, and externship experiences • Real documents—pleadings, contracts, deeds

This conclusion is bolstered by empirical research on the effect on learning of multiple-sense, multiple-method instruction. In general students remember about 10% of what they read, 20% of what they hear, and 30% of what they see in pictures or graphics. With two senses or methods, student retention improves. Students remember approximately 50% of what they see and hear. Since speaking involves both active cognition and hearing, students retain about 70% of what they say. Couple speaking with doing and retention soars to 90%. Illustration 4-5 presents this information graphically.

In every course, some content and skills are more important than others. We should design instructional activities that involve multiple senses and methods for the most important aspects of the course. For example, if a significant learning objective is for students to have deep understanding of the law, policy, and strategy involved in creating security agreements, we may ask students to read applicable sections of the Uniform Commercial Code, discuss cases or problems applying those sections, review a sample security agreement, and draft a security agreement for a hypothetical or real client.

Intertwined with our planning decisions about teaching and learning methods are our grouping choices. We have three basic options—individual, large group, and small group. For example, if we plan to have students analyze a problem that we will present in class, we could have students generate an individual response, ask students to work with a partner or in a small group, or conduct a large group discussion or Socratic dialog exploring the problem.

Most student class preparation activities are done individually, such as reading, responding to problems, drafting, or completing a CALI exercise. In traditional legal education, large group activities make up the bulk of the class—Socratic dialogue, discussion, or lecture. Individual activities in class are common as well—responding to a question, making a comment, or taking notes. We can create additional individual engagement

Illustration 4-5. Senses, Methods, and Retention

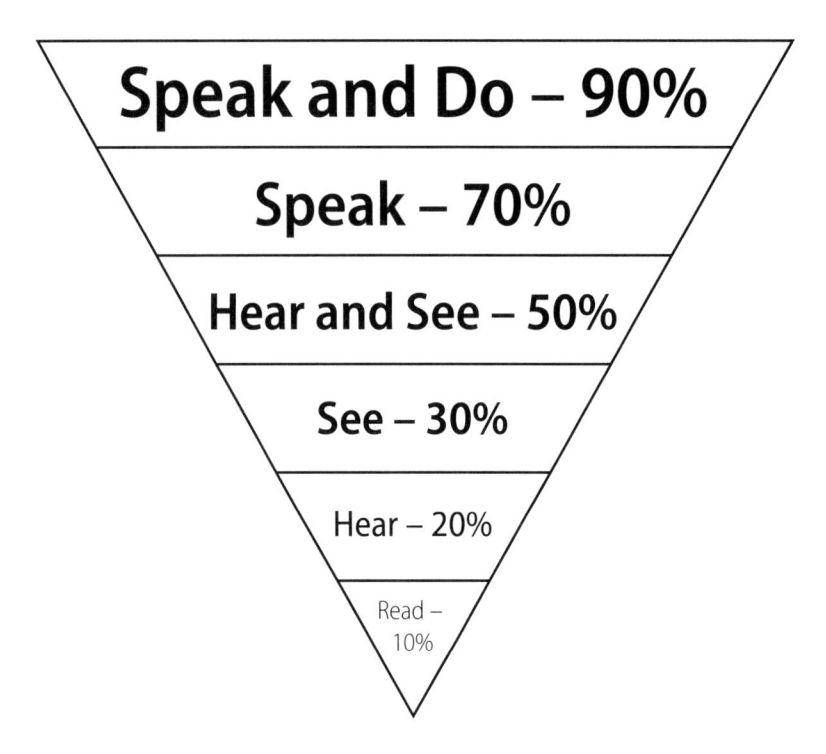

```
Speak and Do – 90%
Speak – 70%
Hear and See – 50%
See – 30%
Hear – 20%
Read – 10%
```

opportunities in a class session by administering quizzes and short, in-class writing exercises, such as generating a written response to a hypothetical projected on a screen or in a handout. Our most significant grouping choice, however, is the use of small groups in class.

More research on small group learning exists than on any other teaching and learning method. Hundreds of studies have established the benefits of collaborative learning in higher education. When compared with individual or competitive structures, collaborative small group learning arrangements result in increased student motivation, higher achievement, more high level thinking, better solutions to problems, more innovative ideas, and greater transfer of learning to new situations.

Our experience using small groups in law school classes is that many students identify it as the teaching/learning method that most enhances their learning. However, some students are frustrated by small group activities, especially when the small group activity lacks sufficient direction and structure. Just as families can be dysfunctional, small group experiences can be dysfunctional—if the professor has not adequately designed the activity. Effective use of small groups in class requires thoughtful planning. Small group design issues include the group type, size, membership, and assignment.

Small groups can be informal or formal. Informal groups are formed quickly and work together for a brief period of time. The group may discuss an issue, analyze a problem, or brainstorm ideas. Formal groups work together to reach a more complex goal, such as developing an oral argument or drafting a document. Formal groups may be together for several class periods or even a whole semester.

Optimum group size depends on the nature of the group, the physical setting, and the assignment. For informal groups, pairs or triads work well because they maximize

Illustration 4-6. Small Group Assignment

> **Climate Change — Briefing Document**
>
> As a class we will create a "briefing document" on climate change science and law. The document should be designed for interested, intelligent members of the public and press. The purpose is to summarize the current science and law of climate change in approximately 3 pages.
>
> The document will have 6 sections. Each section should be about ½ page, single-spaced, 12 point font. It can be in paragraph form, bullet list, or any other format that would be effective. Each group is responsible for one section. Email the section to me at the end of class today.
>
> Group 1. Greenhouse Gases, Significant Sources, Sinks
> Group 2. Projected Major Impacts of Climate Change
> Group 3. Mitigation and Adaptation Strategies
> Group 4. UNFCCC Preamble and Articles 2, 3, 4
> Group 5. Kyoto Protocol Articles 2 and 3, Annex A and B
> Group 6. Kyoto Protocol Articles 4, 8, 12, 17

the involvement of each student and can be formed easily in almost any classroom configuration. Formal groups may have from two to seven members. Groups of seven have more human resources than groups of three, but the larger size is harder for the group to manage and individual members may have little involvement.

Group membership can be determined in three ways. First, students can choose their fellow group members. Student choice is common in informal groups when students simply turn to a neighbor and in formal groups when students sign up to work on a project with one or more other students. Second, groups can be formed randomly. Students can count off in class, receive a playing card at the beginning of the class, or receive a handout with a number on it. Third, the teacher can choose the members, which is a common way to form formal groups. This method allows the teacher to shape the characteristics of the group to achieve balance in terms of gender, ethnicity, experience, expertise, etc.

To maximize the effectiveness of small group activities and to minimize students' frustration, it is critical that the assignment be clear. The group instructions should be in writing, either on the board, a slide, or a handout. The instructions should include the time allotted to the activity, the task the group is to perform, and the product the group is to generate. For example, instructions for an informal group activity could be: "You and your partner should generate an argument on behalf of the plaintiff that includes relevant law, policy, and facts. You have five minutes to construct the argument. Be prepared to give a 60 second summary of your argument." Illustration 4-6 is an example of instructions provided on a handout for a formal small group activity, for which the teacher chose the group membership to balance gender and expertise.

Closing

The last few minutes of class can be a time of significant learning if designed well. When we do not plan a closing, our classes often end with students looking at the clock as we try to cover one more point. Instead, we can plan the last few minutes of class to review, summarize, transfer learning, and re-motivate students.

Students need to consolidate new learning. We have many options to solidify student understanding at the end of class. We can review and comment briefly on the class objectives or articulate the few essential concepts, skills, or values students should have grasped in the class. With a graphic projected on a screen or with a handout, we could demonstrate how the doctrine, theory, or skills fit in the larger scheme or analytical framework. Students can play an active role in the closing by voicing the key concepts they learned in that class. We could ask students to complete a diagram or chart that draws together the learning for that day.

Transfer of learning and re-motivation can be easily melded in the closing. Students need to be able to use the knowledge, skills, and values learned during a class session in the future—in the course, on the bar exam, or in the profession after graduation. We can facilitate transfer by showing students how the learning from the class will be valuable in the future or by asking students to brainstorm about that.

The closing of class can be used effectively for feedback and classroom assessment activities as well. These topics are discussed in the next section of this chapter and in Chapter 7.

> **Thinking exercise**: Reflect on the last several class sessions you have taught. What happened in the last few minutes of those classes? Keep track of what happens in the last few minutes of the several classes you teach. How can you maximize the effectiveness of your closings?

Feedback

Research clearly establishes the central role that feedback plays in effective teaching and learning. We cannot overstate how firmly we believe that feedback should be a part of our course design, class planning, and the teaching/learning activities we use with our students. Nevertheless, we each struggle with the challenge of turning those beliefs into reality in our teaching.

To help you, and to help ourselves, meet the challenge, we have addressed feedback in several chapters of this book. Chapter 5 explores means to encourage students to give themselves feedback through reflection on their learning. Chapter 7 discusses Classroom Assessment techniques, designed to give students and teachers feedback on student learning. Chapter 7 also explains the use of rubrics, quizzes, and practice exams as learning tools and feedback devices. Chapter 8 focuses on formative feedback to teachers through self reflection and information gathered from students, colleagues, and consultants.

Our emphasis here is on the design of class sessions to include feedback on student learning. Our major point is that as we design class sessions, we should look for ways to incorporate formative feedback. By the end of the course, feedback should have been part of many class sessions.

We can design feedback to occur at various points in a class session.

- **Opening.** A feedback activity is an excellent way to gain students' attention and to build a bridge to prior learning. Class could begin with a short multiple-choice quiz that addresses key concepts from a prior classes and important aspects of the current class. The quiz could be on a handout, a slide, or with a "clicker" system. Immediate feedback should follow the quiz.

- **Body.** During the bulk of the class period, feedback can vary from simple to elaborate. For example, when a student performs a skill well, we can call attention to it briefly — "Jan just synthesized a line of cases by …" or "Fran drafted an excellent set of interrogatories that…." Or we could spend half of a class period going over the rubric for a practice exam and involving students in assessing their exam performance.
- **Closing.** By reviewing the class objectives or summarizing the major points for the class (done either by the teacher or students), the students get feedback on the critical content, skills, and values they *should* have learned that day. Or the class could end with a problem that integrates the learning for that day — feedback on the appropriate analysis could be immediate, happen via the course web page, or be part of the opening of the next class.
- **After class.** Feedback on quizzes, problems, hypotheticals, outlines, etc can take place in a discussion on the course web page, via an applicable CALI exercise, or one-on-one in the teacher's office. We can facilitate this type of feedback by initiating the web-based discussion, recommending an applicable CALI exercise, or announcing our willingness to meet with students to review their efforts.

We can design feedback to come from a variety of sources. We believe that a primary obligation of effective teachers is to take the lead in providing feedback to students. Sometimes that obligation means that we will provide the feedback directly: providing clear feedback to students' oral responses in class; drafting a practice exam and a score sheet; composing a hypothetical and going over the appropriate analysis in class; critiquing student performance of an interview; meeting with students outside of class to review a portion of a student outline; or commenting on drafts of papers. Other times we can fulfill our obligation by facilitating feedback from other sources: creating a detailed rubric that students can use to assess their own performance; drafting a form that students can use to provide feedback on one another's oral arguments or presentations; creating an online discussion in which students comment on each other's analysis of a hypothetical; calling students' attention to CALI exercises and exam books that students can use for practice and as sources of feedback.

Materials

In the context of class session design, materials include both print and electronic resources that students will use outside of class or that students and teachers will use during class. Examples include readings, websites, pictures, videos, computer exercises, handouts, slides, objects, and items written on the board or a flip chart.

We can choose and design materials to perform four basic functions:

Achieve class objectives. Just as class objectives drive our choice of instructional activities and feedback, they inform our selection of materials. The primary function of materials is to facilitate student learning of the content, skills, and values that are the focus of the class session.

Guide student preparation. Much of the material we choose is designed to be used by students outside of class to prepare them to participate in a meaningful way during the class session.

Support instructional activities. Once we decide what instructional activities will take place in the class opening, body, and closing, we are ready to select material to support our teaching of each portion of the class.

Facilitate feedback. Except for feedback that happens spontaneously during class, feedback depends on material—quizzes and rubrics for example.

The four functions of materials provide guidance on the types of materials we should select for each class. Different class objectives, instructional activities, and feedback call for different types of materials. Several additional considerations apply regardless of the type of material. Effective materials are selective, variable, focused, and interactive.

Selective. For virtually any topic we address in class, we could find hundreds of pages of text (cases, statutes, articles) along with websites, pictures, and videos. Consequently, for every class session, we are choosing a tiny slice of the available material. What should guide those choices? First, we should select the material that is most relevant to our class objectives. Perhaps the cases, statutes, problems, and articles selected by the casebook authors will be relevant—and perhaps not. Second, we should limit the material we assign to students to a reasonable amount. We believe that the traditional guideline of two hours of student preparation for each hour of class is reasonable. If we expect students to read, brief cases, and generate responses to problems, a sixty-page assignment is not reasonable for a one-hour class. Instead, we can require the most relevant twenty pages and alert students to supplemental material that they can explore if they want to broaden or deepen their understanding.

Selectivity applies to our use of materials during class as well. Research shows that students will copy verbatim anything we write on the board or project on a screen. The words or diagrams we write and project go directly into our students' notes. So we should be thoughtful about those words and images. Less is more. A few key phrases or a clear, simple flow chart will aid student learning more than a board covered with our writing or slides jammed with text.

Variable. Variety in materials is a virtue for several reasons. In modern life, we get information from both print and electronic sources. Our class materials should reflect that reality. We miss opportunities to enhance our teaching and our students' learning if we march through the casebook without incorporating relevant stories, documents, and images. Further, variety makes our classes more interesting. Each time we shift material in the classroom, we grab attention. When we distribute a handout, project a picture, show an object, run a short video, most students are alert and on task. However, most students' attention will wane if we proceed through a dozen slides or show a forty minute video. In addition, because of our students' range of learning styles, different students will respond more favorably to different types of materials. Some students hone in while reading and briefing cases. For other students, a picture really is worth a thousand words. Some students learn deeply through a CALI lesson, while others need to work with real documents (contracts, wills, pleadings).

Focused. One way to facilitate student preparation for class is to provide questions about the material before class. These questions allow students to focus their preparation, just as a lawyer prepares for the issues that will be central to a motion hearing. We will ask other many questions in class as well, just as judges ask lawyers questions in court. We can provide the advance questions to students in writing via a supplement, webpage, email, or a handout. Illustration 4-6 contains questions that address doctrine, skills, and values.

Illustration 4-6. Focus Questions

Doctrine Questions — Case
Parklane:
1. Define offensive issue preclusion.
2. What incentives does offensive issue preclusion give plaintiffs?
3. What test does the Court adopt for offensive issue preclusion?
4. Should the Court have decided to prohibit offensive issue preclusion in all cases?

Doctrine Questions — Statute
Clean Air Act sections 108 and 109:
1. What are National Ambient Air Quality Standards (NAAQS)?
2. What factors is EPA required to consider when setting NAAQS?
3. Why did Congress prohibit EPA from considering cost when setting NAAQS?
4. Should the CAA be amended to allow EPA to consider costs when setting NAAQS?

Skills Questions — Analysis
Identify five elements of statutory analysis that the Supreme Court employs in *Sweet Home*. Apply the elements of analysis to the problem following *Sweet Home*.

Skills Questions — Fact Investigation
Tomorrow in class you will depose Ms. Dominguez. Read the material on conducting and defending depositions at pages 33-35 in the supplement. Prepare at least five questions you would like to ask Ms. Dominguez.

Values Questions
Identify at least three ethical issues you see in *A Civil Action*. Assess the professionalism of Schlictmann, Facher, Cheeseman, and Skinner.

We can use focus devices in material we prepare for use in class. For example, we can focus student's attention in handouts and on slides through any of the following:

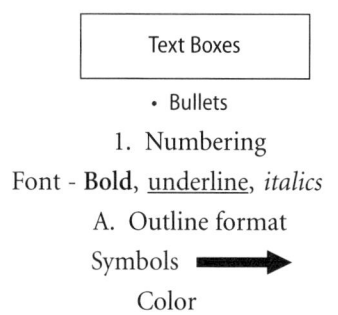

Text Boxes

- Bullets

1. Numbering

Font - **Bold**, underline, *italics*

A. Outline format

Symbols ➡

Color

Most of these focus devices apply to material we write on the board during class as well.

Interactive. Much of the material we assign to students is designed for students to read, such as cases, statutes, and articles. Likewise, materials we use in class are often intended for students to read or view, including slides, handouts, pictures, and diagrams. This type of material is valuable for presenting doctrine, policy, analytical frameworks, and theory to students. To maximize the effectiveness of material in achieving class objectives, we should look for ways to make materials interactive as well.

Simple techniques can add interactive features to many types of materials.

- **Readings.** The most passive use of readings is to simply assign pages. We can encourage more active reading by giving students focus questions (discussed above) or by asking students to do something with the reading—brief a case, apply a statute to a problem, or synthesize the law and policy from the material for the previous several classes.

- **Videos.** Short video clips relevant to the class objectives can be powerful teaching and learning tools. Videos are readily available on websites such as www.youtube.com. Books such as *Reel Justice* describe portions of movies that illustrate doctrine, skills, and values. We can make the clips even more effective by providing students with questions or problems to focus their attention.

- **Slides.** Presentation software, such as PowerPoint, allows us to produce slides that transmit information and images to students. These visual aids are helpful to many students. On the other hand, if we use slides extensively and the slides do no more than present information, many students will become passive receivers. We can change this dynamic by including interactive slides, that is, slides with questions, problems, quizzes, and hypotheticals designed to facilitate active student engagement in the classroom.

- **Whiteboards, flip charts, and projectors.** These basic tools excel at supporting discussions. We can easily capture student contributions to class discussions on the whiteboard, a chart, or a document projector.

- **Word processing software.** We can accomplish the interactive aspects of presentation software and whiteboards by projecting a document on a screen in word processing software. The document can include questions, problems, quizzes, and hypotheticals. We can capture student contributions during class discussion and send the document to students after class if we desire.

- **Diagrams, flow charts, and tables.** These tools, which education experts refer to as graphic organizers, can be excellent devices to organize concepts and illustrate the interrelationships among ideas. Better yet, we can provide students with partially completed or blank diagrams and tables, and have them complete them before or during class. For example, Illustration 4-8 is a simple blank chart that helps students synthesize two cases.

Appendix 4-1 contains other examples of charts, tables, and diagrams.

- **Handouts.** We can accomplish many of the functions of materials with handouts, distributed in either paper or electronic form. Handouts can include readings, pictures, questions, problems, hypotheticals, quizzes, rubrics, flow charts, and diagrams. The interactivity of a handout we design for use during class depends in part on how we incorporate white space. Illustration 4-9 contains portions of a handout designed to support a fifteen minute lecture/large group discussion on three United Nations organizations. Students reported that their active engagement, in terms of taking notes and making comments, was lowest in Section 1, higher in Section 2, and highest in Section 3. This result is consistent with studies that have compared the learning results of (1) students given the professor's notes, (2) students given a bare-bones outline into which they can take notes, and (3) students given nothing. The students in group (2) learned more than the students in groups (1) and (3), and the students in group (1) and (3) learned at about the same level.

4 · DESIGNING EACH CLASS SESSION   81

Illustration 4-8. Case Synthesis Chart

	Hansen (1958)	McGee (1957)
Issue		
Holding		
Defendant's contacts		
Reasoning		
Distinction between cases		

Illustration 4-9. Handouts and White Space

1. Commission on Sustainable Development.
Origin — Rio Conference
Program areas
    Agenda 21 implementation
    Reports on the sustainable development efforts of each country
    Technology transfer
Successes
    Information and Monitoring — e.g., Annual foreign aid target of .7GDP
    Forum for nations to discuss sustainable development
www.un.org/esa/sustdev National Sustainable Development Strategies

2. United Nations Development Program (UNDP)

www.undp.org Millennium Goals

3. United Nations Environmental Programme (UNEP)
Origin _____
Headquarters _____
Funding/Budget _____
Successes
    Environmental Law _____
    Clearinghouse _____
    IEL agenda_____
www.unep.org Thematic Areas

Evaluate and Revise

In Chapter 3 we extolled the virtues of a systematic, reflective, continuous process for evaluating and revising our course designs. We urge you to engage in a similar process for your class design decisions.

The evaluation and revision process can be quite simple. After class, spend five minutes reflecting. Were the class objectives achieved? How effective were the opening and closing? The teaching and learning activities? Would other grouping strategies have worked better? Did you provide feedback to students? Were the materials appropriate and effective? Memorialize your reflections in writing and keep them someplace that you will not lose them, such as with your notes for the class or in a teaching log.

The next time you teach the class, begin your preparation by reviewing your reflections. Then, after considering the new context that will apply the next time you teach the class, make appropriate revisions in the class objectives, instructional activities, feedback devices, and materials.

We believe that there is no such thing as a perfect class session. We do not seek perfection in our classes. Instead, we strive to make incremental improvements in our classes over time. The five-step class design process helps us, and can help you, improve teaching and enhance students' learning class-by-class.

Sample class designs

Illustrations 4-10 and 4-11 are examples of class plans that incorporate the five design elements discussed in this chapter.

Illustration 4-10. Civil Procedure Class Design—Discovery Obligations and Sanctions

Context
Civil Procedure is a two semester, first year, required course with an enrollment of 70 students. This 50-minute class session takes place in the last week of class during the first semester.

Class Objectives
As a result of this class students will be able to:
- Define the obligations the Federal Rules of Civil Procedure place on attorneys when they respond to discovery requests;
- Identify the policies supporting the Federal Rules of Civil Procedure sanction provisions for discovery abuse;
- Evaluate attorneys' discovery behavior and justifications based on the obligations imposed by the Federal Rules of Civil Procedure; and
- Articulate their views of the effects of discovery behavior on professional reputation and responsibility.

Instructional Activities
- Before class. To prepare for class, students read a case and a Federal Rules of Civil Procedure in light of focus questions about the case and rule.
- Opening. Share objectives with students, brief review of discovery sanction law explored in previous classes, describe the substantial national influence of the case.
- Body. Address ten questions about discovery obligations, policy, strategy, and ethics. Divide class into ten small groups — each group addresses one question. Then each group reports to the class their response to the question. Large group discussion of issues raised.
- Closing. Two minute writing exercise in response to the prompt: "The lesson of *Fisons* for me as a lawyer is...."

Feedback
- During small group activity, teacher interacts with groups to keep them on track.
- After class, teacher compiles themes from student responses to writing exercise, posts the document on course web page, and begins next class with teacher and student comments on the themes.

Materials
- Reading — ten-page case from casebook, one-page rule from statutory supplement, and five focus questions from course supplement drafted by teacher.
- Handout with ten questions and writing exercise prompt in a text box
- Word document projected on screen to memorialize student responses to questions
- Document compiling themes from writing exercise posted on course web page

Illustration 4-11. International Environmental Law Class Design — Drafting Fundamental Principles

Context
International Environmental Law (IEL) is an upper-level, elective course with an enrollment of twenty-four. This 50-minute class takes place in the first third of the course. It is the first class of a three-class simulation to draft and negotiate a world environmental charter.

Class Objectives
As a result of this class, students will be able to:
- Define four principles of IEL;
- Develop a negotiation position based on research about a country other than the US; and
- Draft four world charter principles from the perspective of a country other than the US.

Instructional Activities
- Before class. Students are assigned a country to research on the US State Department web site. Students read text about fundamental principles of IEL.
- Opening. Teacher presents overview of the three-class simulation — drafting, bi-lateral negotiations, multi-lateral negotiations. Teacher shares class objectives with students.
- Body. Students work in groups of four, chosen by the teacher to achieve gender balance. Each group drafts four world charter principles from the perspective of their assigned country.
- Closing. Large group discussion debriefing drafting exercise. Teacher previews the next class.

Feedback
- While students are drafting principles, teacher circulates among the groups commenting on draft principles.
- When all groups finish drafting, large group discussion on the challenges of drafting charter principles.

Materials
- Reading. Twelve pages from the IEL text.
- Web research. US State Department website country profiles.
- Handout explaining the details of the three-class, world charter simulation.

Checklist for class design process

Illustration 4-12 is a checklist you can use as you work through the class design process.

Illustration 4-12: Class Design Checklist

❏ **Consider the context of the class:**
  ❏ Course context
  ❏ Student context
  ❏ Teacher context

❏ **Draft learner-centered, clear, concrete class objectives:**
  ❏ Knowledge (doctrine, theory)
  ❏ Professional skills (thinking, performance)
  ❏ Professional values

❏ **Choose instructional activities to achieve class goals:**
  ❏ Opening
  ❏ Body (teaching/learning activities, groupings)
  ❏ Closing

❏ **Provide feedback to students**

❏ **Select materials:**
  ❏ Use outside class (readings, CALI, Internet)
  ❏ Use in class (slides, whiteboard, videos, diagrams, handouts)

❏ **Evaluate your design**

Chapter 5

Student Motivation, Attitudes, and Self-Regulation

Introduction

"It's easy to teach 1Ls. But how do you motivate burnt-out 3Ls?"

"One day in class, I called on three students, and none of them were prepared. I just wanted to walk right back out of the room! What else could I do? "

"I want my students to develop a sense of professionalism and a commitment to the lawyer's responsibility to serve the community. But how do you teach values?"

"My students just want to be spoon-fed. They don't want to do any of the work for themselves. How do I get my students to take control over their own learning?"

Whenever we do faculty workshops on teaching—for our colleagues, at other law schools, at conferences—someone invariably asks us these kinds of questions. In our experience, it is not at all unusual for smart, dedicated, passionate law teachers to express concerns about motivating their students, about changing or developing student attitudes and values, and about training law students to be self-motivated, reflective, lifelong learners. This chapter is our effort to address those concerns.

We have chosen to join these topics in a single chapter because each addresses a different facet of what law professors perceive to be some of the emotional issues in the law school learning process. Motivating students, influencing them to change or adopt new attitudes, and inspiring professional growth all focus on the students as people and our role in the students' personal development.

This chapter addresses these concerns from several perspectives. We start by sharing the research on motivating students. We introduce the research on intrinsic vs. extrinsic motivation and suggest the gold standard for motivation, known as "flow," to which law professors can aspire. We then suggest some concrete things law professors can do to motivate their students to learn and facilitate flow.

After explaining what law teachers can do to motivate their students, we turn to a discussion of the research on attitude change, discussing the spectrum of possible attitude changes, the facets of attitude change, and the techniques law professors can use to facilitate attitude change.

Finally, based on the motivation and attitude change materials, we suggest concrete ways law professors can motivate students to re-think what they know about being learners and to choose to become self-actualized, reflective, lifelong learners.

Motivating students

Introduction

On the one hand, motivating students arguably is not really its own, separate subject but, instead, is a natural outgrowth of adopting the good teaching principles we describe in this book. As you read this discussion of motivation, you will hear echoes of other ideas explored in this book. On the other hand, teaching for motivation and interest is a specialized field in educational psychology. Educational researchers have conducted hundreds of focused studies in an effort to tease out the key triggers of student motivation. Out of the morass created by these many studies, some basic principles have emerged.

Educational experts describe the goal of motivation instruction as increasing the likelihood that students achieve the state known as "flow." In the academic context, flow refers to a mental and emotional state in which the student experiences a task as exciting and challenging yet attainable. The student feels confident yet pressed to grow, engaged yet not over-stimulated. Students who feel a sense of flow immerse themselves in the learning process. They feel less inhibited than normal and also feel in control. Even though the work may be challenging, they experience the work as effortless. In many instances, a student who experiences flow is so engaged in the learning process the student loses track of time. Most of us have had at least a few class sessions in which both we and our students have lost ourselves in the thrill of learning. Wouldn't it be great to have more such sessions? How can we systematically and reflectively teach for flow?

> **Thinking exercise**: When have you experienced flow? For example, you may have felt a sense of flow when you were immersed in preparing for class and figured out how to fully engage your students or while writing a law review article regarding a subject about which you are passionate.

One important distinction experts draw is between teacher efforts fostering students' extrinsic motivation and efforts designed to help students find intrinsic motivation. Extrinsic motivation, which was the early focus of researchers in this discipline, emphasizes things teachers do to reward student engagement and to impose natural consequences for student disengagement. In our experience, law professors interested in fostering student motivation tend to *only* use extrinsic motivational ploys, such as emphasizing grades, administering pop quizzes, considering class participation in assessing students' grades, or rewarding (with a small grade boost) those students whose class participation throughout the semester was extraordinary. Some teachers go one step further, privately thanking, right after each class session, those students who unmistakably engaged themselves in the class discussion.

While extrinsic factors can influence motivation, they seldom produce the long-range satisfaction and sustained interest possible when students are intrinsically motivated. In educational settings, intrinsic motivation refers to qualities and circumstances within the student or the learning activity that stimulate engagement in a course. We all have had students who simply seem to enjoy learning for its own sake (and, we suspect, many law professors fall in that category); such students engage in every one of their classes simply because they enjoy the process. Most of us also have had students who are excited by the subject area either because of their past experiences or their career plans.

Unfortunately, many of our students fall in neither the enjoy-learning-for-its-own-sake category nor the particular-interest-in-the-subject category. Recent studies have focused on techniques teachers can use to stimulate the development of intrinsic interest by these other students. These studies, taken together, prescribe a wide variety of choices for inspiring and motivating students; below, we describe the techniques best supported by this research. As you study these principles, you will encounter many of the ideas addressed elsewhere in this book. Many of the techniques that produce better learning also motivate students. This overlap should be unsurprising; most of us have a sense that our most motivated law students perform better in our classes. Because the discussion below is about motivation, we focus on the motivational implications of the principles we have elsewhere introduced.

Specific techniques

Teacher attitudes that motivate students. Teacher passion and confidence significantly influence student motivation. As we explain in chapters 1, 2, and 6, students frequently describe their most inspiring teachers as passionate about their subjects and about student learning and as confident in themselves and in their students' ability to learn. These attitudes help students discover the excitement that led their professors to become law teachers in the first place and to feel confident in their ability to learn what we want them to learn. While passion and confidence each are independently important, the significance of both increases when a law teacher adopts both attitudes; inspiring teachers make it seem as if their courses are an adventure in which everyone, including the teacher, will learn exciting new things.

Teacher passion for a subject can inspire students to be vigilant for the life- or perspective-changing ideas, issues, problems, and solutions that have excited their teacher. Students take cues on such matters from how we present them. Students are more likely to be excited if the law teacher sounds excited and explains why. The optimal moment for communicating this passion is during course transitions — when a course or a new topic starts; at this moment, the students are still deciding what they think about the subject.

Teachers can show passion for student learning by expressing excitement about students' insights, by making themselves available to students, by actively and explicitly looking for new ways to help students learn, and by treating student learning as the principle goal in their classes. If a student suggests a new insight or a new way of understanding a concept or explains a difficult concept well, expressing delight in this success and acknowledging the student's influence on your thinking can provide significant motivation for students. When a teacher communicates that the students can change the teacher's thinking or approach to teaching course material, the students are more likely to be motivated to engage in the kinds of behaviors likely to produce such insights. (We do have one caveat: Because students are unlikely to learn if they lack confidence in their teacher's expertise, some teaching experts argue that teachers should refrain from acknowledging the ways in which they are learning from their students until they have established credibility with their students.)

Law teachers can show their confidence (or a lack thereof) in themselves and their students by what they choose to teach, by the particular teaching methods they adopt, by the language they use as they teach, and by how they otherwise interact with their students. For example, the choice to teach difficult materials and to ask students to solve challenging problems manifests confidence in both the teacher and the students. The students get the idea that the teacher believes the students can learn anything.

Likewise, when teachers create learning activities in which students develop their own insights and must manifest their developing expertise, such as cooperative learning exercises, peer feedback experiences, and peer-to-peer teaching, the teachers convey their belief that the students are capable. Well-designed cooperative learning experiences show faith in students because they allow students to negotiate meaning among themselves—the students construct ideas among themselves rather than passively receive the ideas. When a teacher who is passionate about student learning organizes learning experiences that place students in the role of teachers—such as asking students to give each other feedback or to teach course material—the students infer that the teacher respects their abilities.

Very simple things, such as our body language in class, how we react to questions in class (as challenges or as learning opportunities), how we deal with student frustration (with encouragement or disdain), and our comfort in demonstrating our expertise while acknowledging our errors also express our confidence or lack thereof. For example, respectfully listening to students, and finding and reinforcing the insights embedded in students' comments, course webpage contributions, and questions show that we are convinced that the students are perceptive and have promising futures in the field.

These confidence-related techniques are crucial because so many students experience law school as overwhelming and become disheartened. By adopting these techniques, teachers can help students develop what educational psychologists refer to as an "internal locus of control" with respect to learning. In the context of learning, the term "locus of control" refers to how a student evaluates the causes of his successes and failures. If the student credits or blames factors outside his control, such as peers, teachers, and other conditions, the student has an external locus of control. If the student learns to recognize that successes (and failures) are products of persistence, effort and strategy choice, i.e., factors the student can control, the student has an internal locus of control. Having an internal locus of control means the student is a confident learner; as a result, the student is more likely to be motivated by the process of learning as an end in itself.

Authentic experiences, variety, and active learning. As we also explain in chapters 1, 2, 4, and 6, students learn more and learn it better when they engage in a variety of authentic lawyering experiences that involve active learning. Authentic experiences, variety and active learning experiences also can be motivational because all three help maintain student interest in the learning process.

By situating students in their new roles as lawyers, authentic experiences explicitly connect students' new learning with their career aspirations. The concreteness of this link attracts students' interest. Students develop the motivation to learn because the connection between what they are learning and what they want to be doing is direct and the consequences of not learning seem more significant. This strategy is particularly effective with law students and other graduate students because their employers, clients, and peers will expect them to use what they have learned.

Variety and active learning experiences can be motivating because they capture students' attention and minimize distraction. Changes in the learning process recapture students' attention and motivate students to continue trying to learn, especially if the overall cycle of teaching methods includes techniques preferred by the students. Active learning motivates students because it prevents them from mentally withdrawing. Instructional designers argue that an unappealing instructional experience is ineffective; students who must constantly sift through passive, single-method teaching are less likely to find the subject engaging and therefore less likely to permanently integrate what they are learning with who they are.

Structuring student autonomy. Student autonomy is highly correlated with student satisfaction. Thus, giving students power to make choices about how the class will be taught and what they will learn is particularly effective for motivating students. Having chosen for themselves what will be happening in the class and what they will be learning, the students willingly engage themselves. They also feel better about themselves because their professor has shown respect for their autonomy and competency, and the experience gives them more energy to invest in the learning process. Giving students choice also increases the likelihood that they will perceive that they are learning things that are relevant to their experiences and goals.

Disclosing learning goals, providing students with mechanisms to self-evaluate their progress, and explicitly explaining the criteria by which students will be evaluated (i.e., creating rubrics) also foster student autonomy. This information empowers students to control their own learning process. Students may also interpret these disclosures as evidence of your confidence that the class will be successful and the students will learn.

Goal-setting. Student goal setting has been a subject of frequent study. Students who set mastery learning goals not only get higher grades than students who set grade goals or who do not set goals at all, but also enjoy the learning process more and, accordingly, act more engaged. Mastery goals motivate students to persist until they learn well and, in fact, probably because they have chosen to persist, the students attach greater value to what they are learning. Consequently, you can motivate students by convincing them to set mastery goals, to monitor the attainment of those goals throughout the semester, and to evaluate their success.

Participation (role-playing). Engaging students in role-plays can be particularly effective for motivating students. As explained above, asking students to assume their future lawyer role helps students identify the importance of what they are learning. But role-playing also can be useful for motivating students in other ways. Asking students to take the various roles involved in a transaction or dispute can motivate them to master difficult concepts by providing context with which they may not be familiar. This technique is especially effective if the students bring strong but incorrect preconceptions to the area of law. For example, many students assume that the proper measure of damages in a breach of contract case is the non-breaching party's out-of-pocket expenses; many do not even consider the benefit of the bargain as a possible measure. By engaging students in a role-play as buyers and sellers, Mike has found that his students not only internalize the benefit of the bargain idea but also gain more robust insights into its limitations. Perhaps most importantly, role-playing can help students understand the perspective of clients, outsiders, judges, opposing lawyers, and others with whom the student will need to effectively interact. Appendix 5-1 includes some of the role-plays we have created in our classes.

Challenge, incongruity and conflict. Of all the techniques educators suggest as tools to motivate students to learn, incongruity and conflict is the one law professors most commonly use. The law school Socratic method focuses heavily on introducing students to considerations and ideas that either actually contradict their viewpoints or seem to do so. This technique effectively stimulates student interest because challenge is one of the two key components in producing flow. However, students cannot develop flow if they perceive success as unattainable. One problem with the law school Socratic method is that, in some classrooms, the law teacher fails to ensure that the students also enjoy success in addressing the incongruity and resolving (or at least understanding) the conflict. Just as challenge is motivating, unending failure is de-motivating. In fact, the research strongly suggests that law students suffer real losses in their sense of autonomy and competence as a result of the law school Socratic approach. Many become depressed, anxious, and disengaged.

Challenge works best as a motivational tool when the challenge is *both* reasonable and continuous. By sequencing course materials and learning activities so that the students' learning tasks are increasingly difficult, law teachers can make sure students get both the benefits of being challenged while also enjoying success and being reinforced for their persistence.

In addition, incongruity and conflict are not the only ways to challenge law students. Authentic lawyering experiences in which students must translate doctrinal concepts into work products lawyers regularly create (such as contracts, wills, pleadings, arguments, letters, etc.) often are more challenging than merely understanding the doctrine. Structuring a role play in which students must find a way to resolve a seemingly irreconcilable conflict not only can challenge students but, also, can inspire them and introduce them to the other, less competition-focused roles that lawyers play in our society.

Most law professors (and certainly Gerry, Mike and Sophie) have taught classes in which some students could more rapidly master many of the concepts and skills than their peers. In fact, each of us have had classes (such as remedies) in which some topics come easily to some students (e.g., the calculation of damages) while others topics seem to be easier for different students (such as weighing the factors involved in determining the appropriate scope and content of an injunction). If your students are mastering the various skills and subjects in your course at widely varying paces, maintaining the optimal balance of challenge and success can be difficult.

The literature suggests a few possibilities for addressing this problem. Many law professors do not realize that, under the stress of law school, praise and attention can keep students quite motivated. Students who are enjoying substantial success feel rewarded, and students who are struggling view such praise as confirmation that they are enjoying at least some success. Finding ways to reward success that seem to naturally flow from the students' success benefits their learning; arranging natural consequences intrinsic to success in learning the material is even likely to be more effective. One possibility is allowing students who demonstrate mastery to move on in a way that doesn't leave the other students feeling even further behind. Consider creating challenging and realistic problems specific to each subject area so that students can learn at their own pace. Another possibility is to ask the speedier students to mentor the students who have not yet finished. This approach benefits both groups of students.

> **Thinking exercise:** What can you do to maintain challenge for your students who have a learned a topic quickly while not overwhelming your students who need additional time to master that particular concept?

Reinforcement. Reinforcements also can be effective in motivating students. In general, however, reinforcement tends to focus students on extrinsic rather than intrinsic goals and therefore is less likely to persist as a motivator. Effective reinforcements include praise, public recognition, and unexpected prizes. Reinforcement also can take the form of eliminating an obstacle or hurdle that is unattractive to your students, such as allowing students to pass their way out of having to complete an exercise. In contrast, threats, surveillance practices, and punishments are less effective in stimulating motivation. These techniques tend to produce student anger, negativity and, in some instances, rebellion.

Two other principles of effective reinforcement are worth noting. Intermittent reinforcement, in which the grant of a reward is uncertain and therefore a surprise, is the most powerful form of reinforcement. If you have gambled money or played golf, you probably already understand intermittent reinforcement. Gambling activities and golf are compelling because the occasional success is exciting and because gamblers and many golfers never know when they will again enjoy success. Thus, rather than always reinforcing student success or effort, consider doing so randomly.

In addition, students need the most reinforcement when they are first trying out a new skill. This early reinforcement encourages them to persist when they encounter difficulty. You can later make the reinforcement intermittent.

Illustration 5-1 summarizes the choices available and our sense of the considerations that can guide your strategy planning.

Illustration 5-1: Techniques for Motivating Law Students

Technique	Keys to Using Technique Effectively	Significant Caveats (if any) in Using Technique
Teacher passion and confidence	• Passion for subject and for student learning • Confidence in teacher and in students • Foster internal locus of control over learning	No significant caveats
Authentic experiences, variety and active learning	• See Chapters 1, 4, and 6	No significant caveats
Fostering student autonomy	• Give students choice of coverage and methods (See Chapter 6) • Disclose objectives and rubrics (See Chapters 3, 4, and 7)	No significant caveats
Goal-setting	• Encourage mastery learning goals	No significant caveats
Participation (role-playing)	• Use law practice experiences • Use to overcome erroneous student misconceptions • Use to expand student perspectives	No significant caveats
Challenge	• May include Socratic-style questioning • Expand to law practice challenges • Create challenge for students who learn quickly by creating additional exercises or structuring mentoring relationships	• Balance challenge and success
Reinforcement	• Use praise, public recognition, unexpected prizes • Reinforce regularly at outset; intermittently thereafter • Avoid punishment	• Risk of emphasizing extrinsic rather than intrinsic goals

Teaching for attitude or value change or development

Law schools and teachers commonly assert that they want their students to develop the attitudes and values of professionalism, commitment to public service, sensitivity to diversity, respect for the rule of law, or belief in the value of reflection and lifelong learning. At the same time (and somewhat ironically), Sophie, Gerry, and Mike also have heard many law professors espouse the view that values cannot be taught or assessed. The research suggests students can be taught values. As you might expect, however, simply telling students to have a value is seldom effective. In fact, even if your students have agreed a particular value is worthy of adoption does not mean they have adopted the desired value.

General principles of attitude learning

Determining whether attitude-focused instruction has changed students' minds is difficult. It is impossible to determine in a direct way whether attitude-focused instruction actually has changed students' minds. While a survey would capture some sense of students' opinions, there is reason to doubt attitude survey results. Students who have received instruction directed at attitude change, especially the very smart students who attend law school, are likely to know how their law schools would like them to respond to such survey questions. Consequently, experts in attitude instruction focus on *evidence* of attitude change; that evidence is measured in terms of student behavior. Students have acquired a desired attitude if they consistently choose to engage in behaviors that express the desired attitude. For example, if the goal is to convince students to be self-regulated learners, students who, without being asked to do so, set mastery goals, reflect on their learning process, seek opportunities for practice and feedback, and adapt their learning approaches based on the task, the time available, and their past results, have acquired the desired attitude.

More specifically, attitude experts conceptualize changes in student attitudes along a wide spectrum as depicted in Illustration 5-2. At one end of the spectrum, the student merely engages in behavior that evidences the attitude. In the context of self-regulated learning, the student follows the professor's directions to engage in self-regulating activities. At the opposite end of the spectrum (a result seldom seen in attitude instruction), the student has become so committed to the attitude that the student has become a role model or advocate for the behavior. A law professor who teaches self-regulated learning would fall into this category. In the middle of this spectrum are lesser degrees of

Illustration 5-2: Spectrum of Behavior Evidencing Attitude Change

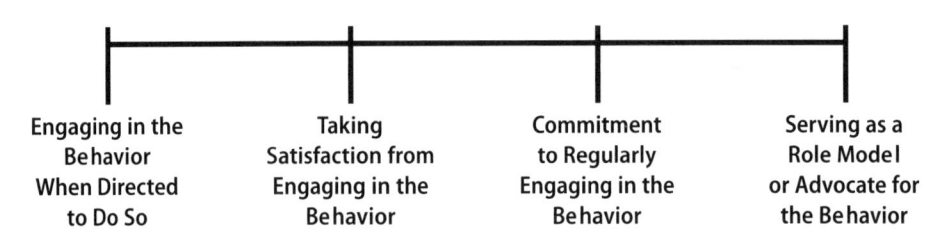

| Engaging in the Behavior When Directed to Do So | Taking Satisfaction from Engaging in the Behavior | Commitment to Regularly Engaging in the Behavior | Serving as a Role Model or Advocate for the Behavior |

dedication to the value, such as taking satisfaction when engaging in the behavior or committing to the behavior (choosing to engage in the behavior when no one else is watching).

It's also helpful to conceptualize attitude change in terms of three fundamental principles or elements: cognition, affect, and behavior. Cognition refers to knowing how to implement the new attitude. To implement the value of providing public service, for example, students need to know what types of public service they can provide as law students and lawyers and need the skills and knowledge necessary to perform those services. Affect refers to knowing why the behavior is valuable and therefore worthy of adoption. Behavior is implementing the attitude, especially if the person chooses to do so in the face of competing demands. Changing an attitude always involves a combination of engaging in the behavior and receiving feedback for doing so. For example, to develop an enduring commitment to public service, students need to engage in providing public service and receive positive feedback when they do so. To become self-regulated learners, students need to engage in self-regulation and receive positive feedback when they succeed. Illustration 5-3 depicts these three elements combining in a funnel because each is essential and interacts with the other two to produce attitude change.

Techniques for producing attitude change

Three commonly-used techniques that have been shown to influence attitudes: persuasion (trying to convince students to change by arguments and other messages), role model-

Illustration 5-3: Elements of Attitude Change

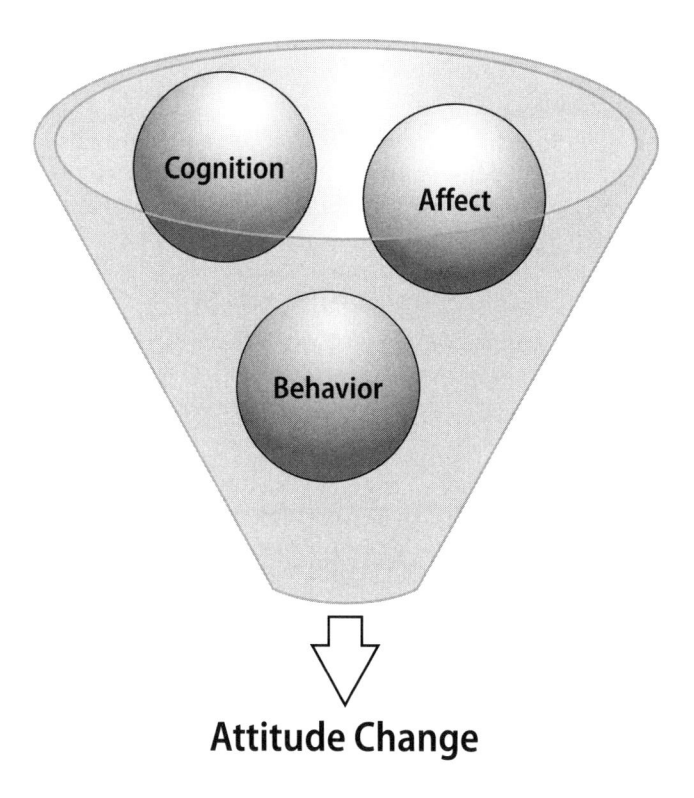

Attitude Change

ing (using others to demonstrate the efficacy of adopting the attitude), and experience (creating an occurrence that juxtaposes the benefits of the desired attitude with students' existing attitudes). The discussion below considers each of these possibilities in the order of least to most effective; that order reflects our sense of the effectiveness of each technique. Persuasion is the least effective technique and, in fact, can be ineffective if the students are highly committed to their existing views. Experience is the most effective technique, especially if the experience positively juxtaposes the desired attitude against the students' previously held attitudes. Role modeling is somewhere in the middle in terms of its effectiveness.

Persuasion. Persuasion has two facets: the characteristics of the arguments and the source of the arguments. Effective arguments for change must be easy to understand, well-structured, and convincing, but the key to success is whether the arguments address a need or problem the students regard as personally significant. Because the students often do not perceive a need or problem, it is helpful to think of persuasion as needing to address two issues: (1) the existence of a need or problem, and (2) the advocated behavior that addresses the need or solves the problem. Finally, the research suggests that persuasion is most effective if the persuader explicitly articulates the attitude change for which he is arguing.

The source refers to the person who is making the argument (the speaker or the author of the argument). A source is most effective when it has one or both of two characteristics: credibility (expertise or education) and attractiveness (similarity to students or fame). The research suggests that teachers can expressly establish the persuader's credibility. Accordingly, if you use a guest practitioner as a persuader, for example, make sure you tell the students about the speaker's expertise.

Upper division students are commonly-used for persuasion because of their similarity to the students. How many times you have had students adopt even crazy suggestions from an upper- division student (usually someone they bumped into in the student lunchroom) who claims to have done well in your class or to know "the secret" for doing well in your class? Using upper-division students allows you to undo some of the damage done by the lunchroom experts.

If you choose to use attractive persuaders, select a diverse group of persuaders and encourage them to open up with the students. A major factor in attractiveness is whether the students perceive that the persuader shares their attitudes with respect to issues other than those about which the persuader is speaking. By selecting a diverse group of persuaders and encouraging the persuaders to be open about themselves, their career goals, and their values, you increase the number of students who are likely to be influenced.

While persuasion can be effective and probably is the most commonly-used attitude-change technique, it typically only addresses the affective elements of attitude change. Persuaders only address why an attitude change is a good idea. Modeling adds in the cognitive element.

Modeling. Modeling, in the context of law school learning, refers to having a former student or a practitioner demonstrating and being rewarded for engaging in the target behavior. Credibility is as important for modeling as it is for persuasion. High credibility role models, people the students regard as worthy of imitation, are particularly effective as role models. Note that the above description of role modeling emphasizes the importance of students not only observing the role model engaging in the behavior but also observing the role model being reinforced for doing so. The combination of demonstration and observed reinforcement emphasizes the relationship between the two. For example, if students see a successful upper-division student engaging in self-regulation and witness the student being rewarded by good grades or exciting career opportunities, they are more likely to adopt the desired behavior. In this way, modeling addresses both the cognitive and the affective elements of attitude change.

Law professors have three potential sources of role models. First, it is important to recognize that you function as a role model. You represent the profession to your students (especially for first-year students), and you therefore serve as a role model whether you wish to do so or not. For example, the way we go about fulfilling our teaching role, in terms of our professionalism and commitment, is an opportunity to communicate our values. Students quickly decide for themselves whether you are engaged, prepared, and committed. In addition, students notice whether we practice what we preach in terms of service to our communities, institutions, peers, and them.

Second, as explained above in connection with the discussion of persuasion, upper-division students are very convincing with other students. Accordingly, having upper-division students demonstrate, for example, their efforts at reflecting on the learning process, and then publically expressing your admiration for their efforts, can be very effective in convincing students to become more reflective about their own studies. It would be hard, of course, for your upper-division students to model (during a class session) behaviors reflecting values such as professionalism and public service. The students may, instead, need to describe what they plan to do outside of class and, afterwards, report what they did.

Third, practitioners can make excellent role models. In particular, we suggest using former students who have become successful practitioners as role models. For example, having an alumnus reflect on something he did in practice (take a deposition, argue a motion, try a case) and brainstorm how he will change his approach the next time he needs to perform a similar task would be an effective way to model the value of reflection. Similarly, having a practitioner discuss his plans to do pro bono work and then report back on his experience can be effective. In this way, the practitioner helps students transfer the adoption of the value in law school to the form the value takes in law practice.

Role models are even more effective if the students try out the behavior themselves. Students are even more likely to adopt the desired value because the activity both engages them and addresses the behavioral element of attitude change and development. Experience, as we explain below, addresses all three elements.

Experience. Experience refers to students actually trying out the desired behavior and experiencing its benefits for themselves. Experiences are most effective if the conflict between the students' existing values and the desired value is readily identifiable and the students receive or discover the benefits (rewards) from engaging in the alternative behavior. Because such experiences expose a discrepancy between the students' existing values and the desired value, many educational researchers use the term "dissonance" to refer to this strategy.

The keys and the challenges are to design experiences that are authentic, give students as much autonomy in the process as possible, and allow students to experience the benefits of adopting the desired value. An experience is authentic if the students are engaging in the behavior in a way that is as similar to what they might chose to do in the future. For example, using actual course feedback (e.g., a grade on a paper, comments on a practice exam) as a springboard for getting students to engage in self-regulation increases the likelihood students will make the connection between the self-regulation activity and their other efforts at learning. An experience gives students autonomy if the students have some choice in the process. For example, asking students to engage in public service but to choose for themselves the particular form of public service in which they will engage gives students autonomy and increases the likelihood that they will value the experience they have chosen. If the students do not experience any reward from adopting the behavior, experience is unlikely to change their attitudes. On the other hand, if, for example, the students get a sense they are learning more by reflecting on their learning process, they are more likely to adopt this behavior as their own. Such natural rewards, rewards inherent in adopting the desired attitude, as you might expect from reading the above discussion on motivation, are more effective than grade or other extrinsic rewards because the natural rewards develop student's intrinsic interest in adopting the behavior.

Experience can address all there elements of behavioral change. Most obviously, experience addresses the behavioral element of attitude change because the students are actually implementing the desired behavior. Experience also addresses the cognitive element because the students are trying out the techniques for themselves and can receive coaching in their efforts in implementation. Experience may most effectively addresses the affective element because, rather than being told about the benefits or seeing someone else get the benefits from implementing the desired behavior, the students actually experience the benefits for themselves. Appendix 5-2 includes material on the use of experience in attitudinal learning.

Conclusion regarding motivational teaching strategies and attitude learning

Taken together, the recommendations explored above suggest a complex set of practices. The discussion below, describing what law professors can do to engage students to become self-regulated learners, reflects an implementation of many of the ideas explored above, both with respect to motivation and with respect to attitude change. Thus, it not only stands alone as an implementation of a commonly-stated law professor goal but also serves as an example of how the ideas might be implemented.

Engaging students to become expert self-regulated learners

This discussion offers some very specific recommendations of things law professors can do to help their students engage themselves in self-regulating their learning and, eventually, choose to be self-regulated learners. Of all the discussions in this book, this section is the only one to focus on a specific goal, getting students to adopt the attitudes, habits of mind, and activities of self-regulated learners. Accordingly, the discussion is very concrete. Because it is relatively easy to teach students the skills involved in self-regulated learning and quite challenging to convince students that self-regulated learning is worth their time and effort, this discussion is organized according to the three techniques for producing attitudinal learning: persuasion, role modeling and experiencing.

Persuasion

Practitioners who work in the field and are respected by the students can serve as credible persuaders and therefore be a useful part of a campaign to convince students to engage in self-regulation. In particular, practitioners can make the link between self-regulation in the context of law school and self-regulation in the context of law practice. Excellent practitioners continuously reflect on their learning and lawyering efforts, treating each oral argument, each client interview, each cross-examination, as an opportunity to improve. Practitioners also engage in reflection while they are practicing. For example, it is common for trial lawyers to take notes both on what witnesses say and on their reflections about the witness' demeanor and about opportunities for cross-examination. This approach increases the likelihood students get the idea that self-regulation is a core skill for lawyers.

Upper-division students who have done well in law school can serve as attractive persuaders. They can be particularly useful for convincing students that self-regulation, when used properly, doesn't mean students must work harder; self-regulated learners just work smarter. They can identify the ways in which self-regulation actually has improved the effectiveness *and* the efficiency of their study efforts. It is particularly important, in this context, that the upper-division students you choose are similar to the students. Choose at least one student with family obligations, one with work obligations, and one who was cynical about self-regulated learning when first introduced to the ideas. Using upper-division students in such a role is probably easier than you might imagine. The students feel flattered to be asked. In fact, a number of law professors around the country already use upper-division students as mentors or small group leaders.

Role modeling

While it is possible to structure learning activities in which a practitioner demonstrates a self-regulation skill, Mike, Gerry and Sophie only have used upper-division students and themselves as role models. Upper-division students can be effective role models because they have developed the desired skills in the same context in which the students need to develop the skills. Sequences in which the upper-division students quickly demonstrate how they continue to self-regulate their learning in their current courses and then supervise the students in using the skills are particularly effective. This approach addresses all three facets of attitude change and directly addresses the possibility that students might perceive that only law professors value self-regulation skills.

Most consistently, all three of us strive to be reflective practitioners of law teaching. We regularly seek information about student learning through quizzes, classroom assessment techniques, student advisory groups, in-class multiple-choice questions, and other mechanisms, and we reflect (explicitly and out loud) on the implications of these data for our efforts to be effective in our teaching role. We teach using graphic organizers and outlines and reflect aloud on their role in our own legal learning (e.g., "I never fully grasped this case until I created this chart." or "I created this flowchart so I could think through all the ways this issue might arise.") (For examples, see the graphic organizers collected in Appendix 4-1.)

The most effective tool for getting students to become self-regulated learners is having them try the techniques and experience how those techniques improve their learning process. Accordingly, the final section of this chapter describes exercises law professors can use to create such experiences. If you choose to implement any of these ideas, you may find it helpful to provide your students with readings about the skill before they try it out and to consider the ideal balance of classroom time and out-of-class work to maximize your limited time with your students.

Experiencing: getting students to take their "metacognitive pulse"

The remainder of this chapter consists of a series of exercises designed to be self-regulated learning "experiences" as we used that term in the above discussion of attitudinal learning. In each exercise, the goal is to engage students in reflective, self-regulated learning in the context of one of their regular courses. We also assume that the exercises would be directed and supervised by one of the students' regular law professors. These two principles are particularly important. Studies conducted both within legal education and outside legal education consistently have found that the best way to get students to make such practices a permanent part of their learning process is to have the students adopt the practices in the context of one of the students' regular courses in a session taught by one of their regular teachers. Stand-alone courses and orientation experiences may be effective in getting a few students to change. For the most part, however, because the students do not see learning experiences in stand-alone courses and orientations as a part of their "real" educational experiences, the students are likely to adopt the recommended practices only for the course or orientation or, at best, only for one semester. Unfortunately, soon afterwards, the students return to their old, comfortable practices.

In fact, students are most likely to permanently adopt such practices if they have experiences in several of their classes. This approach ensures that students do not perceive the experiences (and the suggested activities and attitudes) as idiosyncratic to one professor. If all or most of the students' law professors teach the students to engage in self-regulated learning, the students will perceive that this skill set is at the core of what they should be learning in law school.

We refer to these exercises as getting students to take their "metacognitive pulse" because the exercises are intended to function in ways that are similar to checking your heart-rate while exercising; the students engage in a self-regulation skill and quickly reflect on the implications for their learning (i.e., they engage in metacognition). In general, these exercises have two key components from which law professors can generalize: (1) guided practice, and (2) reflection on results.

One last point about progression is worth considering. As we explained in Chapter 3, instruction should be sequenced from easy to hard so that students receive reinforcement and experience success as they progress towards mastery. In the context of building students' self-regulated learning skills, this progression is slightly modified: students should progress towards independence as they build their reflection skills. Thus, students should be directed to adopt particular strategies early in their process and, later, encouraged to select and implement their own choices of strategies.

Guided journaling. The simplest way to get students to engage in reflection is to ask them to keep a journal about their learning process. Make sure you give them specific writing prompts rather than just telling students to write in their journal or just engage in reflection. Novice self-regulated learners need more guidance, and the research suggests that students perceive unguided journaling as "busy work" or otherwise useless. Generally, for each entry, encourage students to write about three topics: (1) description of the practice—what did the students do; (2) reflection on the experience—how effective was the strategy, how does the strategy compare to other, alternative strategies the students might have adopted; and (3) future planning—how will the students' results and reflections affect future efforts to accomplish the same general task. However, it is also useful to get students to write about and assess their progress towards achieving goals (for the course, for their professional development, for their development of self-regulation skills).

Another crucial condition for productive student journaling is that the students' reflection process must be spread out over time. Sometimes, when busy students are assigned to keep a journal, they choose to procrastinate and complete the entire assignment just before it is due. This approach greatly decreases the chance that students will learn anything of value from the experience and increases the likelihood the students will see the experience as busy work. Consequently, it helps to prompt students to engage in the reflection in a way that reminds them to journal on no less than a weekly basis and encourage them to establish a routine for their journaling.

Moreover, the most significant benefits occur when students look back over past journal entries and draw larger conclusions about their learning processes, strengths, weaknesses, and areas for improvement. Students are unlikely to engage in this behavior absent prompting. Consequently, it is effective to direct the students to look over a series of past journal entries and identify larger themes in their learning processes.

Students also are more likely to value the experience if they know how the journal will be used: Will it count towards their grades? Will the entries be shared with the rest of the class? Will anyone respond to their entries? Who? In particular, feedback on entries is considered a crucial prerequisite to making the experience valuable for students. It's also helpful to assure students will not lose credit for grammatical and punctuation errors. Finally, students may need you to be explicit about the benefits to them of journaling.

Dedicated reflection forum: online class journals. There also is some evidence for the efficacy of a collaborative journal in which both the students and the teacher reflect on the learning process. The easiest way to do so is on your course webpage, but you also could have the tech people at your law school set up a listserv for this purpose. Encouraging everyone in the class to reflect on their learning process with each other may also offset some of the competitiveness common to law school cultures. One major advantage of having an all-student course journal is that it is easier to provide feedback in a way that reaches all of your students. Mike has tried this approach on his course webpage with mixed results; he had one class in which a wide variety of students frequently posted ideas, suggestions, helpful information and links to the "course journal" forum he created, and he had one class in which the students were reluctant to share and seldom did so. Most of his classes have fallen somewhere between these two extremes.

Attention-focusing exercise. This exercise is a quick and simple way to see the value of self-monitoring for attention. As we explained in Chapter 1, attention is a crucial prerequisite for all learning. Chapters 4 and 6 address things law teachers can do to retain or regain student attention. This exercise focuses on the students' role in retaining focused attention. The exercise is most effective at a time when you have been covering some very dry material by lecture or by traditional law school Socratic-style interactions. In the middle of the discussion or lecture, ask the students to write down what they were thinking about in the immediately preceding moment. Encourage them to be honest and communicate that you are looking for people who weren't focusing on the lecture or discussion. Solicit a few examples and then ask the students to write down what the exercise teaches them about self-monitoring for attention.

Reflective reading exercise. A series of five studies on law student reading have found that successful law students read court opinions differently than their less successful peers and much more like successful practitioners and judges. (Interestingly, there are no studies that have found a correlation between case briefing and law school grades.) Two key reading characteristics of the successful students are: (1) they are more likely to argue with the author of the opinion while reading the opinion, and (2) they are more likely to vigilantly monitor their comprehension, by brainstorming examples of the principles discussed in the cases. Consequently, a nice variation on case briefing expectations would be to ask students to come to class with three points made by the courts with which they disagree and two examples of each of the principles discussed by the courts. You may also want to ask students to develop two non-examples (see Chapter 3 for an explanation of the term "non-examples"). In class, rather than doing a typical facts-issue-holding discussion, engage students in comparing, with each other, their critiques and their examples (and non-examples). Conclude by having the students compare how well they understood the cases for which they have done traditional case briefs and the cases they read for this exercise. These reflections will guide students in making good choices in reading future cases. Even those students who feel they learned better by briefing will benefit; their sense of the value of briefing (to them) will be enhanced. You can provide students additional fodder for their reflections by having them take short, three-five question multiple choice tests on both sets of cases.

Note-taking reflections exercise. This exercise addresses two learning process issues. First, a significant number of students treat note-taking as a dictation exercise; they try to write down every word rather than trying to understand and take notes with an emphasis on writing down what they need to remember and focusing on comprehension. Second, students also learn more in class when they engage more deeply with the discussion. Consequently, starting a class by asking students to divide their handwritten notes or laptop page between space for notes and space for reflections and asking them to use the reflections space to come up with examples of the concepts or questions they have or reflections on things that are helping them learn. Asking students, at the end of class, to review their reflections and comment on whether taking notes in this way helped or interfered with their learning process can help them see the benefits of reflection for productive note-taking.

As an alternative, you simply can ask students to look over their notes at the end of class and identify any gaps in their understanding. It's particularly helpful if you also ask students to decide for themselves how they will remediate any confusion (e.g., e-mail the professor, ask a peer, review a supplemental text).

Organizational strategies exercise and debriefing. A particularly effective exercise for teaching students the value of imposing structure on their learning and for taking time to process the course material is to have 25 or 30 students each name one concept the class has studied and, as they do so, write the name of the concept on the board (in random order). Then, cover up the list and give the students two minutes to see how many of the items they can recall from memory. After the students correct their answers, conduct a class discussion in which you and the class create a mind map or hierarchy chart in which you structure the concepts into categories, sub-categories and sub-sub-categories (you also can create an outline but that alternative is the least attractive one because students already frequently are told they need to create outlines). After you have done so, cover up the list and the mind map and give the students another two minutes to see how many of the concepts they can recall. Most students will do better the second time (although you often will have one or two outliers who do worse or do the same). Conclude the exercise by having students write or discuss why most students do better the second time—because they have imposed structure and because they have mentally processed the materials.

Time management/self-monitoring logs. In a frequently-replicated set of studies, professors have asked students only to add one additional practice to their study practices, keeping a time management self-monitoring log such as the log reproduced below. The key components are: getting students to focus on mastery goals, on consciously deciding how they will study, and on evaluating their learning as it is ongoing. Other possible topics on which students can reflect include: where and with whom they will study, the presence or absence of distracters, when they will take breaks, and how they will remediate any confusion (if they were dissatisfied with their results).

Concept and Mastery Learning Goal	Study Strategy(ies)	Planned Time and Place for Study	Actual Study Time and Place	Ability to Focus	Results of Study Efforts

An expanded version of this time management/self-monitoring chart is available in Appendix 5-3.

Comparison of strategies exercise. To become expert self-regulated learners, students need to become experts in knowing which strategies work best for them. This goal requires students to try and compare their results in using the wide variety of strategies available to them. Thus, if you have students outline one week and do hierarchy charts three weeks later, having each student compare how well each strategy worked for that student (either as a free write exercise or in small groups) will reveal to the students not only their individual preferences but also the variety among their peers.

Exam or paper results exercise. Returning an exam or paper presents a particularly apt moment to engage students as self-regulated learners. At this moment, students are most interested in continuing those things that worked for them on the exam or paper and changing those things that did not work. Unfortunately, getting students to self-assess their work isn't easy. You may even need to establish some sort of a reward system: for example, you can ask students to complete a reflection exercise and promise those who do so access to a model answer to the exam or you can provide the model answer to facilitate student self-assessment and offer an additional practice and feedback opportunity to students who engage in appropriate reflection.

There are several keys to maximizing student learning in this context. First, a crucial skill of productive learners is their ability to self-assess their learning; expert learners "know when they don't know." Consequently, before the exam, ask the students to predict their results and, afterwards, ask them to compare their results with their predictions and grapple with the inconsistency (if any). Second, expert self-regulated learners attribute learning successes to effort and persistence and struggles to insufficient persistence or strategy choice errors. Accordingly, provide students with a list of possible causes of their failures to learn—all of the items should be related either to persistence or to strategy choice. Third, based on their results and their assessment of the causes of those results, students need to plan how they will improve their studying efforts in the future. For most students, it is also useful to ask them to remediate any confusion, i.e., correct any errors in their original paper or essay. A post-exam (or post-paper) student self-assessment and reflection form is available in Appendix 5-4.

Free writing re lessons learned. This lesson focuses on helping students self-assess what they have learned in a class session as they are finishing the session. Ask students an open-ended prompt, e.g., write about class today or, somewhat more narrowly, write about what you learned in class. Give the students a few minutes and encourage them not to edit or otherwise limit themselves. The idea is to do a true free write in the hope that their concerns and ideas about the class session will come to the forefront of their minds. This exercise works best with students who already are fairly sophisticated in reflecting on their learning.

Conclusion regard self-regulation exercises. Generally, you can ask students to engage in any self-regulated learning experience. For example, you can ask students to set and reflect on their attainment of mastery learning goals; you can ask students to invoke self-efficacy by recalling a similarly-challenging learning task and why they succeeded in learning, or you can ask students to take online or pen-and-paper assessments of their learning style preferences or personality types and then reflect on the implications of what they have learned for their law school studies. The key conditions to developing students' self-regulation skills are integrating these exercises into students' regular coursework, providing them with the opportunity to reflect, and giving the students feedback.

Checklists

Illustration 5-4 includes three checklists you can use to implement the ideas in this chapter: a motivation checklist, a teaching values checklist, and a teaching self-regulated learning checklist.

Illustration 5-4: Motivation, Attitudes, and Self-Regulation Checklists

Teaching for Motivation Checklist

This checklist summarizes things law professors can do to better motivate students.

- ❏ **Adopt attitudinal strategies**
    - ❏ Passion and enthusiasm
    - ❏ Confidence
- ❏ **Create authentic lawyering experiences**
- ❏ **Use variety of teaching techniques**
- ❏ **Structure opportunities for student autonomy**
- ❏ **Encourage student goal-setting**
- ❏ **Create non-threatening challenge, incongruity, and conflict to spark interest**
- ❏ **Provide reinforcement**

Teaching Values Checklist

This checklist lists the three techniques law professors can use to facilitate student attitudinal change.

- **Persuasion**
- **Role Modeling**
- **Experience**

Teaching for Self-Regulation Checklist

This checklist summarizes the things law professors can do to build students' self-regulated learning skills.

- **Persuasion**
- **Role modeling**
- **Experiences**
    - Guided journaling
    - Free writing
    - Attention-focusing exercises
    - Reflective reading exercises
    - Reflective note-taking exercises
    - Organizational strategies reflection exercises
    - Time management/self-monitoring logs
    - Comparison of strategies exercises
    - Exam or paper results exercises

Chapter 6

Teaching the Class

You've planned the course and the class. You have worked out the student learning objectives, materials, timing, and active learning exercises. You have a clear class plan (see Illustrations 4-10 and 4-11). You are ready. In this chapter we look at the nuts and bolts of "live" teaching. If you skipped to this chapter without reading the earlier ones, we gently suggest you go back.

There is a good reason that *Teaching the Class* is only one of eight chapters in this book. The in-class teaching experience is like the performance of a play, where you are the director and the actors onstage are the students. A good performance occurs after lots of planning and rehearsal. (Even the best improvisations come after extensive preparation and practice improvising.) Like a good performance, a live class session is both technique and art. Understanding the basics of teaching and learning, considering students' perspectives, and being thoughtful about course and class objectives inform what you do during the few minutes you and the students are all physically present in one location.

Keep in mind that each class is really four classes—the one you planned, the one you experienced, the one you wish you had, and the one your students experienced. As teachers we all have good days and bad. And we aren't always correct in our assessment of what are good and bad days. The three of us don't think there are "perfect" classes. At the same time, we occasionally experience that wonderful sense of flow.

There is also no single way to effectively teach the class. There are classes that are effective for some students some of the time; we hope to have effective classes for most students most of the time. But we can't be sure. We recommend that you intentionally engage in the process and learn as you go. (Chapter 8 has great ideas for efficiently using a "teaching journal"—one of the most effective ways to learn from and build upon your teaching practices.)

A few years ago, an expert on teaching and learning came to one of our institutions and sat in on classes for several days. At the end of each class she asked the teacher one question:

"Who in the room was acting like a lawyer?"

Certainly the teacher was, most of the time. Usually a handful of students were: the ones who were called upon, and the ones who volunteered. In most classes, that meant many students were not acting like lawyers. We may have wished that they were all vicariously engaging in the Socratic dialogue between teacher and individual student; the research does not support that hope. (Interestingly enough, the teachers responded with frustration to the outside consultant's question: "Why can't she just tell me what three things I need to do to improve my teaching?" Hmmm. Sounds a bit like our students' question, "What *is* the right answer?" and our answer, "It depends ...")

If you keep this fundamental question in mind as you teach your class—*who in the room is acting like a lawyer?* (Yes, this repetition is deliberate)—you will be more likely to stay focused on your learning goals and maximize students' experience. As shown in Illustration 4-5, when students act like lawyers they are likely to remember and develop higher-level cognitive skills. We'll say it again: the more the students are *engaged in acting like lawyers- speaking and doing -the more they are likely to learn.*

Another question to ask about live teaching is,

"Who is doing most of the talking in class?"

Too often, we perceive teaching to be about *what the teachers do* in the classroom. The focus is on what the teacher says and how the teacher presents information or questions. If we are not doing a lot of the talking, we fear that we are not teaching. We suggest that you adopt a different image of teaching when thinking about what you do in the classroom: **Teaching is creating a place in which students learn.** Creating a place in which students learn means that your role in the classroom is less about what you say and more about what students are doing.

From Chapter 3 and 4 you know students will likely learn more if you divide the course into units and sequence classes as part of those units. Within the actual classes, the most effective approach is to focus on one to three learning objectives per class. As you teach the class, try to ensure that most students are acting like lawyers as they engage in applying the learning objectives you have identified. This chapter suggests ways you can make this happen.

Create a positive learning environment where students feel that it is safe to take risks.

Before we get into the nuts and bolts, we suggest you focus on the "art" side of live teaching, the ineffable "feel" of the class. As you know from previous chapters, creating a positive learning environment is critical to student learning and self-efficacy. Across all domains, one of the key components of effective learning is being "community-centered." Having a positive classroom affect takes more than teaching technique and subject matter expertise. Creating and sustaining a place in which students learn means that we need to consider our values, attitudes, and the nonverbal cues we send students about our social and emotional engagement in the class. We want to build a classroom community where students experience flow. (See Chapter 5). Below are some suggestions and reminders about what you can do to help build a positive classroom environment.

Know and use students' names.

If you have a hard time learning names, practice with flash cards, make a video of students talking about their interests, or use other devices. If learning students' names is not feasible, we recommend that you use name tents (see Illustration 6-1) so that you can regularly use students' names during the class.

Be conscious of the messages you send.

Experts in communication tell us that 75% of our message is delivered by body language. (No wonder email works poorly for some messages—we can't read the cues!) When in the classroom, be aware of what your body language may be conveying to students. Eye contact, listening attentively, and projecting a sense of confidence and openness are as important as any specific technique.

Most of us aren't terribly good at faking strong emotions. If we are annoyed, angry or frustrated, we may well be transmitting that message through eye contact, tone of voice, or gestures. Students pick up on those messages. Are those the ones you want to send? Even if you are annoyed or frustrated, we encourage you to act *as if* you were happy to be in the classroom. Research shows that when we act *as if* we are positive and happy, our ever-flexible brains rewire our emotional systems so that we actually become more positive and happy.

Find an image of students that helps you visualize them positively. You may think of them as friends you have invited to a dinner party, offspring, or young relatives (how would I respond if my favorite niece asked that question?) Consider them future colleagues in practice or on the bench. Whatever you do, try to find something to be positive about.

Illustration 6-1: Name Cards

Using Name Cards

In classes of more than twenty, we find it helpful to have students bring "table tents" or "UN Name Cards" to class. These name cards have students' names printed in large font on the front and back. With the names on both sides, students can learn each others' names.

These cards are printed on heavy card stock paper so that they stand up and last for at least a few weeks. A faculty administrative assistant can print these off your rosters. On the first day of class, you distribute the name cards and make a heavy black marker available to those who want to be called by a different name.

Alternatively you can bring in photocopy paper, ask students to fold in half lengthwise and write their names in ALL CAPS on both sides, using a heavy black marker.

Encourage students to bring the name cards to class until you know all their names—even better, wait until all students know each others' names. (Sophie asks students to put the name cards in a book they regularly bring to class or tape to the back of their laptop so that they always have them with them.) The table tents help you and the students attach names to faces starting on the first day of class.

Practice students' names outside of class—a few minutes a day. Regular practice, a commitment to learning students' names, and using name cards enables most teachers to learn students' names within a few weeks, even in classes of over 100 students.

Be enthusiastic.

You may be sweating inside (we are often nervous before class) but your students need you to project confidence and enthusiasm. If we don't care to be in the classroom, students wonder why they should care about our classes. You can always find something to be enthusiastic about teaching. You may love the subject matter. Or love learning and being a teacher. Really appreciate that you are privileged to be a law teacher and have the benefits of that career. (After all, you worked to become a teacher and chose this profession, right?) You don't have to be ragingly enthusiastic about the particular subject so long as you are enthusiastic about students and their learning. You can show enthusiasm with small gestures: starting the class with a smile and "Good afternoon!" makes a difference.

Experts tell us that moods are catching and have serious health consequences. Most of us suspected this already, and now scientific studies back this up. Being around positive, empowered, and cheerful people builds confidence and self-efficacy. Being around grumpy, anxious people does the opposite. We don't mean to suggest that you should slap a fake smile on your face and keep it there; we do suggest that you find something you like about teaching that you can focus upon. Having sat in on many classes, we know how enjoyable it is to be taught by teachers who clearly enjoy students and teaching.

Model taking risks and acknowledging weaknesses.

It's ok to say, "Great question. I never thought of that. I'll have to think about it and get back to you." In fact, students greatly respect and appreciate teachers who are self-confident and excited enough about student learning to acknowledge students who come up with a new insight or question. Or you could say, "I'm going out on a limb here. I am not sure if this exercise will work, but I am going to ask you to engage in a different kind of learning activity today."

If you made a mistake (we've all made tons), tell the students. "Last class I gave you some misinformation. Let me try to clarify." It also helps students to know that you struggle. Let them know that you, too, have to work at writing complex prose, speak in public, and teach effectively. Apologize when you err. Apologies are not a sign of weakness. Admitting your errors and asking for students' pardon treats students with respect.

Envision yourself less as the "sage on the stage" and more of a "guide on the side."

Actively engaging most students in the class can be more work than teaching in the traditional way, but it is worth it if our students learn more effectively. In the effective live classroom, we are in the roles of coaches, managers, directors, and choreographers. We have expertise, but our main role is to help students learn, not demonstrate how much we know. (One educational expert uses the image of teacher as white water rafting guide. The guide has to safely navigate the boat through treacherous white water rapids but the guide alone can't do the job; the others on the raft have to paddle hard.)

As the coach or guide, let students know that you have high expectations for them, but that you do so because you believe that they can meet your expectations and that you will coach them to get there. As you know from the earlier chapters, these kinds of statements show students that you have confidence in them and helps them develop intrinsic motivation to learn.

Be transparent.

Explain to students what you are doing and why. Even if students want a concrete answer to an unresolved issue, explain why the answer is "it depends" and what it depends on. When you use different instructional activities, explain why, at least the first few times you use them. Be honest. You may say that there is no right answer, but you mean there is no *one* single right answer. Instead there is a cluster of right answers and a group of wrong ones.

Be authentic.

As the educator Parker Palmer says, "We teach who we are." If your style is to be self-deprecating and you are good at telling jokes, do so. But don't try to be someone you are not. Experienced teachers often say that it takes three years of teaching to develop your teaching persona. Pay attention to what feels right for you in helping students learn.

> **Thinking exercise**: Consider a few recent classes. Who in the room was acting like a lawyer?

The Nuts and Bolts

We've broken this part of the chapter into the following four main sections:
- Pre-class—the fifteen minutes before class starts
- Openings—the first five minutes
- Body—the heart of the class session
    - Instructional activities
    - Lectures
    - Questioning techniques
    - Addressing controversial issues
    - Visuals
    - Discovery sequence instruction
    - Timing
- Closings—the last five minutes

In your class, you want to tell the students what you want them to learn (opening of class), engage them in instructional activities to help them learn (body), and summarize what you wanted them to learn (closing).

Pre-class: the fifteen minutes before class starts

First, arrive early.

We recommend you arrive at least 15 minutes before class. If this session is the very first class of the course or you are new to the room, check out the room in advance. Identify how you plan to use the room. Practice using the technology (including chalk or markers) before you go live. (Will you need to bring your own markers?) If you plan to have students work in small groups, how will you arrange them? Are there columns in the room that might impede students' views of the board or projection?

During those pre-class minutes, re-check the room. If you are lucky, all systems are working, chairs are in place, and you can calmly set out any materials, handouts, project first slides, or write your objectives on the board. In the remaining minutes, you can casually chat with students who have arrived early, review your notes, take a deep breath, and focus on your learning goals.

Having such a smooth start doesn't always happen. We've arrived in classrooms to hear jackhammers blasting, experienced 95-degree heat, found computers and screens not working and, sometimes, discovered fruit flies buzzing around the trash can. Not the most conducive learning environment. You may be much more adaptable than we are, but we find encountering these kinds of problems disconcerting and stressful. Arriving early doesn't eliminate any problems but showing up early in the room allows you to learn about any problems and try to fix them before class. Even if you can't solve the problems, you have at least a few minutes to figure out how to work with them.

Arriving early is not always possible. Some classrooms are scheduled with only a few minutes between classes. In that case, you can arrive early and chat with students in the hall. Your effort to do so shows that you are interested in the students and committed to their learning, factors that help engage and keep students motivated.

Openings: the first five minutes of class

Consider the message you are sending to your students at the start of class.

In thinking about the beginning of a class session, where you make a powerful first impression, consider five of the elements of effective teaching and learning from Chapter 1:

Good teachers:
- Show respect for students
- Have high expectations
- Support and coach students to reach high expectations
- Are enthusiastic and passionate
- Are prepared and organized

Arriving early, giving students a roadmap for the class session, identifying the learning objectives, and being enthusiastic help students learn.

Provide students with the objectives at the beginning of class.

Because most students benefit from having the information in more than one medium, it helps to have a "road map" or outline of the course objectives provided visually *and* verbally. Visually, this goal can be accomplished on a slide, a handout, or on the board. Verbally, you can flesh out the objectives and provide the context of this class in the learning unit and in the course as a whole. Include the transition from the previous class and the context overall:

In the last few classes we were looking at a range of crimes, ending with murder. We looked at what a prosecutor would need to prove to charge a defendant with negligent homicide, manslaughter, felony murder, and first- and second-degree murder. In groups you made arguments applying the elements of those felonies to different factual situations.

Today we are moving from those crimes to conspiracy. Specifically, today we are investigating prosecution and defendant arguments for conspiracy and attempted conspiracy. We will be building upon the same skills—articulating the law, facts and policy—in making and responding to arguments.

You can further explain what will be happening in the body of the class:

Today you will be working with one partner to compare and analyze your individual responses to Problem 7-A, using cases A, B, and C.

It also helps to acknowledge when a particular set of cases or concepts or your objectives are challenging to a significant number of students. The students who have struggled and are feeling anxious will feel less stressed, and the students who mastered the materials will feel proud.

It helps here to see if students have any questions arising from the previous class sessions.

Questions or clarifications you would like at this point?

Pause. Practice being still and quiet. Mentally count to five to allow students a chance to gather their thoughts. If you don't want to respond to any questions, and are in a rush to move on, you are better off not asking.

If there are a lot of questions and you don't have time to answer them, you can answer a few of them and then move on, encouraging students to email you, talk to you after class or during office hours, or post questions or comments on a course webpage.

Alternatively, as suggested in Chapter 4, to assess whether the students are ready to move on, you could administer a short quiz or pose a series of questions before moving on.

I am handing out a quiz/problem/hypothetical scenario. Read through the facts and jot down your answer. When you have completed this, turn to two classmates sitting next to you and compare your answers. Then compare why you arrived at those conclusions.

You can then ask for responses or give students the answers to the problem. Clickers are a great tool for assessing how much students have retained from the previous class or classes.

Modifications—first day of the course; other significant classes.

On the first day of the course, your opening may well be longer. You may want to lay out more of the landscape, or tell a story about the course, the students, law practice, or yourself. It helps to recognize and honor that these days are the beginnings of a course. You may feel like you are just teaching another course in personal income tax; for your students, your course is likely the students' only such course.

Explain any policies for attendance, seating and using names. Some teachers like to be called "Professor X," others are comfortable with a range of names. One of our colleagues introduces himself by saying something like:

> *My name is Pat Davis. You can call me Pat, Mr. Davis or Professor Davis. I will call you by whatever name you prefer. Today I will go through the roster; let me know if I have mispronounced your name or if you have a different name you would like to use.*

If your class is different from the culture of other classes at your school because you don't call on students, have them work in teams, or involve them in course design, let them know why you are taking a different approach. As you know from Chapter 3, it's also a good idea to put this information in your syllabus. Use the time in class to reinforce major points.

> *One of the course goals is to have fun. This is because experts on learning have found that people learn better when they have fun. Humor, it turns out, lubricates the learning process. Sometimes students assume that having fun in class means they can expect easy grading. In this class, I have high standards and expectations for your performance, but I will do my best to see that we have fun learning. Let's not take ourselves seriously, but let's be serious about learning.*

You can further explain your views on teaching and ask for students' help:

> *We'll be using a variety of teaching and learning strategies in this class. I will lecture, ask you to do group work, in-class exercises, team-based exercises, and practice other lawyering skills. You all have different learning preferences and not all techniques may be ideal for you. I ask for your forbearance when we are using a style that works for others, but not for you.*

On days when students have experienced a crisis, you may want to delay the formal opening to allow a time for reflection, silence, and a chance to discuss. Whether a student has become severely ill or lost a family member, flooding has jeopardized area homes, or violent outbreaks have affected your students, you may not want to jump right in with the elements of copyright infringement. Instead, you could acknowledge the crisis and give students some quiet time.

> *As most of you may have heard, last night terrible storms attacked the west coast. I know that many of you have been concerned about family and friends who were in the area and whom you have had a hard time contacting. Let's take five minutes to sit in silence or write. At the end of that time, anyone who wants to can share thoughts about this tragedy.*

If this isn't your style, you might just want to acknowledge the event and move on. Be authentic and remember that students crave to connect with our humanity.

> *I heard about the shooting in City X yesterday and am very sorry for all those involved. If any of you would like to talk to me about it outside of class, I would be happy to do so.*

While not exactly at the same level, there are times when students are facing significant challenges, and it helps to acknowledge their distractions. We've noticed that many students hit the wall in November and March. As they face the pressure of final exams and the need to put together weeks of material, many students become tired and stressed. (Until she spent a year teaching in Arizona, Sophie thought that this only happened in the northeast and was due to the long, cold and dark winters.) You could say something like:

> *I realize many of you are in the middle of moot court arguments / interviews / extracurricular events / journal applications / midterms / writing assignments — let's take a poll. Raise your hand if you are feeling overwhelmed.*

Students frequently come to class with many other things on their minds. Taking the time to acknowledge that stress and then inviting them to focus on the class will help them engage in their learning.

> *OK, so many of you are preoccupied. For now, I am going to ask you to set those concerns aside for the next 55 minutes and practice being corporate lawyers.*

The beginning of class sets the tone and provides a map for the rest of the class. Use it to help your students prepare for their learning.

Body — the heart of the class session

The body of a class session is where you will be spending most of the class, focusing on your core learning objectives. What is it that you want students to learn by the end of the class? How can you make it happen? Think of yourself as having the total class time minus about ten minutes (five minutes for the opening and five for the closing.) Having a visual of your learning objectives comes in handy; if your learning objectives are present on a handout, slide or board, you are less likely to try to cover too much material or go off on tangents. Instead you will be more likely to honor your implied promise to help students achieve those objectives.

In thinking what you want students to learn, we encourage you to follow the suggestions in this and earlier chapters and focus on one to three learning objectives per one-hour class session. As we have explained, once you have identified the clear and concrete learning objectives for each class, you can work backwards to design effective class sessions. For example, if you want students to outline the steps involved in registering a new trademark, identify what they need to do and how you will know whether they have correctly outlined the steps. Sketch out how much time you want to have students work on each class objective. Remember that they are more likely to retain a deep understanding of this process if they are actively engaged.

Most teachers spend the body of class lecturing or engaging students in a discussion or both. For example, in a trademark course, the teacher lectures students about the requirements for registering a new trademark, providing a lot of content and information, and then asks individual students to verbally outline the steps for registering a different kind of trademark. You may also ask students about the legal authorities assigned for class, "Why in *Case B* did the court deny the registration after the lower court held...." Working through a series of authorities through questioning, students might be asked what rules, principles or policies they gleaned from the authorities. Under both these approaches, students would have been exposed to the material, and some students will actively have engaged in talking about it. A number of students, however, become disengaged during lectures or during the teacher's discussion with one or more of the students' classmates.

Instead, you could start the main portion of class with a question that encompasses your objectives. "How can a party obtain injunctive relief?" Tied to your learning objectives, one or more key questions can provide a unifying theme to the class. Like a musical refrain, the repetition of key points and concepts can keep students aware of what you want them to learn. Use the majority of the class time to engage as many students as possible in a variety of instructional activities. During these activities, repeat and flesh out your main question to keep students focused on the main learning objective. Provide closure to students as you go, summarizing and repeating important points.

Instructional activities

Use instructional activities that engage students, helping them practice acting like lawyers.

Students are engaged when they are:

- Writing
- Talking and listening
- Reading
- Reflecting

Illustration 6-2 lists five active learning instructional activities you can use in the body of your class. Each of these activities is described briefly below. When they are engaged in these activities, the students, and not just the teacher, are "doing the work"—practicing acting like lawyers. They are actively solving problems, thinking, talking, listening, taking notes, reading, and writing. When you use these techniques, watch the energy, volume, and activity in the class soar.

Illustration 6-2: Instructional Activities: Active Learning Selections

- **Think-write-pair-share**
- **Small group discussion**
- **Student-to-student group discussion**
- **Small group role-playing**
- **Point/counterpoint**

You don't need to be an expert in these activities to be an effective teacher. There are many simple, quick techniques that can be included in law school classes. Multiple sources list a range of techniques and how to use them. Start simple, start small, and give yourself time to work these into your classes and learn from experience. For each class, remember to ask yourself, "Who in this room is acting like a lawyer?" *and* "Who in this room is talking?" *Choose one or two new instructional activities a semester. Don't give up just because they didn't work as well as you hoped the first time or some students didn't like them.*

Ideally, use three or more different instructional activities per class. As you know from earlier chapters, variety is key to student engagement and learning. Variety keeps the class interesting, engages students in different levels of thinking, and addresses different learning preferences. When we recommend colleagues try different instructional activities, we often hear, "OK, but I already did that activity last month." The implication is that any approach other than the traditional Socratic-style questioning is a gimmick, and should be used sparingly. We suggest that you consider Socratic-style questioning as one kind of instructional activity (more about how to use Socratic-style questioning effectively below) and mix it with a variety of other instructional activities.

Think-write-pair-share. This technique is one of the quickest, easiest, and most versatile activities. Pose a question verbally or in writing. (Consider doing it both ways.) Ask students to think about the question for a minute and then jot down a response. Once they have completed their responses (one-to-three minutes depending on the complexity of the question) ask students to exchange their ideas with a neighbor. Ask them to discuss their answers and the reasons for them (one-three minutes).

Call on a few students to provide responses, or ask one or two students to volunteer his or her neighbor's response. Note responses on the board, enter and project them on a screen, or verbally reinforce responses. We have found that after students have talked with a neighbor, who has either confirmed the difficulty of the question, acknowledged confusion with the issue, or affirmed the student's response, a much greater range of students volunteer and are comfortable being called on.

Small-group discussion. Pose a question or problem that students must work together to solve. Students can collectively discuss and answer questions at different levels of thinking, e.g. What are the elements of the statute? Which element is at issue in this client's case? How would you describe federal preemption to a lay person? Contrast the courts' different tests for issuing preliminary injunctions.

As the groups work, you may decide to circulate among them, be available as a resource for students to call upon, sit in and listen to a few groups, or allow them to work on their own. There are trade-offs of each choice. If you circulate, you can identify and address any common areas of confusion and get a sense of how the groups are functioning. If you allow the groups to work on their own, at least some of your students may be more likely to take risks. Once groups have discussed their responses, call on a couple of different students — ideally those who have previously not contributed to the large group discussion — to talk about the group's responses. Once you have a response, invite students who had a different response to contribute.

A word about using small groups effectively. As noted in Chapter 4, small group assignments must have crystal clear directions. Specify an amount of time for students to work in groups. Allow less time than you think students will need, and add time if students are still focused and more time would help them attain the learning goals. You can gauge how things are going by asking the class as a whole or circulating and asking different groups whether they would like another couple of minutes. If all the groups are working on the same problem, avoid having groups do a "reporting back" where each group gives a presentation on the same topic. (The reporting back group responses get tiresome and most students disengage after a few minutes.)

Student-to-student group discussion. Ask the students to lead the discussion by calling on each other. For example, after posing a question about a rule, holding, factual analysis or other teaching objective, explain to students that the goal of the next few minutes is for them to achieve that objective by talking to and calling on each other without your involvement. You can start the discussion by asking a student, perhaps one who has previously not spoken, to respond to the question you have posed. After she or he has contributed, each subsequent student must call on the next one to further the discussion. While students talk and refine their understanding, you or another student can serve as scribe and note responses on the board.

Small group role-playing and simulations. Divide the class in sections, and assign a role to each. For example, in an employment law class, you might assign one group to the role of employees, one to employers, one to in-house counsel, and one to legislators. In small groups, ask the students to collectively outline the large-scale structure of their positions, using notes or bullet points. Tell them to think about the big picture, not get stuck on the particular words or polished language and note that they may want to start in the middle or end and bounce around as they work through the outline. One or two groups from each section could write their outline on chart paper, overheads, board or laptop, and then show the analysis to the whole class.

Point/counterpoint. From different sides of the room, ask students to take turns making their arguments. In this portion of the session, a participant on one side of the room will be asked to make one statement about the argument, and then identify someone on the opposite side of the room who will make the counter-argument. Continue for a few minutes as both sides of the room explore the analysis. At the end of this portion, students will be asked to raise their hands about whether they think, given the materials they have, what the strongest arguments are. (This one can also be done with a small prop, such as a squishy ball or soft toy that students toss back and forth across the room. Emphasize that the idea is to toss gently to another student, calling upon them by name, rather than demonstrate throwing prowess.)

Additional points about instructional activities.

<u>Keep track of the time.</u> Active learning instructional activities can take on a life of their own. Help keep students on task and focused on the learning objectives. If individual or groups of students finish an activity early, have additional instructional activities they can engage in.

<u>Close the loop.</u> After students have engaged in learning activities, help bring closure by explaining what they have done and reinforce the learning you have observed. You can summarize main points, engage in a whole-class discussion, invite students to share what they learned from the activity or clarify questions students have as a result of being engaged in active learning.

Common misperceptions about active learning instructional activities.

If you aren't sure about using these techniques, you are not alone. Many of us haven't been engaged in these techniques as students, and, when we have been, have not always been aware of what was going on. As a result, we tend to default to the teaching techniques we were exposed to. Before we discuss other instructional activities, we want to address some negative ideas teachers may have about using active learning activities.

<u>Active learning takes too much time in class.</u> A related concern is that we will be able to cover less material if engage students in active learning. Well-designed active learning exercises have been shown, however, to maximize students' deep learning of knowledge and skills.

<u>Active learning is touchy-feely.</u> As with any role, we have to be authentic to be effective. Some active learning techniques ask students to reveal more of themselves than they do in many other classes, such as when we ask students to write reflective journals or work closely with others. Reflection and cooperation are critical skills for success and satisfaction in law practice.

<u>Active learning requires a degree in advanced psychology.</u> Asking students to work together to solve a problem does not require extensive knowledge of group dynamics. What is important is to be explicit about directions and expectations.

<u>Active learning means that all control in the classroom is lost.</u> Creating situations where students are engaged may mean that the classroom "looks messy." Students are gesticulating, the noise level is high, and the professor doesn't look like she is doing anything. But, in fact, active learning requires more advance planning and allows exercises to proceed in a controlled fashion.

We admit that sometimes it is hard to reconvene the class as a whole once students have engaged in active learning. Briefly turning on and off the lights, calling students' attention to the class, giving students a warning about how many minutes they have left, and using their names "I see that Elizabeth's, Carlos's, and Kim's groups are ready to discuss their responses with the class.... Others?"

Lectures

Lectures can lead to significant student learning. They are most effective when they are:
- Short (fifteen minutes max)
- Adding valuable content
- Surrounded by other activities
- Supported by visuals
- Delivered effectively

Use mini-lectures.

Students have short attention spans. Studies show that, within ten minutes, students' attention considerably drops off. And no matter how interesting and dynamic we are as speakers, few people retain more than a small portion of any lecture. Make your lectures mini-lectures: limit them to fifteen minutes. Even better, keep them to ten.

Mini-lectures are highly effective in addressing students' misconceptions about a concept, giving feedback to students, or summarizing a portion of the class. Many teachers think they are effective when they give students a mini-lecture and then follow it with questions or problems for students to solve. Instead, mini-lectures are more effective when they are given to students *after* they have done some initial preparation and engaged in problem solving. Then students are primed to pay attention; they realize where they have questions and need guidance.

Add valuable content.

Anything you can deliver in print should not be included in a mini-lecture unless doing so will likely help students learn. Instead, in the mini-lecture build upon what you have assigned students to prepare in advance, or highlight important points that were not in written material or may need emphasis.

Surround mini-lectures with other activities.

Sandwich mini-lectures between a mini-quiz, problem, small group discussion, active learning technique, or other activities that engage your students. Include pauses between main points to allow students to catch up on notes, review, and consolidate their thinking.

Include visuals.

A picture says a thousand words, a movie even more. Use sounds, pictures, cartoons, graphics, charts, props and other material to embed the important points. With the abundance of images available on the internet, it is easy to find visual enhancements for your mini-lecture. It also is helpful to provide students with a bare-bones outline or chart into which they can take notes; the mental effort the students use to fill out the outline or chart helps hold their attention.

Deliver mini-lectures effectively.

Follow the basics of effective public speaking. Use a voice audible from the back of the room. Vary your phrasing and allow for pauses. Avoid speaking in a monotone. Move around. Make eye contact with students. Periodically include students' names, "So if Marcella was deciding to file a Section 1983 claim, she would..." Tell students which points are especially important and encourage them to write them down. Even better, repeat main points during the mini-lecture to reorient novice learners.

Questioning Techniques

Using questions or engaging in "Socratic" dialogue is what most law teachers think about when they teach classes. And for good reason. Questioning techniques can be one of the most effective ways to engage students in achieving all levels of critical thinking. (We're not going to get into the difference among the different kinds of "Socratic" dialogue, such as questioning the way Socrates did it vs. any other modification; we're just going to refer to it as Socratic-style questioning.) As with any other aspect of teaching and learning, we believe an intentional approach to designing and using questions will enhance student learning.

Like any other technique, Socratic-style questioning can be effective or ineffective, depending on how we do it. One of the greatest weaknesses of traditional law school Socratic-style discussion is that most students are not engaged. Certainly, the selected student is actively engaged in the one-on-one conversation with the teacher and receives feedback on her learning process. For all the other students in the class the learning process is vicarious at best. We hope that each student is playing along in his mind, comparing his answers to selected student's answers, and evaluating, based on his peers' and the professor's reactions, whether his own ideas and the selected student's ideas reflect insight or confusion (or a state of mind somewhere between insight and confusion).

Unfortunately, many of our students are not playing along in their heads. Yes, some of our students are shopping electronically, e-mailing other professors, or sending each other text or instant messages that may have little to do with the skills, knowledge, and values we think we are teaching them. (If you doubt this assertion, wander into some classes and see what you notice from the back of the room.) We have observed, even in classes taught by masterful practitioners of law school Socratic-style teaching, that students disengage in such classes, especially if they know they will not be called on. Fortunately, there are ways to make Socratic-style questioning effective.

Questioning techniques work well when you:
- Prepare students in advance
- Ask clear questions
- Ask one question at a time
- Ask a range of questions
- Elicit different levels of thinking
- Allow sufficient wait-time (three seconds or more)
- Encourage and promote effective responses
- Respond appropriately to ineffective answers

Prepare students in advance.

From handouts, web pages, syllabi, or other formats, give students enough information in advance so that they are prepared to discuss the questions. (See Chapters 3, 4, and 5.) Particularly for more complex thinking skills, giving students advance notice of the kind of thinking you want them to discuss will help them target their out-of-class studying. Not all questions have to or should be given in advance, but giving students core questions before class will help them focus and deepen the level of discussion in class.

Model the kinds of responses you are looking for. For example, if you want students to analyze and evaluate a defendant's response to a negligence claim, first show them how you would do so. For example, you can present students with a problem (even better, invite students to provide you with a hypothetical on the spot) and then model the steps you would take in solving the problem, talking through each step, and admitting where you are stumped in the process. Pause as you go, allowing students to catch up with you and take notes.

> *Ok, I have these facts. I am considering what defenses I have and which ones are the strongest. I am going to address these in order of the elements of negligence: duty, breach, cause and damages. Right now, because I haven't fully analyzed the situation, I don't know if my client has a good defense or not. So I don't yet know whether it would be better to fight this claim or to arrive at a settlement. I also don't yet know what the damages are and that would factor into any recommendation for how to proceed.*
>
> *First, I am going to look at duty. As the driver of the car, the defendant definitely owed a duty of due care to the injured pedestrian. Nothing in the facts suggest otherwise, so I am going to concede this element and move onto the next.*
>
> *Second, it looks like the defendant breached the duty of care. He was trying to change the CD in his car and failed to look fully and completely to the right as he pulled out of the gas station. There may be an argument here that the defendant was acting reasonably, but I don't see it yet; I'll come back to this one. . . .*
>
> *Now coming to the element of proximate cause or scope of liability. Hmmm. Let me see. I think the defendant has a potentially strong defense here. . . .*

This technique, called a "cognitive think-aloud" stems from the research on the nature of expert performance. Because experts tend to skip steps and quickly make and discard hypotheses, make sure you are vigilant about your own thinking process. Having a colleague in the room, who can ask you questions about skipped steps and discarded hypotheses, adds to the richness of students' experiences.

Ask clear questions.

This aspiration is harder to achieve than we think. As authors of the questions, we know what we are looking for. The students, some terrified of "getting it wrong" in front of their peers, may stumble and have little clue what we are asking. Writing down the questions ahead of time and being sure that they align with your class learning objectives will help improve the clarity of the questions you ask, and allow you to determine what types of thinking you are looking for. For students who are not auditory learners, projecting your questions on a PowerPoint slide will allow the students to more readily process the question and focus on answering it. Avoid questions that suggest you really are asking, "What am I thinking?" If you have a definite point you want a student to make, you may be effective in stating a proposition and asking students whether and why they agree or disagree.

Some education experts advocate asking no question to which you know the answer, as those are inauthentic questions that stifle rather than stimulate dialogue. But part of what we are doing as law teachers is ascertaining whether students have learned the material that we seek them to learn. So, while *we* know the answer to: "What major factors did the court use in allocating punitive damages?" we are really asking students to tell us whether they identified those major factors. We could help students engage in the dialogue by naming what we are seeking to learn, such as by asking, "The court used a number of factors in rejecting the claim for punitive damages. I'm wondering if you all identified the same factors, or interpreted this opinion differently. Phil, please start us off by identifying one of the factors that the court seems to use?" If you don't wish to call on a particular student, you could invite any student to respond, "Could someone start ... ?"

Ask one question at a time.

Most of us have had the experience of asking a question, seeing blank looks on the faces of our students, and therefore following up with other questions, revising the question, or even tacking on additional points. This approach seldom results in great student learning. Discipline yourself to staying with one question at a time. While it is ok to repeat a question if it is long or complex, adding questions compounds student confusion. Having written the questions out in advance is particularly helpful for avoiding such problems altogether.

Ask a range of questions.

Open-ended questions are more likely to generate discussion than yes/no questions. Vary the kind of question and the length of time it takes students to respond. Some questions are effectively posed in a quick and ongoing repartee — think of a lively dinner table conversation — rather than a long question followed by a longer answer.

Elicit different levels of thinking.

Ask students questions along the range of thinking hierarchy. (See Illustrations 4-2 and 4-3.) Depending where you are in the learning unit (see Chapter 3) and the context of the class, develop questions from lower and higher levels of thinking. As you progress through the course, ask students questions at increasingly more complex levels. Embed material about a concept studied earlier in a question about the current class topic, for example: "Let's review the tests administrative agencies use to … [name tests briefly]. Let's apply those factors to …"

Allow sufficient wait-time (at least three to five seconds) after you ask a question.

Most of us struggle with silence in the classroom. We ask a question and default to the usual students who raise their hands. Alternatively, we may call on students, expecting their immediate responses. The research shows that we usually wait only a second or two before we fill the silence with our own voices by making a comment or rephrasing the question. One second is not enough time for most students to generate a meaningful response. Giving yourselves and students time to process the question usually results in more students being able to answer your question. You can explain this fact to students to address the awkwardness of the quiet. "I am going to wait for 5 seconds to give you time to think," or, "I see that Jenny, Ee Ming, and Rafael all have answers to this question. How about some others? I'll wait."

Another way to provide students with time to process the question is to ask them to write a response in 30 seconds or to engage in a think-write-pair-share exercise as described above. These processes allow students a chance to reflect and work through their thinking for a particular response.

Encourage and promote effective responses.

Actively listen to students' responses. Looking elsewhere, leaning away from the students, fiddling, or interrupting the students suggests that their responses don't deserve your attention. Acknowledge students' effective responses, both at the time they respond and later, e.g. "Louis made an excellent point. Remember how he said that…." Be encouraging and coach students to develop their responses. "Great start! Now can you help me out by explaining how you arrived at that answer?" Smiling, nodding, being quiet, and making eye contact encourages students to elaborate. Leaning forward, writing students' responses on the board, and inviting others to help their classmates can all help build student confidence in responding to questions. Show delight when your students develop particularly insightful points and be sure to acknowledge insights that are new to you; your students will remember those moments, both as a sign of your respect for them and as a reflection of your own self-confidence in your expertise.

Respond appropriately to ineffective answers.

When students do give a "wrong" answer, help guide them to a better response, if at all possible. Focus on the answer, not on the student, and acknowledge any positive aspect of the response. Using a gentle sense of humor can help diffuse a potentially uncomfortable moment for the student, "Oh, good, that is so-o-o close! But I am wondering if that answer might be missing something. How about taking a look further down the page where it says …" Try hints (e.g., "Why do you think the court mentioned _____ fact?") or cues (e.g., "Is there anything in the federal rules that you might use as a basis for support in making your argument?"). You can also invite the student to ask for "co-counsel" to assist, and then return to the student to have the student end the discussion with a positive contribution. (For more suggestions on giving corrective feedback, see Chapter 7.)

Use the "live discussion" course webpage tool to engage students in law school, Socratic-style discussions.

This short discussion adds a technological tool to the mix of options during those instances when you choose to use the traditional law school Socratic method. It is another way to engage more students than just the one responding to your question.

On both the Lexis-Nexis (Blackboard) and West (TWEN) platforms commonly used by law professors, you have the ability to establish a live discussion. This live discussion can occur at any time of the day or night, and the discussion lasts as long as the professor wishes it to last. The students open up the course webpage, click on the live discussion button, and then can join the discussion by posting comments. Each comment adds to the discussion at the moment in time when the student posts the comment; students therefore cannot insert comments wherever in the discussion they wish. The fact that the discussion is live, that it lasts only for a prescribed time, and the inability of students to insert comments wherever they want distinguishes the asynchronous discussion boards also available through both Blackboard and TWEN. (For a detailed discussion of the benefits of asynchronous discussion boards, see Chapter 3.) The best analogy for this "live discussion" tool is the actual classroom setting, in which the students and professor make comments throughout the class discussion.

The live discussion tool can be used in or out of class. When used outside of class, live discussion is an excellent tool for conducting reviews, remediating student confusion, and otherwise interacting with students at a time when you are not available or do not choose to be available in person.

It also can be a tool for engaging students to learn vicariously and teach each other during class. By establishing a live discussion that operates during class and asking students to respond to your questions by posting comments to the live discussion, you can greatly enhance their learning experience in the context of a law school Socratic-style discussion. Typing their responses engages students in the process. In fact, the act of writing their responses engages them more deeply in the process than merely mentally answering your questions engages them. When students articulate their thoughts in writing, they have the opportunity to refine them, rethink them, and expand upon them. The process of responding to your hypothetical questions gives them practice in performing the very skill on which you will assess them on your final exam (and midterm). In effect, they are quickly answering mini-practice exams. Moreover, if you give students permission to give each other feedback, you greatly expand your students' opportunities for practice and feedback, providing the formative assessment (see Chapter 7) they need to develop their skills.

The challenge in using this technique is in how you implement it. It is very helpful to define for students what types of comments are appropriate. (Mike learned this lesson the hard way.) It also is important that you monitor the discussion while it is ongoing. In other words, it's very helpful if you periodically interject verbal comments about the students' postings such as, "Nice insight, Jamie" or "Bill, you didn't consider a crucial fact" or "Could someone please explain what makes Alice's analysis is so convincing?" "Is Samantha right?" These kinds of comments let students know you are invested in this learning process and provide some immediate feedback to students who often feel starved for feedback. Of course, the mental energy needed to simultaneously engage with the selected student, read student postings, and generate effective feedback is quite significant.

Discovery sequence instruction

One powerful tool you might consider is discovery sequence instruction. This technique involves providing students a series of examples and non-examples of a concept and labeling each as either an example or non-example and then asking students to infer the principle or principles that reconcile the examples and non-examples. For example, you could provide students a set of examples and non-examples of contracts to which Article II of the UCC would apply or of activities for which a person successfully could be charged with conspiracy and then ask students to infer the principles. You even could provide students with a set of effective and ineffective responses to a hypothetical or draft contract terms and ask the students to explain the principles that distinguish the effective responses.

Discovery sequence instruction can readily be combined with a think and write-pair-share experience or other small group learning activity. Studies suggest that, because the students must figure things out for themselves, such experiences effectively capture students' attention and produce strong and lasting memories.

Appendix 6-1 provides examples of discovery sequence exercises.

Using real-life experiences

Another powerful instructional technique is bringing real life scenarios into the course. Bringing real life into the course can be done in a wide variety of ways, including:
- Photos
- Videos
- News stories
- Documents (contracts, pleadings, tax returns)
- Interviews of practicing lawyers and judges
- Field trips (court, agency, business)
- Service learning experiences (domestic violence shelter, low income tax advice)
- Research papers applying the course to real-life).

Having real-life examples or experiences allows students to think about abstract concepts and written material in a different way. For example, a photo of a nuclear waste facility located next a river may have a powerful effect on students' understanding of environmental law. Similarly, inviting an attorney to class to discuss and answer students' questions about a consumer protection class action suit allows students to see how litigation strategies play out on a daily basis. Inviting students to research current issues and events, and having students follow new legislation or community issues also involves students in applying their classroom learning to practice. As with other instructional techniques, using real-life experiences can be included with other exercises to engage students in a variety of learning approaches.

Using simulations to promote deep learning

As with real life scenarios, engaging students in simulations can lead to deep learning of values, skills, and knowledge. Research on teaching and learning supports the value of simulations. Simulations are particularly effective for some students; students who struggle with learning through verbal discussion and reading and writing often excel when they are asked to simulate the role of an attorney.

Simulations range from the comprehensive and complex to more discreet applications. Some teachers engage students in semester-long simulations during which students experience a wide range of challenges lawyers encounter in practice. Other teachers have students engage in shorter simulations, such as drafting and negotiating a contract, making oral arguments, making a presentation for a simulated client, or conducting a mock client interview. Computer-assisted learning also can provide students with ways to practice solving the kinds of problems lawyers face.

Simulations can add to the variety of techniques used in class to engage students. Just as with other instructional techniques, we need to be clear about our learning objectives, provide clear directions and outcomes, and sequence the activity so that students learn effectively.

Address controversial issues

Sensitive issues or challenging behaviors arise in almost every course. Reading a court opinion with offensive language, students rolling their eyes when a classmate speaks, and discussing polarizing issues are all part of a class dynamic. According to students, one of the worst things we can do as teachers is to ignore these sensitive issues of race, class, politics, religion, gender, and sexual preference. (See Chapter 2.) Instead, we can acknowledge the challenge and invite students to engage in a respectful discussion about the topic.

How do you structure a class session to facilitate such discussions? Sometimes, such as when an assignment includes polarizing issues, we can anticipate an emotionally-charged discussion in class. But, frequently, "hot topics" are unpredictable, such as when students engage in behavior or use language that offends their classmates. Either way, our job as teachers is to provide a safe, respectful environment in which students can learn. This obligation does not mean that we can avoid all discomfort, but we can help students learn from the discomfort. If we have worked at creating a positive learning environment, addressing challenges will be much easier. We may have managed to prevent offensive comments in class by having developed and modeled a classroom culture where students treat others with respect.

In facing challenging issues, we first need to be aware of our own responses. In these situations, students especially need to see us model calm and constructive leadership. Think of yourself as someone responding to a health emergency or 911 call. The first rule is to stay calm. Take a deep breath. Try to disengage for a minute and consider the view of the classroom dynamic from above the class. What just happened? Why might a student have reacted that way? We can name the challenge, use silence, and ask students to pause and reflect on what just happened in the classroom. "I see that many of you are uncomfortable with the opinion just stated, that health insurance should never cover the cost of an abortion. Before we continue, let's pause for a minute to think about why some of us might hold that view." We want students' to learn how to listen to controversial views and to try to understand others' perspectives.

Another way to provide time for reflection and processing is to ask students to engage in one of the instructional activities noted in Illustration 6-2. Students could take a few minutes to write down their thoughts on the controversial issue, talk to a neighbor or discuss the topic in a small group, or be assigned to articulate different perspectives. Depending on the class, you may also want to delay the conversation for the next class.

> *An important issue has just come up in class. We don't have enough time to do justice to this right now, so I would like you all to think about this issue. We will talk about this issue in the next class. I invite everyone who would like to stay after class to talk about this issue to come talk to me. I am also more than happy to talk to you about this during office hours, via email, or on the course webpage.*

This approach allows you and students time to reflect, shows that you are not avoiding the issue, and provides a definite time when the issue will be addressed. (Note: Adopt this approach only if you will actually deliver on your promise.)

While you want to provide a place to discuss hot topics, we don't believe in allowing students to be personally attacked. If a student says something pejorative, such as, "Anyone who believes that praying in public school is OK is an idiot," you can rephrase the comment to make it one for general discussion, such as stating, "In fact, many smart, thoughtful people believe that there is a place for praying and spirituality in public education. Why might they think so?" After class, you might want to talk to the student who made the offensive remark. What did she experience during the class that prompted her to make the remark? None of us are on our best behavior when under pressure. Students who might never say offensive remarks may do so for reasons we are unaware of. Talking to students and asking them how they might feel if they were in a group labeled "idiot" allows them to reflect on their actions and how they might affect others.

With any hot topic, it is often very helpful to talk to students after class. It is hard enough to discuss controversial issues with a small group of acquaintances; having an audience of 20 to 100 is even more difficult. Trying to understand individual students' experiences, reactions and suggestions for how they can learn from the experience may often be best done outside the class. If a student becomes very upset in class, we urge you to talk to the student outside of class. If unavailable right after class, we suggest you email the student noting that you were aware that the student was involved in a controversial discussion and encouraging him to talk to you about it in person. In some cases, such as where a student is extremely upset, you may want to contact your administration or dean of students to find out what other steps you can or should take.

You may be concerned that addressing controversial issues will take up valuable class time that could be otherwise used to help students learn. We suggest that understanding others' perspectives and learning how to address controversy with respect and dignity is an important learning objective in any class. If you have created a positive classroom environment, anticipated issues in advance, and seek to have students learn from these discussions, you will have done your students a service.

Visuals

In this section we address a couple of visual attributes of the classroom, including PowerPoint and dress.

PowerPoint and other visuals

Visuals are like any other aspect of teaching. They can be highly effective, disastrous, or somewhere in-between. There is a wealth of information about how to effectively use visual media, including PowerPoint. Any of these tools can work really well; we suggest (again) that you use these tools intentionally and thoughtfully. Think about your learning objectives in the class. Consider how visuals may help students meet those learning goals. Then learn about and practice using the technique, and reflect on how well visual and other media worked in class. There are terrific classes that include lots of visuals and other media; there are wonderful classes that use considerably less. You can spend hours and hours developing beautiful and media-rich classes, but if your choice to use media means that you are the one doing all the lawyering in the class, it is probably not the best investment of your time.

Rather than give you all the specifics about using visuals, we want to focus on a few essentials. For any visual device, whether a computer projection, movie clip, or black or white board, the key is whether all students can "read" the visual. Check out the sight lines from all points in the room. Do students have to crank their necks to read a PowerPoint slide? Can students decipher your handwriting on a board? Is a screen large enough that students can accurately read and interpret the content? These considerations translate into a principle you've read elsewhere in this book: Less is more. Use bigger letters, numbers, and images. Have fewer of them.

When projecting text, use principles for effective graphics:

- As suggested in Chapter 4, projecting text using text boxes, bullets, white space, numbered lists, and color helps students get the most from the visual.
- Use a font without feet like Arial or Helvetica. While fonts with feet (like the one on this page) are easier to read in a document, fonts without feet are easier to read when enlarged. (You'll notice that most road signs use fonts without feet.)
- Limit yourself to six lines of type or less. Six lines is not much text, but this limit increases the likelihood your students will be able to read your text. Limit your text to the important points. You can allow students to fill in the gaps, put essential points on another slide, or amplify verbally.
- Unless there is a good reason for doing so, when you are in the classroom, don't look at the projected text and read it. Students can do that. Instead, face the students, use the text as a focal point, and then engage students in discussion.

If you are using any kind of a projected image, practice with the technology in advance and be prepared to have an alternate plan when what worked before doesn't work again. No one enjoys watching someone fuss over problematic technology.

Recent literature on using PowerPoint has argued that clipart is passé, that you should not include such images in your slides. On the other hand, for some students, such visual metaphors may provide an excellent memory hook. Consequently, we are not yet prepared to suggest that you abandon clipart entirely. Of course, as you might expect, we do encourage you to use clipart judiciously.

One final though about using PowerPoint is worth considering. It is tempting to use PowerPoint slides solely to transmit information — e.g., the language of a statute, an excerpt from an opinion, three points you want to make in a lecture. If you only transmit knowledge using PowerPoint, however, your students may conclude that your course is mostly or exclusively about acquiring knowledge. Just as writing on a board can send a message about what you think is important, what you include in your PowerPoint slides can influence your students' sense of your course. By including questions, problems, visual metaphors, or even a checklist that addresses the process of using a skill you are teaching, you communicate a much different message about what's important in your class.

Dress

Dress is an issue for all teachers and is especially important for teachers who are women, of color, relatively young, inexperienced, or otherwise don't fit the traditional profile of a law professor.

We have colleagues who wouldn't dream of showing up in the classroom without the power suit. Others teach comfortably in khakis and a casual shirt. What you choose to wear will depend on your personality, your comfort level, where you are in the semester, and what is going on with your students. We urge you to be yourself. There is no one right way to dress for the law school classroom. Here are some things to consider.

If you tend to be an informal person, don't suddenly start wearing conventional and formal dark suits. On the other hand, at least for the beginning of the course, you may want to lean towards the more formal side of your personality. Likewise, if you tend to be more formal and conventional, stick with who you are. Your school may have a dress culture; consider how others dress and, if you have questions, talk to your colleagues about these unspoken norms. If you want ideas about how your students might perceive teachers your age, you can find helpful images in the news or TV. How do politicians dress? TV anchors? Other people in public positions of authority whom your students respond positively to?

We suggest that the best clothing to wear is that which is comfortable and makes you feel confident. For some of us, putting on the suit is part of how we create a sense of confidence: "Even if I am scared out of my wits, I'll at least look the part of a law professor." Some women feel most confident wearing pants; others feel they project a desired image of professionalism when they wear skirts. One of our friends, a young woman new to teaching, feels that she needs to look as much like a 50 year-old as possible. Her approach is to wear the power suit, heavy jewelry, and silk scarves associated with top women business executives. Similarly, some men feel better wearing a jacket; others feel confident so long as they wear a collared shirt and tie *or* jacket but don't feel a need for both. Whatever you decide to wear, we recommend that you try it out before you wear it in the classroom. (You never know when that nice jacket will make it hard to reach up high to write on the board or will become beastly hot with all your gesturing.)

Most of us tend to be more formal at the beginning of the semester. Some of us think of the first class as analogous to a professional job interview: What will make the best first impression with the students? As the semester continues, and students start to show signs of stress, we may want to shed the power suit, jacket or other formal attire and adopt more casual and comfortable dress. One teacher deliberately pulls out his cardigan sweaters for the days when his students are most stressed out. Mike has a colleague who, to the great delight of his students, pulls out his red and white seersucker suit on such occasions. You may also want to deliberately choose more formal dress when teaching a large class and be more casual when conducting office hours or teaching an upper-division seminar.

Timing

When in the live classroom, we suggest that you keep track of chunks of time along with your learning objectives. For example, you might divide a 50-minute class into three sections of 13 minutes each , leaving 10 minutes for the opening and closing of the class session. Rather than setting the exact timing for each instructional activity (hard to do unless you have experienced the instructional activity several times), we suggest that you consider what you want students to have been doing for each 13 minute chunk of time. Remember, you want students to be the ones acting like lawyers in the class.

Because many of us worry that we have enough to "fill the time," we plan far more instructional activities than the class time allows. If you are focusing on what the students are doing and how they are learning the material, you will be less concerned about having enough material. Instead you will wonder how you can help students learn sophisticated skills within the body of class. We suggest that you map out and prioritize the timing along with your learning objectives.

For example, you have 40 minutes for the body of class. You plan the following instructional activities:

- Small group discussion: 7 minutes
- Whole class discussion: 6 minutes
- Mini-lecture summarizing and clarifying: 10 minutes
- Think-Write-Pair-Share: 3 minutes
- Whole class discussion: 5 minutes
- Point/counterpoint: 9 minutes

In the classroom, however, you find that students need more time in the small group discussions. Because students seem engaged and on task, you decide to extend the time to ten minutes. The whole class discussion similarly reveals a number of questions and misunderstandings. You allow that to go on for 15 minutes. It's now 25 minutes into the class you are already more than 10 minutes behind your plan. What do you do?

Go back to your learning objectives. What is it that students should learn by the end of this class? Of the instructional activities you have planned, which one is most likely to help students achieve those learning objectives in the remaining 15 minutes? We suggest that, rather than cramming all the instructional activities into the remaining time, you ditch one or more of those activities and focus on the one that you think will be most effective. If you plan for this in advance, you can determine which instructional activities you definitely want students to engage in, which ones you would like to have students engage in, and which ones are not essential, but would be lovely to use if time allows.

Consider how you can use time effectively for most of your students. Often teachers don't limit discussion or questions because they fear that doing so is disrespectful to the one student whose questions or comments are being limited. However, it is disrespectful to the entire class if the discussion meanders off on tangents unrelated to the learning goals and objectives. Several techniques help keep students on task and allow you to limit discussion. One is saying something like, "Last comment goes to Josef," even when three other people have their hands in the air. Another is stating, "Let's hear two more contributions. I'd like to hear from students who have not yet contributed to the class discussion." If you have decided not to call on volunteers who are the most frequent contributors, we suggest that you talk to them outside of class, letting them know that you appreciate their eagerness and enthusiasm, and that you want to be sure a variety of students' voices are heard in class.

Sometimes we have the opposite challenge, having extra time. You plan a number of activities, and, much to your surprise, students complete them and are ready to move on well ahead of schedule. Now what? Again, we suggest you return to your learning objectives. What will help students understand the material at a deep level? We have found that students claim to be "done" with a group assignment after they have discussed it verbally. Because being able to articulate ideas in writing is such an important lawyering skill, ask students to prepare an outline summarizing the group's key points. When students have to move beyond talking to writing and organizing, they frequently identify gaps in their analysis. Another solution is to prepare an "extra" instructional activity that you use during the class if you have time.

A final word about timing. Some teachers find it extremely helpful to actually practice their class sessions. They spend time before class rehearsing, refining and tracking how long it takes. No matter what else you do, end the class on time. Track the time during class so that you leave five minutes at the end to summarize and provide closure.

Closings: the last five minutes of class

Some of us find it easy to skip this step. The students are busily working on different instructional activities. We look at the time and see that we have three minutes left. We rush through a few final points as students start nosily packing up.

Instead, as suggested in Chapter 4, use the last five minutes of class to consolidate students' learning. In many ways, closings mirror the openings. We tell them what they have been working on and what they have shown us about their learning. We can summarize important points, preview how this class will fit with the next, or provide them with feedback. We can also ask the students to play the leading role at the end of class, asking them to complete a minute paper about the most important point they learned in class (see Chapter 7), invite them to summarize material individually or in small groups, or spend a few minutes quietly writing notes to themselves about what they learned.

As with any aspect of teaching the class, variety is helpful. We suggest you develop a number of approaches to closing class. Three examples are below.

Summarize key points.

In the last few minutes of class, summarize the key learning points of the class. You might do this by using a skeletal outline on the board or a slide and verbally adding to it. (This may be the same outline or slide that you used at the beginning of class.)

> *Today you focused on the skill of identifying ambiguity in contracts. You noticed ambiguities in the words used, such as "damage to property or physical injury." The phrase was ambiguous because "damage" alone included physical and economic damage.*
>
> *You also noticed ambiguity created by grammatical use ...*
>
> *You noticed the problem with terms of distance, such as "within 25 miles" which could mean a traveling distance or a physical radius.*
>
> *You noticed ambiguities I hadn't seen and other classes hadn't seen. You've analyzed obvious and more sophisticated ambiguities. You learned that, while this effort may seem picky in a class, it can cost a party millions of dollars. You've discussed what steps you could take as lawyers to identify ambiguity in drafting contracts.*
>
> *You've worked through all but the final problem, which is the most complex. Please review that for Monday's class; we'll start the next class with that problem and then move on to the next topic....*
>
> *Thank you and see you Monday.*

This effort takes less than five minutes, but you get the point. The worst that can happen is that you allow five minutes for a closing and end up letting students leave a minute or two early. Alternatively, you could invite anyone to ask a final question.

Give students time to consolidate their learning.

Instead of you summarizing and providing the guidance, involve the students. You can ask them to spend the time reflecting and consolidating the class objectives.

> *Today you had a chance to evaluate different proposed temporary restraining orders. In your groups, you saw five different examples of how these might be drafted, and evaluated the advantages and disadvantages to different versions.*
>
> *Now I'd like you to take a minute to write a few notes to yourself. If in practice or on an exam you needed to draft a proposed temporary restraining order, what important things would you want to remind yourself to do?*

Allow students a few minutes to write. You could then ask students to compare their notes with someone outside their small group, or invite the class as a whole to contribute a few important points.

Allow students to reflect on their learning.

This technique allows students to practice the skills they need to become self-regulated learners.

> *Today, you were assigned to play the roles of constituents seeking to resolve a toxic landfill problem. Some of you represented the landowner, others the neighbors, the city, legislators, the company that produced the toxins, and consumers who would benefit from the toxins. Take a minute to think about what you learned from this exercise. Then, write down one thing you learned from this exercise.*

As with the previous suggestion, you could then invite students to compare their notes with each other, share with the whole class, or thank the students for participating and let them leave when they have finished writing.

Closing modification: the very last class.

The last class, like the first class, is special. It is nice to provide some sense of closure to the end of the semester. People pay attention to openings and closings. For some students, this last class moment may be the last time they are with you in a class. The last class session is your chance to leave a final impression. You might want to leave ten to fifteen minutes for the very last closing.

Some teachers like to give words of advice to students, telling them to remember why they are in law school and what their dreams are once they are in practice. Many teachers like to summarize the course, talking about what the students have learned, thanking students for their efforts, and revealing what the teacher most appreciated about sharing the learning with this group of students. One of our colleagues uses the last class to provide a "best of" review, where she describes some highlights of the course, and then invites every student in her large class to name the one most striking thing that happened to them all semester (inside or outside of class).

Other teachers use the last class as a chance to build students' confidence. They may tell students about the mistakes they made in their lives, and give ideas about how to navigate the stress of final exams. They may tell stories about practice and life. They may offer their assistance and support for future years. They may ask a final question. One of our colleagues stands at the door and shakes the hand of each exiting student. None of these may suit you. Like any other aspect of teaching, be authentic. Do something you enjoy doing. Try different approaches to ending the course. Reflect and learn from the experience.

Final notes on teaching the class

Remember that all teachers have good days and bad days. We urge you not to seek "perfection," but to increase your awareness of how you add value to the few minutes when you are physically present with your students in a classroom. You are the single most expensive, most adaptive, most empathic educational resource available to your students to learn what they need to learn in your course. Consider the small steps you can take to help students act as lawyers in the classroom. Try to find something you can celebrate in every class. As we suggest in Chapters 2 and 8, learn from your students and engage in the ongoing process of developing as a teacher.

Checklist for teaching the class

Illustration 6-3 is a checklist you can use for teaching the class.

Illustration 6-3: Teaching the Class Checklist

Teaching the class: Who in the room is acting like a lawyer?
　　　　　　　　　　Who is doing most of the talking in the class?

❏ **Create a positive learning environment**
　❏ Know and use students' names
　❏ Be conscious of the messages you send
　❏ Be enthusiastic
　❏ Model taking risks and acknowledging weaknesses
　❏ Envision yourself as a "guide on the side"
　❏ Be transparent
　❏ Be authentic

❏ **Openings — the first five minutes**
　❏ Arrive early
　❏ Consider the opening message you send
　❏ Modify for first and other special days

❏ **Body — the heart of the class session**
　❏ Use a variety of instructional activities
　❏ Use activities that engage the students
　❏ Use mini-lectures surrounded by other activities
　❏ Use effective questioning techniques
　❏ Address controversial issues
　❏ Use visuals students can "read"
　❏ Prioritize you timing according to learning objectives

❏ **Closings — the last five minutes**
　❏ Summarize and consolidate students' learning
　❏ Modify for the last class

❏ **Engage in ongoing practice, reflection, and evaluation**

Chapter 7

Assessing Student Learning

Introduction

Despite what you may have heard, assessment can be interesting and—dare we say it—even fun. For many teachers, assessment is synonymous with grading, and you've probably heard the saying about that popular topic: "We teach for free; we get paid to grade." Even when not associated with grading, assessment is often viewed as the onerous, external imposition of arbitrary and meaningless measurement—think regional accreditation requirements and standardized testing. But spending a little time on assessment can transform your thinking about teaching. It can even make grading and assessment engaging, efficient, and rewarding.

The truth is, as teachers, we already conduct ongoing assessment: *collecting information about student learning.* Although we may not have been calling it assessment, we assess student learning all the time. We are engaging in assessment when we read and grade papers and exams, listen to students' comments, consider students' behavior in class, or view students' questions on course web pages. In all of these settings, we are trying to see if our students are "getting it."

In this chapter, we suggest ways to use effective assessment approaches and instruments. As with planning the course or teaching a class, we believe that an intentional approach to assessing student learning can help students develop more significant knowledge, skills and values. We also believe that approaching assessment in this way can increase your satisfaction with teaching and grading. We strive to be like one of our colleagues who was able to say in the years before she retired, "My students now write really good exams."

As with all aspects of teaching and learning, there is a vast literature on assessment. Books, web sites, journal articles and conferences are devoted to assessment. Much of this literature has been produced over the past decade, as constituencies have begun to clamor for evidence of how well students are learning. In this chapter, we focus on the basics of assessing student learning in individual classes.

Assessment and learning are intricately connected. Just as we've asked you to shift your focus from what you are teaching to *what students are learning*, we ask you to keep student learning foremost in your mind when thinking about assessment. In our view, and in the view of educational experts, there is no such thing as good teaching when students aren't learning.

Illustration 7-1: The Assessment Cycle

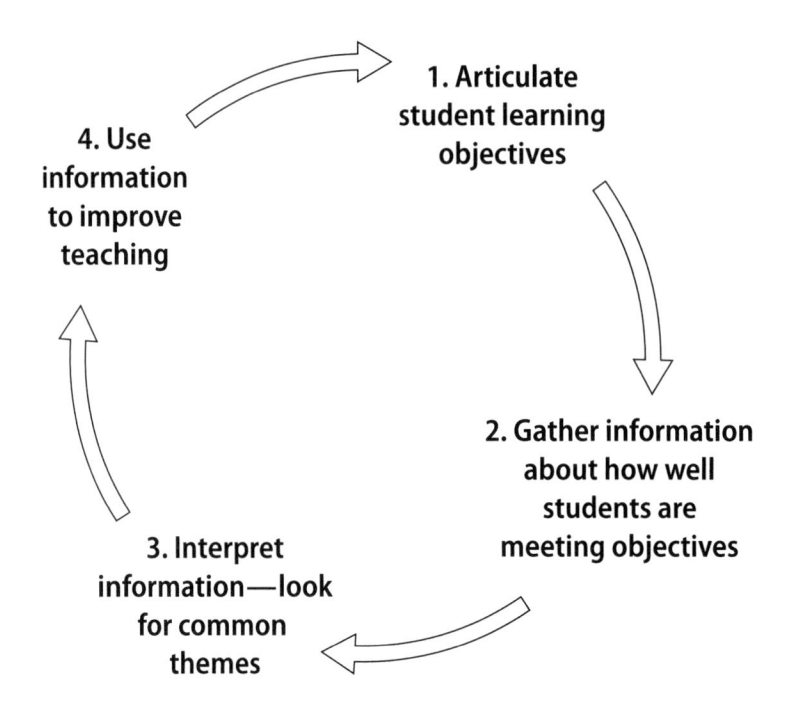

1. Articulate student learning objectives
2. Gather information about how well students are meeting objectives
3. Interpret information—look for common themes
4. Use information to improve teaching

The Assessment Cycle

Assessing student learning during the course and using that information to improve your teaching is part of the assessment cycle as seen in Illustration 7-1. Just like almost every aspect of teaching and learning, assessment is an ongoing and recursive process. Ideally, we conduct a variety of assessments and go through this cycle throughout the course and our teaching career. During the semester we have students perform a number of different tasks to demonstrate their progress in developing the knowledge, skills and values we want them to learn. Looking for trends and patterns, we see areas where most students are competent, and areas where a significant number of students are struggling. We reflect and try new ways to help students learn. We give students more tasks to see if these new teaching strategies have helped the students develop greater competency. The goal is not perfection; just starting to pay attention to how your students are learning can improve your teaching considerably.

Consider the alternative to engaging in this process. Each year you teach the same course. Each year you give one final exam. Most of the students' exams are pretty disappointing. You repeat this cycle for decades. It's no wonder teachers hate grading!

Of course, law schools could and should apply the same assessment model at program and institutional levels, but that goal is beyond the scope of this book. Imagine if your entire institution was collectively engaged in trying to improve the quality of student learning over three years! Now *that prospect* is exciting.

This chapter provides concrete suggestions for assessing student learning in three areas:

1. Assessing students to improve their learning during the course

2. Assessing students to improve your teaching — using classroom assessment techniques
3. Evaluating students to assign grades

These three areas overlap — the same assessment instrument can be used to help students learn, to improve teaching, and to assign grades. The key is to make assessment ongoing, effective and sustainable. In this chapter we will offer a number of suggestions for ways to develop effective assessment instruments and methods. We don't expect or advise you to implement all of them immediately. Try the ones that resonate with you. Like all aspects of teaching, assessment is an ongoing work-in-progress.

Assessing students to improve their learning during the course

The best way to assess what your students are learning — and, hence, what you have effectively taught them — is much like drafting your will: do it early and often. As you know from Chapter 1, students need to have many opportunities to practice showing us what they are learning so that we can give them feedback and they can improve. This type of assessment is often called *formative assessment* — where the purpose is to help students learn rather than to assign grades. Having students complete a variety of tasks — assessment instruments — during the course will allow them to approach knowledge, skills, and values from different perspectives and allow for deeper learning. Having students engage in multiple and varied assessments will also help them develop the independent, self-regulated learning skills that will allow them to succeed after the course is over (see Chapters 1 and 5 for more on self-regulated learning).

Think about the value of having regular practice and feedback. Imagine that you were trying to learn how to cook Indian food. You went to a class one night a week. During class sessions, the teacher talked about cooking, showed the class how to prepare different dishes, and questioned you and your classmates about ingredients and techniques. As the course progressed, the teacher engaged you in increasingly sophisticated discussions about Indian cooking. Never once in 14 weeks did you practice cooking or receive any feedback. To get your cooking certificate, you had to cook an Indian meal in front of the teacher. You might still get your certificate, but your chance of success is pretty small. In contrast, imagine the class engaged you in practicing cooking and the teacher provided regular feedback on your efforts. Do you have any doubt you'd do better in this second version of the course?

Research shows that the need for ongoing practice and feedback applies to all education, across multiple disciplines. One of the four ingredients essential for learning is an "assessment-centered" environment. In an assessment-centered environment, students have repeated opportunities to practice and receive feedback. If we want students to learn, we need to give them multiple opportunities to practice lawyering skills and to get feedback on how they are learning.

In this section, we walk you through three steps in using assessment to improve student learning during the course. Illustration 7-2 identifies these steps, which are essential to any assessment process, and which we will refer to in the later sections of this chapter.

Illustration 7-2: Designing Effective Assessments — 3 steps

> **Designing Effective Assessments**
>
> **3 STEPS**
>
> 1. Identify what you want to assess (learning objectives)
> 2. Prepare and give assessment instruments
> 3. Give feedback to students

> **Thinking exercise**: Consider your career. How have you benefited from having opportunities to practice and get feedback on your professional development?

Step one: Identify learning objectives

In the ideal world, you have followed our suggestions and have mapped out clear learning objectives for your course and your individual classes. You have a good sense of what students should learn and how they will show that to you. And you have done all of this before the first day of class, just as the educational experts recommend. Look at the examples of learning goals and objectives in Chapters 3 and 4. If defining objectives seems like hard work, it is. Clearly identifying what students need to learn is one of the hardest parts of course design.

Even if you are somewhat unsure about specific learning goals, you can still engage students in ongoing practice and feedback. Consider what you ask students to do on final exams. If it is your first time teaching, look at others' exams and talk to colleagues about what they are seeking on their exams. The kinds of intellectual skills and knowledge you test on your final exams are often good indicators of what you think students should learn in your course. Even if you are unsure of the discreet learning goals, go on to the next steps; often, you will recognize what you wanted students to do when you see how they perform on an assessment instrument.

Assume that you are only a few weeks into the course and that your goals for an ungraded assignment are modest. You decide to focus on having students demonstrate the three objectives in Illustration 7-3.

Illustration 7-3: Classroom Assessment — Learning Objectives Example

> **Class assessment — Assignment 1**
> **Learning objectives**
>
> 1. Identify the elements of _____;
> 2. Apply given facts to the elements of ____; and
> 3. Write coherent prose.

This exercise may seem simple. After all, the students have been discussing elements and facts for weeks. You may worry that you are not being rigorous enough; you may believe you will insult the students by giving them "busy work." Try and see. We have learned that this simple assignment can reveal that many first-semester students are struggling with basic legal analysis and writing skills.

Step two: *Prepare the assessment instrument*

There are many different kinds of assessment instruments you can use in law school. Illustration 7-4 includes some of these.

Illustration 7-4: Assessment instruments

Assessment Instruments
1. Multiple-choice and short answer quizzes
2. Analytical, issue-spotting, and advocacy essays
3. Outlines, charts and matrices
4. Legal documents such as wills, articles of incorporation, injunctions, statutes
5. Journals
6. CALI exercises
7. Role-plays — simulations with students engaged in practice-related performances
8. Verbal presentations
9. Oral arguments
10. Skits, movies, games, artwork, ... and on and on.

The nature of the assignment will vary according to your learning objectives. The most common assessments ask students to respond to a verbal or written question or solve a problem in writing, but you might also ask students to engage in a simulation, prepare an oral argument, design a graphic, or perform a skit.

Regardless of the kind of assessment you are doing, as you prepare the instrument, consider the factors described below and listed in Illustration 7-5.

Illustration 7-5. Common Factors to Consider When Preparing Assessment Instruments

Common Factors to Consider When Preparing Assessment Instruments
- What is the rationale for this assessment?
- What do you want students to do?
- How much time will it take for students to complete?
- Will the assessment be completed in or outside of class?
- What is the assessment's content?
- Is there a particular format students should use?
- How much can students collaborate on the assessment?
- How will you provide feedback?

By providing answers to these questions, you can focus the students' learning. Students can more efficiently use their time if they know on what they should focus. We prevent a lot of wasted time and effort—ours and the students'—if we are explicit about what we want and why we want it.

Provide the rationale for the assessment.

Make sure your students know *why* you are asking them to perform the assessment and what feedback they can expect. We typically clarify our reasons for administering the assessment when we administer it:

Let's figure out how this rule applies. I'm going to give you some facts and ask you to make a decision. After you make your decisions, we'll discuss a number of valid responses. This interaction will give you practice and verbal feedback on applying this rule.

OR

Please prepare <u>Assignment 1</u> for next Monday. Completing this assignment will give you a chance to practice using the material we have been discussing in the past few classes. The exercise will also give you practice in doing the kinds of things lawyers do and what I will ask you to do on your midterm and final exam. The exercise will also help me understand what you understand and what we might want to review.

Depending on the complexity of the assessment, you might also want to include the rationale as part of the assessment. You also may include information about assessments in the syllabus, along the lines of: "In this class you will be completing a number of ungraded assignments. Each of these is designed to deepen your understanding of the course material. Unless instructed otherwise, please bring written responses to these exercises in a form that can be read by a classmate. Your responses may be handwritten or may simply be saved as a document on your laptop."

Identify what you want students to do and give clear directions.

What do you want students to do? The task should relate to your learning goals. Be clear. It is more effective to ask something like, "Is this a valid contract? Why or why not?" than asking students to "Discuss plaintiff's claims." To a novice, the word "discuss" might suggest that the student should regurgitate knowledge, a common task when writing college essays, rather than articulating and evaluating the arguments reasonable lawyers would make while analyzing the factual dispute.

You'll provide a more effective learning experience if you do the assessment yourself, revising your directions and the assessment based on what you want to emphasize. Remember that you may have a very clear idea of what you want students to do, but, as novices in your field, they need more clues, especially because what you want students to do may be quite different from what your colleagues ask them to do. One way to realize how specific you need to be is to consider giving a basic instruction to a stranger. If we were to ask our significant others to pick up milk on the way home, they would likely know whether we wanted no-fat, 2%, soy, or lactose-free milk. If we asked a stranger to do the same errand, however, we would have a great chance of not getting what we wanted. Help your students by giving them clear guidelines.

Take another look at the three learning objectives in the above assessment (Illustration 7-3). Consider what you might really want students to focus on when presented with a hypothetical problem. Do they need to identify *all* or just some of the facts that apply to the element? Would identifying one key fact be enough? Do you want students to be selective about what facts they apply or should they identify as many as possible?

The longer and more complex the assessment, the more helpful it is to have specific directions or identified outcomes, such as "Identify the best argument this employee can make in her claim for gender discrimination." Depending on where you want students to focus, you may also find it helpful to specify what students should *not* do. For example, you might want to suggest something like:

> Please focus on the defendant's duty of care. **Do not** discuss the elements of breach, causation, scope of liability or damages.

Education experts might characterize such instructions as a "scaffold;" scaffolds are particularly useful for novices. As your students develop their abilities, you gradually can withdraw the scaffold until the students can handle the task on their own. Much as a painting scaffold holds up painters so they can do their work and not fall, an instructional scaffold helps novice learners stand up to the struggle of performing challenging intellectual skills.

How much time will it take for students to complete?

A good rule of thumb is that students will take twice as much time as you would to complete an assessment. When you prepare an assessment, *do* the assessment yourself. How long did it take you? If you are fortunate enough to have one or more teaching assistants, ask them to complete the assessment and keep track of how long it took. Ask a colleague to read the assessment. How long did it take to just read the material? If the assessment is completed outside of class and takes more than a few minutes, consider what else you have assigned students to do for that class. If you are giving students class time to do the project, budget the class time to allow most students to complete the assessment.

Determine when students will complete the assessment.

Some assessments work well in class; others are better if completed outside of class. Also consider the other demands on your students' time. If they are in the middle of midterms in other classes, an ungraded assessment will get considerably less attention than if students have fewer other deadlines. Of course, it is easier to determine competing demands when all your students have the same required classes, but, even in a large, upper-level class, you can ask for a show of hands to find out about students' other deadlines. Asking students to solve a complex problem over the weekend when 75% of the class is taking an exam that weekend is not likely to be a positive experience for you or your students.

Determine the content of the assessment.

Keeping your learning goals in mind, focus assessments on the foundational aspects of the course. Our formative assessments and our final exams should address the most important skills, content, and values in our courses.

As you progress through the course, consider adding complexity to your assessments. Our tendency is to design discreet problems related to a particular class topic. "Oh, I just thought of a good hypo on injunctive relief. We'll work on that today and, then, next class they'll work through contempt." Remember that the goal of having students practice is to improve their skills. If you are like most teachers, your final exam will ask students to analyze a complex set of facts and its relation to many different areas of the course. So give students the opportunity to practice integrating different areas of the course. Embed material from an earlier section of the course in a new assessment. Allow students to revisit and practice recognizing and integrating material.

In designing the assessment, you may be one of those gifted and creative teachers who excels at crafting interesting stories and problems. Others of us are more limited. We find it helpful to consult casebooks, court opinions, restatements, journals, and current events for ideas about assessment content. We also ask students to prepare problems and sample answers, embedding a concept taught earlier in the course in the problem. In the process of writing hypothetical scenarios and possible answers, students learn a ton.

When preparing an assessment, try to omit distractions that could impede students' learning by leading them astray. Avoid using unexplained references or making assumptions about students' cultural experiences or background knowledge. For example, including sports references or names of TV shows from your youth will be meaningless to a number of your students. Keep the actors' names simple unless you want students to consider biases and question their assumptions about names and roles.

Is there a particular format students should use?

It helps students to have guidelines if you are asking students to do more than supply a verbal answer. How many minutes should their presentations be? Can students use props in their simulations? Should they dress up? Are they expected to speak loudly enough to be heard at the back of the room? Do you have preferences about margins, font type and size, page length, spacing and organizational structure? (Single-spaced essays in 10 point font with 1/2 inch margins are really hard to read.)

Alternatively, you may want to leave the options wide open to allow for a greater range of student creativity. For example, Gerry asks students in civil procedure to work in small groups to create a graphic as follows in Illustration 7-6.

Illustration 7-6: Joinder Graphic Assignment

> **Joinder Graphic Assignment**
>
> Prepare a graphic of all or part of joinder. A graphic is a visual representation of concepts. Typical examples of graphics are flow charts and diagrams. However, a graphic could also be a picture, cartoon, board game, or many other visual representations. Use your imagination. The purpose of this assignment is to help you organize and synthesize the law that applies to joinder.

Decide whether students can collaborate on the assessment.

The research shows that students learn a tremendous amount from each other. They benefit from being part of learning communities where they can brainstorm and solve problems together. But, in most courses, students will earn an individual grade. To help students see how well they are progressing towards the course learning goals, it's helpful to have them complete at least some of the assessments individually. To maximize the benefits of collaboration, some assessments can be group projects, and some a hybrid, such as asking students to prepare an assessment individually and then collaborate with others who have similarly prepared. Another hybrid possibility, suggested by the cooperative learning experts, is to have students take an assessment individually but to award a bonus to all the members of a group if everyone in the group performs at or above a predetermined level, such as 80% correct.

Determine how you will provide students with feedback.

Many teachers hesitate to give students assessments because they fear that doing so with any degree of integrity or usefulness will involve hours of reading and commenting upon individual student work. Such detailed feedback is one way, but there are lots of others. You could give "global feedback" where you read all assessments to get a sense of the class and then provide comments on common themes. You can select excerpts from a few sample answers and comment on the common errors reflected in these papers to the whole class; make sure you emphasize how common the errors are and preserve the anonymity of the authors of the papers you use as examples. You could provide a sample answer that students can compare with their submissions. Students could review and comment upon their peers' work and you could provide a checklist or rubric students can use to self-assess. (More on rubrics below). If you're new at providing feedback, you may want to tell students that you will provide feedback and will determine the particular method after you've seen their work. Sample assessments are included in Appendix 7-1.

Step three: Give feedback to students

Before we get into the nuts and bolts, we want to suggest the "Rule of 3s." (Like any rule, it has exceptions and nuances.) In general, give students feedback in three areas. These three areas can be pretty broad, like "law," "facts," and "organization and coherence," with more feedback within each of the three areas. People learn better when the feedback is organized, focused and concise. Learners can focus effectively on three things; a list of a dozen errors tends to be overwhelming. In addition, bear in mind the principles from Chapter 1: the most effective feedback has four characteristics. We'll address each of these below.

1. **Specific.** Students get information about specific criteria they have or have not met.
2. **Positive.** Students find out what they are doing well.
3. **Corrective.** Students learn about their weaknesses and are given strategies to improve them.
4. **Prompt.** Students get feedback while the assessment is fresh and in time for the next assessment.

Provide students with specific feedback.

General statements, such "Good job!" or "Needs work" don't tell students much if they lack supporting details. While an "excellent!" suggests that everything is great, a competent response may demonstrate a mix of skills and knowledge. Most students excel in some areas and are weak in others. Because our goal is to have students practice and get some feedback, even general feedback is better than none at all. As you know from hearing the students' perspectives in Chapter 2, students welcome any practice and feedback, even if they just get a "check," "check plus," or "check minus" on their work. If you know what you are looking for, you can whip through a lot of one-page responses pretty quickly, putting checks on them and returning them to students in the next class.

Sometimes giving specific feedback is harder than giving general feedback, particularly with more complex assessments. As many teachers say, "I just know what feels like a 'B.'" You might, but your students don't have the expertise to understand why their performance on an assessment was above a "C" but below an "A." You have to spell it out for them. It takes more time and energy the first time, but, if you build a library of effective

Illustration 7-7: Sample Formative Assessment Checklist

Sample Formative Assessment Checklist

❏ Notes that D will have a duty of care
　❏ Identifies reasonably prudent person standard of care — law
　❏ Apply key facts to standard

❏ Posted speed limit — Is statute relevant? — Go through 2 part test
　❏ Is P in the group of people meant to be protected by the statute?
　　❏ Apply facts to test
　❏ Is P's kind of harm the kind of harm that was meant to be prevented?
　　❏ Apply facts to test

❏ If statute is relevant, how will courts use it?
　❏ Negligence per se or evidence of negligence — what effect?

---

assessments, feedback methods, and feedback instruments, you will save time and agony later. Even better, your students will learn more.

As with designing an assessment instrument, the best approach is to take the assessment yourself, analyze your response, and then make a list of specific things you want students to do on this assessment. What are they supposed to be learning and how will they show that to you? (Yup, we're right back at that thorny question, *what **are** your learning goals?* Sorry but, no, you can't keep avoiding this question.) Make a checklist of what you wanted students to do.

As an alternative to taking the assessment yourself, you can read about ten sample student responses and start to generate your list from there. Start thinking in categories. Are you looking for rules? Exceptions? Factual applications? Policy? Illustration 7-7 is a sample checklist with specific information sought on an assessment.

You also can give specific feedback verbally in class. For example, in class, you might say,

> *"Excellent! Jake just articulated a number of significant facts in analyzing this rule. Each of those facts helps show why the plaintiff was unsuccessful in this case. In practice, and on exams, it is essential to not just give the conclusion but to show how the facts apply to the law."*

This type of feedback shows everyone in the class how important this skill is and gives them a specific example. Similarly, giving students mini quizzes, using electronic response devices (clickers), having students vote by raising their hands and then providing oral responses provide students with specific feedback. If given verbally, these techniques help to reinforce students' learning and the value of the feedback, especially if students write down the correct response or the specific feedback.

Another way to provide specific feedback without having to spend hours going over individual students' work is to give students a rubric — a grid with a set of detailed written criteria used to assess student performance. Illustration 7-8 shows a sample rubric from a criminal procedure course. Students and teachers can assess performance more effectively when they have a rubric describing specific criteria and levels of quality. No time to prepare a rubric? You're not alone. (Sophie has a colleague who tells her that he loves using rubrics — "when you prepare them for me.") Even if you don't think you have enough time, we recommend that you try. Research has proven rubrics to be effective in

Illustration 7-8: Sample rubric

The categories to the right do not necessarily correlate with end of semester grades. → **Description of what is being assessed** ↓	**Levels of quality**		
	Exemplary	**Competent**	**Developing**
Identifies basic and complex criminal procedural issues—"Issue Spotting" 40%	❏ Accurately identifies *all* basic procedural issues *21-30 points* ❏ Identifies *most* of the complex issues *7-10 points*	❏ Accurately identifies *most* basic procedural issues *11-20 points* ❏ Identifies *some* of the more complex issues *4-6 points*	❏ Accurately identifies *some* basic procedural issues *0-10 points* ❏ Identifies *a few* of the more complex issues *0-3 points*
Analyzes the facts 40%	❏ Accurately and explicitly shows how the law applies to important facts *27-40 points*	❏ Accurately shows how the law applies to most of the relevant facts *14-26 points*	❏ Accurately but minimally shows how the law applies to some of the facts *0-13 points*
Identifies and applies the policy for the rules of criminal procedure 20%	❏ Identifies and applies competing policy goals to facts in predicting results *14-20 points*	❏ Somewhat identifies and applies policy to facts in predicting results *7-13 points*	❏ Minimally identifies and applies policy to facts in predicting results *0-6 points*

helping students learn and develop accurate self-assessment skills. More about how to use and develop rubrics follows under the *Evaluating student learning to assign grades* section of this chapter.

Returning to the Rule of Threes mentioned earlier in this section, regardless of how and when you give feedback, we recommend that you identify no more than three areas for providing feedback, and one specific example from each.

Provide students with positive feedback

Unfortunately, much of law school feedback tends to be a tad on the negative side. We train law students to become skilled at critiquing ideas and analysis. Developing a sharp sense of how something could be improved has real advantages, but hearing only about what you need to do to improve can get tiresome and even depressing. It's true that some students love the thrill of being critiqued and challenged. Most of us, however, do better and learn faster when we are validated for what we do well. The research shows that learners do best in an environment where they are challenged *and* affirmed.

As a general rule, it always helps to give feedback by starting with what students are doing well. There is almost always something a student has done well on an assessment. Find what the student has done well and tell the student about it, even if all you can say is "Nice job using the accurate regulation" or "What is effective about this is that it is very concise—no wasted words." One of Sophie's favorites is "Great mistake! You did exactly what you were asked to do—make factual inferences. Now let's talk about whether these are reasonable." (These kinds of comments are also specific.) Even if the student has done excellent work, it helps to identify *what* is excellent so the student can build upon that excellence. As novices, students aren't often aware of what they are doing well.

Give students feedback about their weaknesses and provide strategies to improve them.

We recommend that you sandwich the specific corrective feedback in between the positive feedback. We believe in being honest and direct, but also gentle and compassionate. Whether students outwardly communicate distress, it's not easy for them to hear that their work was ineffective. In addition to being specific, corrective feedback is more likely to help students learn when it:

- Focuses on the work, not the person;
- Avoids making normative judgments;
- Encourages students to become responsible for their learning; and
- Provides strategies to improve.

Providing feedback on a student's performance is very different from providing feedback on the student herself. Talking about the work diminishes some of the intense emotional responses that arise from receiving corrective feedback. It empowers students to see that you have not given up on them as people, but are dispassionately critiquing the quality of their work. It provides them with a slight but powerful shift—the focus is on the student's work and learning rather than on the student or her abilities.

Frame corrective feedback in terms of what is effective and ineffective. For example, "Your mock client interview would have been more effective if you had stated your advice in simpler language." Getting feedback that a performance is "poor" or "bad" or "unprofessional" is not helpful. Those words are loaded. Try to avoid making unfounded assumptions. You may be dismayed to see a student's performance, assume the student blew the exercise off, and become very irritated. In fact, the student's performance may need significant improvement because the student was facing a crisis, because the student needs additional coaching, or because you weren't specific about how to complete the assessment.

Giving students specific feedback about their weaknesses is only half the process. The other half is to provide them with concrete strategies they can use to improve their performance. One effective approach is to provide specific guidance on a select area. For example, a student has just engaged in a role play where she has demonstrated how she would introduce a photo into evidence. Throughout the role play, the student has spoken in a way that suggests a lack of confidence; each of her sentences end in the rising tone of a question. "I'm showing you what has been marked as Exhibit A? This is a photo?" Telling the student that her voice goes up diagnoses the problem; explaining how to practice deliberately lowering her voice at the end of a sentence, and then modeling a sentence for her gives her the strategy.

Sometimes it is really hard to provide students with a helpful strategy. Telling them that they needed to identify more issues in an assessment tells them *what* is missing but not *how* to fix the problem. In that situation you might suggest that the student prepare an outline or checklist that he can work through when solving problems and suggest he practice issue spotting problems and compare his efforts with peers. If you are stuck, colleagues and other students often have lots of ideas. Don't avoid giving corrective feedback if you can't provide a strategy. Every little bit of feedback helps.

As part of being honest and respectful, we also believe teachers should let students know when their work suggests that they may be in danger of failing a course. It is never an easy message, but it is far more difficult to have the conversation after the student earns the D or F than it is to give the student the heads up early on.

Give students prompt feedback.

The best feedback is immediate. Immediate feedback powers the learning cycle. Students learn if they can remember what they did, get the results, and can adjust accordingly. Completing an assessment and getting feedback three weeks later has the opposite effect. Students may not recall what they did on the assessment and have a hard time processing the feedback. Even worse, if students don't receive feedback for a particularly long time, they may have spent weeks continuing to use learning strategies they need to change.

As a general guideline, the shorter the assessment, the sooner students should receive feedback. In addition, the fewer the students, the sooner they should receive feedback. Feedback on a short quiz or hypothetical done in class is most effective when students get specific feedback during that class or the next. If students complete a longer or more complex assessment out of class, feedback within a week or even a couple of weeks is ok.

So there you are, sitting at your desk, having just collected written assessments from each of your 80 Remedies students. Each of them has drafted a one or two page proposed temporary restraining order. You are committed to giving them practice and feedback during the course, and you recognize the value of giving feedback promptly. It's 4:00 p.m. You read the first one. Seems ok. You put a couple of comments on it and go to the next. It is very different, but adds helpful information not included in the first. You put comments on number two, and then go back and comment on number one about the things missing. You repeat this with the third and fourth assignments. It is now almost 6:00 p.m., you have commented on only four assessments, and you are exhausted.

You realize that, if you keep going at this pace, it will take you 38 more hours. If you can reduce your commenting time from 30 minutes to 20, it will take you 25 hours. Even if you get it down to ten minutes per draft order, it will still take you more than 12 hours. You decide to deal with the drafts in the morning. In the morning, though, you have another class to prepare, a committee meeting to attend, and research to complete on an article. Digging into that pile of drafts feels like entering the valley of doom. In fact, you may feel this deep compulsion to spend the day cleaning out your office and reading all those articles you have collected for the past few months.

Giving prompt feedback does not need to be this onerous. Remember that our goal is to make assessment ongoing, effective and sustainable. It is easier to give feedback promptly if you have prepared for it in advance and leveraged your resources. If you have identified your goals, provided clear guidance on the assessment, and have a sense of what you want to see, you will have frontloaded the feedback process. It will be relatively quick for you to process students' assessments and give them feedback. You have your checklist, rubric or sample handy, use it in evaluating student work, and, voilà, you're done. Even better, you can reuse the assessment and the feedback instrument next time.

You can also leverage your resources by enlisting others to help. Do you have access to teaching assistants? If so, you can provide them with a checklist, sample, or rubric and guide them on providing feedback. If students are engaging in simulations, you can invite practicing lawyers to your class to provide feedback. You can also enlist students. Students can read and comment upon each other's work or their own work, comparing assessments with samples, checklists or rubrics that you provide. It is amazing what students learn when they see how someone else performs. From watching classmates' engage in simulations or present arguments or from reading their peers' drafts, students learn a lot about their own work. They can self-assess and, then, you can review their assessments of their work. You don't need to do assessment in isolation.

Teach students how to use feedback

Some students are adept at using feedback, others benefit from guidance on how to interpret and use feedback effectively. (Refer to Chapter 5 for ways to teach students to use feedback.) Giving feedback is crucial to our students' success in law school and in practice. There are certainly tradeoffs between giving specific individual feedback and getting feedback to students promptly. We recommend that you start small, use a variety of feedback methods, and continue to reflect on what works, as suggested in Chapter 8.

Illustration 7-9 provides a list of some of the different ways you can provide students with feedback and how well each of these methods rates on the characteristics of effective feedback.

Pick an assessment strategy and start helping your students learn. The list of feedback mechanisms discussed above is not exhaustive; electronic response devices "clickers" can be extremely effective in providing immediate feedback. Equally effective are short quizzes

Illustration 7-9: Different ways to provide students with feedback

Feedback Method	Specific	Positive	Corrective	Prompt	Main Benefits ✓	Main Drawbacks ↓
Individual written comments on student work	✓	✓	✓	↓	• Very helpful for individual student — tailored to particular learning	• Takes a long time; may delay students getting feedback • Exhausting for teacher if large class or long, complex assessment
Checklists	✓	✓	✓	?	• Efficient way to provide specific feedback • Can be used later to help with future assessments	• Takes time to prepare
Rubrics	✓	✓	✓	?	• Efficient way to provide specific feedback • Provides more information than checklist	• Takes time to prepare
Teacher gives verbal feedback in class	?	✓	?	✓	• Immediate • Takes little time	• Not as specific — verbal comments generally less specific • Engages fewer students
Students give each other feedback and self-critique in class	✓	✓	?	✓	• Immediate • Develops students' self assessment skills	• Results vary; more effective when combined with samples, checklists or rubrics • Students may need help with providing corrective feedback and strategies

corrected in class, electronically scored forms used to give feedback on multiple-choice questions, on-line quizzes, and CALI exercises.

Assessing students to improve your teaching—using classroom assessment techniques

Classroom assessment is designed to evaluate the effectiveness of a particular class or unit of instruction. While many classroom assessments can be pretty elaborate and involve students in long-term projects conducted outside of class, this section focuses on short, in-class assessment techniques.

With these assessments, we regularly invite students during class to inform us about what they are learning, what teaching methods are effective, and how we can help them learn more effectively. Is our teaching working? The focus is less on shaping individual students' development and more on getting a sense of the collective learning progress of the whole class.

Even though students appeared to be engaged in class and comfortable with the material, they may not have developed the knowledge, skills and values you thought they had developed. We want to identify and remedy learning gaps well before the end of the semester and any graded evaluation. We also want to know about strongly held attitudes and views. We want to know:

1. Where are they most confused?
2. Where are they excelling?
3. What are they learning and at what level?
4. What are their biases, preconceptions, and attitudes?
5. What are we doing in this course that is effective and we should continue?
6. What are we doing that is ineffective and we should stop?
7. What other suggestions do they have about how we can help them learn?

This section focuses on the first four questions. Suggestions about assessing questions 5, 6, and 7, in which ask about students' perceptions of our teaching, assignments, and tests, are introduced in Chapter 2 and developed more fully in Chapter 8. We encourage you to learn about students' responses to questions 1-4, even if only in an incremental way. The benefits can be enormous. Students appreciate our interest in their learning, which in turn motivates them to develop self-reflection and independent learning skills. We learn a lot about our teaching, information we can use to improve. Many teachers also report regaining energy and excitement about teaching from this process.

The process of using classroom assessment techniques, or CATs, follows the same steps as in Illustration 7-2:

1. Identify what you are trying to assess;
2. Prepare and give assessment instruments; and
3. Give students feedback.

We use CATs in class to get an easy, quick, and frequent flow of information about student learning. CATs are shorter and simpler to administer than some of the more com-

Illustration 7-10: Suggestions for new users of classroom assessment techniques

> Suggestions for new users of classroom assessment techniques from Thomas A. Angelo and K. Patricia Cross, *Classroom Assessment Techniques: A Handbook for College Teachers* (2d. ed. 1993)
> 1. If you don't like a classroom assessment technique for any reason, don't use it.
> 2. Don't turn classroom assessment into a chore; go for ongoing incremental change.
> 3. Try the classroom assessment technique on yourself first.
> 4. Allow for more time than you think.
> 5. Give students feedback: What did you learn? How will you use it to help them?

plex assessments you might give students in preparing them to master course learning goals. Co-authors of the leading book on classroom assessment techniques, Thomas A. Angelo and K. Patricia Cross, include 50 different CATs designed to apply across multiple disciplines. Their vetted CATs assess knowledge, skills, values, attitudes, self-awareness, creativity and students' reactions to teaching, assignments and tests. Angelo and Cross helpfully provide guidance on how long each CAT takes, how others have used it, and how to interpret data. If you are new to using classroom assessment techniques, review the suggestions in Illustration 7-10.

As with any assessment you give, tell your students what you are doing and why. We find it helpful to give a brief explanation about CATs along the lines of:

> *Today, I am seeking information about my teaching. The research on teaching and learning shows that teachers often have misperceptions about what their students are actually thinking, feeling and understanding. I want to know. I therefore am asking you to complete this three-minute exercise. Please complete this exercise anonymously because I am looking for general information about the class as a whole, not for information about you as individuals. I will review your responses after class and tell you what I have learned in the next class.*

Specific classroom assessment techniques

Below are three kinds of classroom assessment techniques: minute papers, student surveys, and analysis charts. We chose these three because you can use them to assess a wide range of skills, knowledge and values. These three are relatively quick and easy to use in class, and can be used at any point in a course. For each CAT, we include information about how to prepare it, the materials you need to administer it, samples, and an estimate of the time you will need to prepare and administer it. (Refer to Illustrations 4-2 and 4-3 for descriptions of levels of thinking—e.g. comprehension, knowledge, evaluation—and verbs you can use to assess those different learning objectives.) For more specifics about preparing CATs, refer back to the earlier section of this chapter on using assessments to help students learn. If you are comfortable using electronic response devices ("clickers"), these devices simultaneously can serve as formative assessment tools for your students and as CATs for you.

Minute Papers

Minute papers are one of our favorite classroom assessment techniques. The name comes from the amount of time students have to respond to a prompt. Although minute papers actually take more like two-to-five minutes, these assessments are quick and easy.

Preparation: Identify a discreet question or prompt to which you want students to respond. Depending on what you want to find out, decide when to administer the minute question (you can do these at any point in a class session). If administered at the beginning of class, and the teacher has time to skim through the answers, these minute questions provide information about what students understand going into a lesson. If most students understand the material, the teacher can proceed to build upon it. If students show misunderstanding, the teacher can summarize and redirect. Administered at the end of class, the teacher can quickly get the same information about that day's discussion.

Materials needed: It helps the students to have the question in a written form on the board, computer slide, or handout. Some teachers also like to have the question printed on a small strip of paper, like a quarter or half sheet of paper; this approach reinforces the idea that students should keep their responses brief.

Sample minute questions:

These questions are designed to assess students' understanding of specific content, usually material discussed in that class or the previous class. Tailor these for your own course.

- "What is the burden of proof necessary for a criminal conviction?"
- "Identify a major factor in determining the 'best interests of the child.'"
- "How does the IRS Code classify a keynote speaker's honorarium?"
- "In your own words, define "hostile work environment."
- "Explain the policy of deterrence in products liability."
- "How can an inventor respond to the Patent and Trademark Office's rejection of a claim?"
- "If the plaintiff's complaint fails to include facts for each of the elements of a claim, what should the defendant do?"
- "A company is dumping toxic waste in the soil. What kinds of relief can the neighbors seek?"
- "Give an example of an offer and an example of a non-offer that is similar to your offer in all trivial respects but lacks an essential feature of an offer."

Other more "global" minute questions that teachers find very helpful include the following. These questions allow students to give you information that they might not otherwise volunteer.

- "What are the three most important things you learned from today's class?"
- "What one or two questions do you have?"
- "What was the muddiest point of today's discussion?"
- "I am most comfortable with the following topics in this course …"
- "I am least comfortable with the following topics in this course …"
- "My biggest question/concern about what I will be asked to do on the final is …"

Minute questions can also be used to assess students' attitudes and levels of confidence. They can be used to help students focus and self-reflect:

- "What does professional behavior look like in this class?"
- "When working in small groups, how do you want your classmates to behave?"
- "Which of the following words describes your dominant feeling today? Love, fear, anger, sadness, or frustration?"
- "How confident are you about your ability to learn environmental law?"
- "What can you do to prepare yourself for the next assignment?"
- "How prepared were you for class today- unprepared, prepared, well-prepared, or able to teach the material yourself?"

Giving feedback: As with any assessment, give feedback. Because minute papers are so short, you can quickly scan through nearly a hundred responses, jotting down notes as you go. Look for general themes and common questions. You may be surprised at what you see, and, depending on how well the question is posed, you may end up with interesting but different information than you anticipated. Make sure you tell students what you found: "Almost everyone had a question about federal preemption." "Most of you showed an understanding of the commerce clause." "The five most common responses were …"

Estimated time to prepare and administer: Fifteen to thirty minutes: one-to-five minutes to generate a question and answer it yourself, five minutes to give it in class, five-to-twenty minutes to review the responses and summarize the main points. Just start small and learn from experience. Don't let perfectionism get in the way of the good.

Student Surveys

Surveys or opinion polls are effective in gauging a range of student responses. More detailed than minute papers, you can similarly adapt them to assess a wide variety of knowledge, skills, or values. They can be especially effective when assessing students' reactions to controversial or highly emotional issues, areas where their views could influence their understanding.

Preparation: Identify a few questions to which you want students to respond. Avoid overkill; asking three -five questions is more likely to be effective than asking 20. You might want to use a Likert scale, asking students to respond to statements by checking whether they:

- Strongly disagree
- Disagree
- Neither agree nor disagree
- Agree
- Strongly agree

You also can ask them to take a position on a topic. For example:

Sixteen year-olds who commit murder should be prosecuted and sentenced:

A. As adults
B. As juveniles
C. As adults or juveniles on a case-by-case basis

D. As juveniles unless the prosecutor presents evidence justifying treating the teens as adults

Materials needed: Written surveys or projected survey questions and scantron forms. You could also administer surveys as on-line quizzes or in class with clickers.

Giving feedback: We recommend that you approach giving feedback on survey responses in much the same way suggested above for minute paper feedback. Get a general sense of the students' responses. In that class or the next, via email or web page, tell the class what you learned. In a professionalism survey Sophie conducted with a class of nearly 70 students, she and the students learned from using electronic response devices that nearly everyone in the class thought that some students were acting rudely. Because the vocal students in the class had said that everyone was acting professionally, this information provided an excellent opportunity for the class to discuss what it meant to act respectfully in a classroom.

Estimated time to prepare and administer: Twenty-five to thirty minutes: ten-to-fifteen minutes to generate questions and field-test them on yourself and someone else, five minutes to administer the survey in class, ten-to-fifteen minutes to review and summarize the main points. Of course, if you have done one before, you can complete these tasks much more quickly. You can also give students feedback on how other classes have responded to the survey.

Analysis Charts

Analysis charts, where you provide students with categories and then have them fill in information, can help students connect pieces of a course. These charts can be especially effective after students have completed a section of a course.

Preparation: Identify multiple categories and kinds of information you want students to organize. As with surveys and minute questions, you can ask students to complete a relatively simple chart in class to get a sense of the knowledge, skills and values students are comfortable with. Ask them to fill in the chart starting with the easiest parts first. You also can ask students to complete these charts in small groups or teams.

Materials needed: Handouts with blank sections of charts on which students can write. Alternatively, you could send the charts to the students electronically before class.

Giving feedback: By walking around the room and looking at students' charts, you can get a quick sense of their responses. You can collect the charts at the end of class and quickly review the responses. During the class, you could also have the students compare their charts with one or more classmates and then submit a group chart. Once you have a general sense of the students' responses, tell the class what you learned.

Estimated time to prepare and administer: Twenty-five to forty minutes: five to ten minutes to generate chart categories and complete the chart yourself, ten-to-fifteen minutes to administer the exercise in class, ten-to-fifteen minutes to review and summarize the main points. As with other classroom assessment techniques, if you prepare one of these for one course, you can reuse it or reuse it with slight tweaking next time, gradually building up a number of analysis chart classroom assessments.

Sample analysis charts

Personal Jurisdiction	**Jurisdiction**	**Facts**
Identify where a court would have jurisdiction over a defendant and list the supporting facts	New York	D has business office in NY

DISCOVERY CHART — Medical Malpractice

Rule number and name	**Kind of evidence gathered**
	Medical records
	Medical examination

Pro and Con Chart

Identify three advantages to having strict liability claims and three disadvantages

Advantages	**Disadvantages**
1.	1.
2.	2.
3.	3.

Evaluating students to assign grades

Grading, or *summative assessment*, which focuses on evaluation rather than practice and development, is the hardest part of assessment to do well. Grades are "high stakes;" students' law school grades can greatly impact their opportunities in school and afterwards. Not all students do well under that kind of pressure. Consequently, unlike using assessments to help students learn during a course or employing classroom assessment techniques to help you improve your teaching, grading requires that we pay much more attention to what we are evaluating and how we doing so. Fortunately, we can apply decades of research to make grading much more effective for our students and less onerous for us.

Illustration 7-11: Evaluating Students to Assign Grades — Essential Elements

> **Evaluating Students to Assign Grades — Essential Elements**
> 1. Use multiple assessments
> 2. Use a variety of assessments
> 3. Evaluate fairly:
>   - Test what you teach
>   - Provide students with grading criteria in advance
>   - Provide students with opportunities to practice meeting criteria before they are graded
>   - Use explicit criteria to ensure consistent grading
>   - Show students how they met grading criteria — make the grading process also a learning process

First, some preliminaries about grading in law school. While some law schools are progressing towards a competency system, where students earn either a "pass," "no pass," or "high pass" instead of letter grades, most schools use letter or number grades. Given that grades are a reality at most law schools, we should find ways to use grading to our students' advantage. As one educator said, "grades are among the most powerful learning and motivating tools we have." We can work within our institutions' required grading systems, including mandatory means and curves, and still improve our grading practices.

For our grades to have any integrity, our graded assessments must be valid and reliable. Students should only earn a grade after having multiple and varied assessments which are fairly administered (see Illustration 7-11.) No research supports the idea of determining grades based solely on one exam given at the end of a semester. We recognize that we are asking you to do more work and perhaps even change the culture of your law school, but we urge you to give your students more than one graded assessment.

We know how important it is for students to have multiple opportunities to practice and get feedback. The same is true for graded exercises. Not all students demonstrate proficiency in the same way. For example, while some students do well on traditional, objective analysis exam questions, others do better if they are asked to use the material as an advocate might use it or to apply what they have learned in drafting a document a lawyer would draft. If we want to be fair, we have to give students a variety of opportunities to show us their success in learning what we have tried to teach them.

In this section we address each of the three essential characteristics of effective grading.

Use multiple assessments

Illustration 7-4 lists different assessments. Any number of these can be used to assign a portion of students' grades. (We address how to calculate grades below) For example, you could have students earn the grades as follows:

- 10% of their grade for class contributions (professional engagement in and outside of class);

- 30% on a midterm exam (containing half essay and half multiple-choice questions);
- 10% on an oral presentation; and
- 50% on the final exam (containing some essay questions, and some multiple-choice).

If this list feels too daunting, consider breaking it into two assessments:

- 25% on a writing assignment and
- 75% on the final exam (containing both essay and multiple-choice questions).

We recognize that this idea may be antithetical to your school culture and that, depending on your risk-taking comfort level, you may balk at increasing the number of assessments used to grade students. Remember, though, that the point of our teaching is to help students learn and that grading is meaningful only if it accurately reflects student capabilities. If you don't adopt multiple assessments, your grading will probably not help your students learn and will risk inaccuracy.

To prepare summative assessment instruments, refer to the list from Illustration 7-5, Common Factors to Consider When Preparing Assessment Instruments. All of these issues are equally important to consider in the summative assessment context, especially because the results can have a major effect on students. A few of these are particularly important, which we highlight below.

Writing test questions and directions

Because of the high stakes involved and the problems if your graded assessment has flaws, you cannot be too careful in constructing your test questions and directions. Sometimes we ask teaching assistants to field-test our graded assessments. Almost always, we have a colleague review them. As the author of a graded assignment, you know what you want students to do, but students frequently answer questions in different ways than we anticipate.

Provide ultra-precise and clear directions. We can't emphasize this recommendation enough. It may take more paper, but giving students plenty of white space, using bullets, numbers and different forms of emphasis help them stay on task. Directions should be written in plain English, using sentences of 25 words or less and paragraphs of 4-8 sentences. Consider what it would be like for someone to translate your directions into a foreign language. Unless you intend an ambiguity, there should not be any doubt about what students are expected to do.

If at all possible, give students the directions before the graded assessment event. It can reduce a lot of needless stress if students know what they will be expected to do and are aware of the exam's format, number of questions, time allotted, and format requirements. Also make sure students know, well before the exam, what materials they can bring to the exam room and use.

How much time will it take?

Few of us do our best under high pressure. The same is true for our students, particularly when we give them little practice. Accordingly, we recommend that you take any test or other assessment that you plan to grade. Assume it will take students at least twice as long or longer.

If the summative assessment is being done under time constraints, such as a one-hour midterm or three-hour final exam, help your students by giving them suggested amounts of time for each section. For example, how many minutes do they have to complete a series of multiple-choice questions? How many minutes per question? Tell them. Students have a hard time budgeting their time; these suggestions help keep them on track. The same is true for any other assignment. It may seem ridiculously obvious to you that a student should spend 75% of their time on 75% of the test's points, but it doesn't hurt to remind students.

Giving take-home assignments.

There are advantages and disadvantages to take-home assignments. If you give take-home graded assessments, we recommend that you either give students a lot of time, such as handing out the assessment a week before it is due, or giving students 8 to 9 hours, particularly if the assessment counts as a large part of students' final grade. When faced with a 24 to 72-hour, high-stakes assessment, some students panic for the whole time, barely sleeping and ending up more stressed than they would be if they had 8 or 9 hours to get the assessment done.

Content.

With graded assessments, humor is rarely effective. Teachers sometimes love to get creative on a final exam, using their names or names of their colleagues in fact patterns and trying to be funny by using jokes or witty turns of phrases. Students rarely find jokes or attempted humor funny on an exam; you are better off avoiding it. Trust us, we love humor. Using humor in the classroom is fun for us and has been found to enhance learning, but using it on a graded assessment doesn't work.

The same is true for distracting content. Do you need to test rape on a criminal law exam? Perhaps, but if the goal is understanding and applying the law, there are lots of other crimes that won't provoke a powerful and negative emotional response in students who may have been raped or abused. Whenever you can, it also helps to make the content realistic and related to practice. Students may use graded assessments as writing samples; having to prepare a license agreement using the law from the fictional planet Marculon is a needless distraction.

Names can be similarly distracting. Avoid names that sound the same, such as Donald and Doreen. The name of every person in a scenario or question should have a name that sounds different from any other person. We like using one-syllable names that start with "P" or "D" when we want to make it clear who the plaintiffs and defendants are. We also don't want to have students spend time and energy on writing names if that is unrelated to our learning goals. As with factual scenarios, it helps to have realistic names of corporations, towns and statutes. ("Big Bad Corp." is not so helpful.) Have a hard time coming up with diverse names and scenarios? Just look on the web or your local paper.

When you design an assessment, consider alternatives to providing content in text alone. Including a photo, a map or other visual can help students more quickly understand the scenario you want them to analyze. Talk to colleagues and check out different websites to get ideas about graded assessments. Exam-writing is one area where we recommend you never do it alone.

Use a variety of assessments

As we know from the science of teaching and learning, students perform differently on different kinds of assessments. We've all had the experience where the students who are most articulate in class struggle with written work; the students who ace multiple-choice and issue-spotting tests have a hard time engaging in effective client counseling simulations. Because the practice of law is multi-dimensional and because students can demonstrate competency in many ways, we urge you to use a range of graded assessments. Use the list in Illustration 7-4 to select a variety of ways to allow students to show their learning.

Evaluate fairly

To evaluate fairly, identify the specific learning objectives you want to measure, establish the grading criteria you will use to evaluate student performance, and provide those criteria to students in advance (see Illustration 7-8 for an example of criteria that could be given in advance). Use explicit criteria when grading to ensure consistency across all students' work and show students how they met those criteria.

Test what you teach

As suggested in Chapters 3 and 4, designing the course and designing the class, you should set your learning objectives and create your assessment instruments before the class has started. If you know what you want students to learn by the end of the course, you can constantly check to make sure your class sessions work towards those goals. As you construct your assessment instruments, review the goals to ensure that you test students on those goals.

Provide students with grading criteria in advance

It is only fair to evaluate students on explicit criteria that you have provided them in advance. When we make his suggestion at our law schools, some colleague always exclaims, "But everyone would get an 'A'!" We have not yet had that experience. Every year, our students' performances have been sufficiently varied to allow each of us to produce grades well within our schools' mandatory grading requirements.

Giving written criteria in advance is not that hard; you can provide students with a list of criteria or a rubric, such as the rubric in Illustration 7-8. If you further explained the relative weight of the different criteria, students could more appropriately focus their performances based on what you say is most important. Giving students explicit criteria encourages students to be metacognitive, or reflective, independent learners (see Chapter 5). Students can also use a rubric to self-assess their own performance.

For example, if you are using oral presentations as an evaluative assessment, you might tell students that the grading criteria and relative weights are the following:

- Content—clear, organized and coherent – 50%
- Visual aids—handouts, slides, props used to enhance content – 20%
- Delivery—audible, clear, varied, responsive and within time limits – 10%
- Creativity—shows innovation in presenting and engaging classmates – 20%

You could describe these criteria to students verbally, as many of us do. But it helps students to have this information in a tangible and reliable format to which they can refer. Using the list above, students would know to focus less on actual delivery and more on creativity. The rubric in Illustration 7-8 also shows students explicitly the breakdown among identifying issues, applying facts, and using policy. Such rubrics provide the criteria and their relative weights, but not the content, and so could be distributed in advance.

Going through the process of articulating the criteria in writing forces us to engage in the same process that we go through when we identify specific learning goals. We have to name what we mean by "analyze the following problem." Usually, we find out that we are expecting far more from students than they (or even we) realize.

Law students often spend an inordinate amount of time struggling to understand unfamiliar material *and* what the teacher wants. They know that we want different kinds of responses to questions and look for different levels of performance. By providing them with clear criteria, examples of previous graded assessments, sample rubrics, and examples of student work, we give them that guidance. Rather than letting students waste time and effort trying to figure out what we want, we can communicate our grading criteria. Appendix 7-2 provides a number of examples of grading rubrics.

Provide students with opportunities to practice meeting criteria before they are graded

As we urge you to do in the earlier portion of this chapter, give students plenty of practice and feedback before you grade them. Practice exams, quizzes, paper drafts, and mock performances, coupled with feedback, promote student learning and allow them to be fully prepared for graded assignments. Grading students on their performance when they have had no opportunities to practice just isn't fair.

Use explicit criteria to ensure consistent grading

Grading without explicit criteria can be unfair and usually is inefficient. Teachers in every discipline are notoriously inconsistent in grading complex student performances when they lack criteria. A single teacher might score the same test differently at different times, and teachers who verbally agree on standards often widely fluctuate in their evaluations of student work. In contrast, when teachers have explicit criteria, such as when using checklists and rubrics, they grade consistently and reliably. In addition, professors can maintain high expectations by modifying criteria according to the level of the course.

Having a rubric, checklist, or scoring guideline also makes grading far more efficient. We have found that one of the hardest things about grading has been spending lots of energy worrying about whether we had graded Exam #123 using the same standards as we used for exam #72. The order in which we grade assignments, our energy level, emotional state, and health may affect how we interpret students' work. When we have explicit criteria, though, we know what we are looking for, and find that we are much more consistent. Sure, creating a rubric takes time but the early investment pays off big time during the actual grading. And once you make one rubric, the next ones are much easier.

Show students how their work met grading criteria- make the grading process also a learning process

Several weeks after they have completed an exam or assignment, students get their grade. For most students, that is where it ends. Students may be delighted or disappointed, but usually have little clue why or how they earned the grade. Some teachers will offer to meet with students to show them the criteria they used to grade the assignments but won't allow a student to keep the student's own copy of the exam question or of the student's answer.

We encourage you to structure your graded assessments so that they also are opportunities for formative assessments; make a graded assessment a learning experience. If the graded assessment occurs before the end of the semester, hold a review session to go over the exam or spend time in class reviewing it. Allow students to see or have the checklists or rubrics you used to assign their grades. Ask several students who have done well for permission to use their work as examples. Let students learn what good exam answers can look like. Even if you want to reuse part of an exam, consider having a window of time, say two or three weeks, when students can view their exams, your comments, scoring sheets, and sample answers.

Talking to students about grades

Talking to students about their exam results and grades can be difficult. Students may be upset, frustrated and angry, whether they earned a B+ instead of an A- or a C. Bear in mind that they may have received grade increases when they talked to their college teachers, and have similar expectations in law school. We have found several practices help make these discussions manageable and productive. The list includes these six practices.

1. *Meet with students in person.* It is easier to read body language, empathize and try to help students learn when you meet with them in person. Talking about grades over email and the telephone is sometimes unavoidable. In those situations, it helps to have students initially let you know what their questions are and then schedule a time to talk or have an electronic exchange.

2. *The 24-hour rule.* Talk to students only after they have had their graded assessment for 24 hours. The time gives everyone a little breathing space.

3. *Have students review all materials and prepare questions before meeting with you individually.* Asking students to review their exam or other graded performance, the scoring criteria, and any other feedback before they meet with you makes the experience much more manageable and specific. If students are given a rubric, and challenge your evaluation of their ability to meet criteria, ask them to show you where in their assessment the criteria were met, "Help me understand where the exam answer analyzes the policy behind patent law reforms."

4. *Almost never change a grade; if you do, only do it slowly and very carefully.* Your school likely has rules about grade changes. We never change grades unless there has been a computational error. We've been known to make mistakes in our math, no matter how closely and carefully we have checked and rechecked. Because grades are such high-stakes, once they are released, any changes are likely to be quickly known by the whole class. If you learn of a mathematical error, it helps to review that exam and score sheet as well as the practice that may have contributed to the problem. If the error is in more than one place, consider how you can fix the problem across the board.

5. *Limit the number of weeks in which students can talk to you about a graded assessment.* Here we are referring to talking about the particular graded assessment, not talking about student learning in the course. One reason for this policy is our limited memories. Having reviewed and graded assessments, they are relatively fresh in our minds. After a few weeks, though, we become less effective in talking to students about their individual efforts. The second and more important reason for imposing a time limit on such discussions is that the sooner students review the graded assessment, the greater its potential as a learning exercise.

6. *Try to make the meeting a learning experience.* We encourage students who wish to meet with us to self-assess their studying and exam preparation process in ad-

vance of the meeting, and we explicitly set, as one goal of the meeting, helping the student discover ways to improve her or his performance on future exams.

Designing and using rubrics

There many ways to develop a rubric and evaluate student work. In fact, we believe that we all have some form of a "rubric" in our head whenever we grade student work; the goal is to make these criteria transparent so that we can improve our grading and our ability to enhance student learning. If you are new at grading law school exams, and haven't developed a rubric in advance, you can still prepare one after the students complete their graded assessments. Below is one method we've used in preparing and applying a rubric. (For shorthand, we are using the term "exam" to mean a graded assessment.)

- Start with students' completed exams.
- Working off a calendar, figure out how much time you have until you want to or are required to submit grades to the registrar. Remember that giving feedback sooner is always more effective for student learning.
- Read quickly through about ten exams, developing checklists for what is effective and what is ineffective. Start your checklists as soon as possible after the exam ends. It is tempting to procrastinate but waiting doesn't make grading any easier, and you will be more stressed. If you must, clean off your desk to make a clear space, but don't indulge your procrastination inclination more than a few hours.
- Read through a few more exams, refining the checklists. Analyze the checklists— what are common themes? What do the effective exams have that the ineffective answers don't?
- Determine how to weight the different effective components—is spotting tricky issues more important than spotting basic issues? How important is the number of issues the students have spotted? How important is the number of facts the students have used in their analysis? How important is the quality of the students' efforts to explain the significance of the key facts?
- Draft the rubric or scoring sheet. Consider this first effort a draft; you may need to change it as you go—students always surprise us.
- Include a "bonus" category; if a student does something really well that makes the exam really thoughtful and rewards what you have taught in class, you can use the "bonus" category to award points.
- Use the draft rubric to score ten exams. Revise the rubric as necessary. Set aside these first ten exams; track their numbers.
- Keeping a list or spreadsheet or other method to track exam numbers or names, start using rubrics to score student exams.
- If the exam has more than one part, such as three essays, grade all students' Essay #1s only. When you have scored all Essay #1s, grade the Essay #2s. This approach helps reduce "drift," where a student's performance on one part of an exam influences your evaluation of another part of that exam.

- Vary the order in which you grade the exams. So if you started grading the first essays starting with low exam numbers, start grading the second essays with the middle or highest numbers.
- Use a pencil or have white-out handy.
- Take breaks every hour, even if only for a few minutes to stand and stretch and even if you don't think you need it. You'll be fresher and more efficient in the long run.
- When you have finished grading all your exams, revisit the first ten you graded. If their scores reflect what you would grade now, having worked through the entire set, you are good. If you have changed your approach (such changes usually are quite slight if you have a detailed rubric), revise the grades. If you notice significant discrepancies, review the next ten, revising accordingly. Keep going until you find that the scores you gave the first time are consistent with the ones you would give the second. Sound hard? Yes. But we want to be fair. If you have a detailed scoring sheet, you will find you are far more consistent.
- Total all the scores. You may want to review the handful of highest and lowest scores.
- Look for trends in scores. Notice where students are doing well and where their scores as a whole reflect that they have struggled. Store that information with your notes on the course (see Chapter 8) so you can consider how to help students avoid those errors the next time you teach the course.
- Submit grades.
- Once you have submitted your grades, you may want to identify a few students who earned high scores on different parts of the exam. Request their permission for you to use their unidentified answers as samples of high quality student work.
- Make a page of notes for yourself about the grading process to help you the next time. What worked? What did you learn? What do you want to remember for the next time you design and use a rubric?

We encourage you to engage in the recursive assessment cycle. Gather information from students about their learning, interpret information, and make changes to your teaching. Repeat.

Checklist for assessing student learning

Illustration 7-12 is a checklist you can use as you work through the assessment process.

Illustration 7-12: Assessing Student Learning Checklist

Using assessment to improve student learning and your teaching

❏ **Identify discreet learning objectives**
  ❏ What knowledge, skills and values do you want students to show they are learning?

❏ **Prepare and give assessment instruments including CATs**
  ❏ What is the rationale for this assessment?
  ❏ What do you want students to do?
  ❏ How much time will it take for students to complete?
  ❏ Will the assessment be completed in or outside of class?
  ❏ What is the assessment's content?
  ❏ Is there a particular format students should use?
  ❏ How much can students collaborate on the assessment?
  ❏ How will you provide feedback?

❏ **Give feedback to students**
  ❏ **Specific.** Students get information about specific criteria.
  ❏ **Positive.** Students find out what they are doing well.
  ❏ **Corrective.** Students learn about their weaknesses and are given strategies to improve them.
  ❏ **Prompt.** Students get feedback while the assessment is fresh and in time for the next one.

Evaluating students to assign grades
  ❏ Use multiple assessments
  ❏ Use a variety of assessments
  ❏ Evaluate fairly:
  ❏ Test what you teach
  ❏ Provide students with grading criteria in advance
  ❏ Provide students with opportunities to practice meeting criteria before they are graded
  ❏ Use explicit criteria to ensure consistent grading
  ❏ Show students how they met grading criteria — make the grading process also a learning process

Engage in ongoing assessment

Chapter 8

Developing as a Teacher

The central aim of this book is to produce significant student learning by designing, delivering, and assessing law school courses and classes. An underlying premise is that teachers play a meaningful role in students' learning. The focus of this chapter is on our continued professional development as teachers. How can we enhance our students' learning by continuing to improve our teaching throughout our careers?

Sustaining a teaching practice

Empirical research demonstrates that university professors are motivated primarily by the intrinsic rewards of academic work, including teaching. Faculty want to feel competent and have a sense of self-determination. The need for self-determined competence leads us to engage in activities that interest us, that provide challenges, and that lead us to learn and achieve. Self-determined competence spurs us to seek feedback on our performance and new strategies to improve our teaching.

Although continued professional development as teachers can provide great satisfaction and reward, we should acknowledge the institutional and personal obstacles. Many law schools value research and publication over teaching excellence. If the quantity and quality of publications is the primary criteria for tenure, promotion, and salary increases, many faculty members will choose to exert more effort on scholarship than teaching. Faculty misconceptions about teaching and learning present obstacles as well. Misconceptions include that (1) if you know the content well, you can teach well; (2) you should master one teaching technique that suits your style and stick with it; and (3) good teachers are born, not made. Research debunks all of these myths: (1) effective teaching requires knowledge of content coupled with pedagogical skill; (2) no single teaching method works for every student or accomplishes every educational goal; and (3) successful teachers learn how to teach and continue to improve their skills throughout their careers. Finally, continuing to develop teaching skills, a complex, human activity, is not easy. As we learn more about teaching and learning, we may uncover shortcomings in our current philosophy and practice. It is common for us to struggle and make mistakes as we implement new methods. Sustained development in teaching requires hard work and perseverance.

The challenges and rewards of ongoing efforts to improve teaching apply to all faculty, not just new teachers or those who are struggling in the classroom. All of us can en-

Illustration 8-1: The Teaching Development Cycle

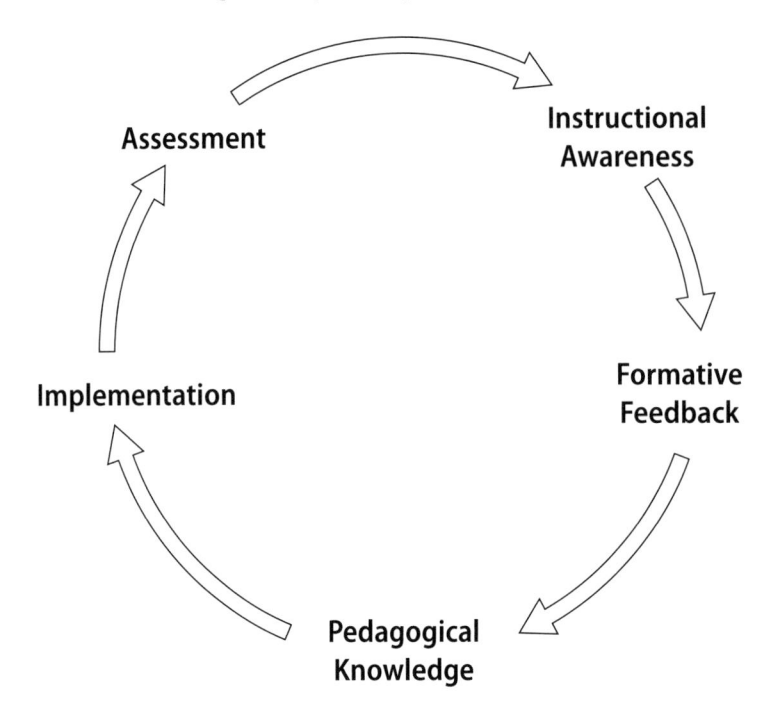

Assessment → Instructional Awareness → Formative Feedback → Pedagogical Knowledge → Implementation → Assessment

hance our effectiveness through reflection, feedback, and innovation. Most models of teaching development are cyclical and involve several stages: instructional awareness, formative feedback, pedagogical knowledge, implementation, and assessment.

Instructional awareness

The first step in the process of improving instruction is to increase our understanding of our own teaching philosophy and practices. What do we believe are the purposes of legal education and our roles as teachers? What assumptions do we make about teaching and learning? What behaviors do we exhibit when we interact with students in and out of the classroom? Are our teaching methods consistent with our educational philosophy?

Formative feedback

Formative feedback is critical to improving teaching and learning. To make effective changes in teaching, we need to know the strengths and weaknesses of our current practices and their effect on students' learning. We can gather that information from ourselves, students, colleagues, and consultants.

Pedagogical knowledge

Deeper understanding of student learning and teaching methods can help us put the feedback we receive in context. We can gain valuable insights from research and scholarship about learning theory, student motivation, learning styles, and factors that inhibit or improve learning. Knowledge about students and learning provide a foundation from which we can examine our current educational philosophy and practices. Likewise, the extensive literature on teaching methods, instructional design, educational technology, and assessment of student performance inform our choices about appropriate adjustments in our teaching.

Implementation

Teaching improvement occurs through changes in our teaching philosophy, attitudes, and behavior. Numerous resources are available to assist us at this stage—books, articles, websites, and videotapes on teaching; discussions with colleagues; working with consultants. To be effective, these changes should be incremental and systematic. A good start in teaching improvement could entail one or two small changes implemented throughout a course. For example, incorporating more small group activities and more ungraded feedback for students throughout the semester would be an ambitious, but achievable, teaching development agenda.

Assessment

The final stage is for us to evaluate the effectiveness of our teaching improvement efforts. Did our changes in philosophy, attitudes, and practices improve our teaching and our students' learning? We can gather this information from the same sources for formative feedback—ourselves, students, colleagues, and consultants. This information forms the basis for the next cycle in our teaching development.

Types of teaching development activities

Many types of faculty development activities are available for teachers who want to increase their effectiveness. In 2006, we surveyed law teachers throughout the United States regarding their participation in twenty-two types of activities to improve teaching. The chart below summarizes the percentage of faculty members who engaged in each type of faculty development activity in the previous five years.

Engagement in Faculty Development Activities to Improve Teaching

Faculty Development Activity	Percentage of Respondents
Thinking about effective teaching methods before and after class	97%
Reviewing student evaluations of own teaching after the course	95%
Talking with colleagues about teaching	94%
Reviewing students' performance on exams, papers, and assignments	93%
Reading articles on teaching and learning	82%
Reviewing teachers' manuals	75%
Observing a colleague's class and providing feedback	58%
Gathering and reviewing feedback from students about own teaching during a course	51%
Attending a workshop on teaching and learning at own institution	51%
Having a colleague observe your class and provide feedback	46%
Attending a session at AALS Annual Meeting on teaching and learning	43%
Making a presentation on teaching and learning	33%
Reading books on teaching and learning	33%
Reviewing institutional data on student engagement and learning	25%
Attending a national or regional conference or workshop on teaching and learning	24%
Writing a journal or newsletter article on teaching and learning	17%
Reviewing a videotape of own teaching (alone or with others)	17%
Reviewing student performance on bar exams	15%
Reviewing websites on teaching and learning	15%
Review a videotape of another's teaching (alone or with others)	11%
Keeping a journal about teaching	9%
Conferring with a consultant about own teaching	5%

These faculty development activities fall in five categories: (1) teachers engaging in faculty development on their own, such as reading books and articles on teaching and learning or keeping a teaching journal; (2) receiving information from students, including reviewing student evaluations or gathering feedback from students during the course; (3) collaborating with colleagues, for example viewing one another's classes or participating in discussion about pedagogy; (4) working with consultants; and (5) attending a workshop or conference on teaching and learning.

Each of these categories of teaching improvement activities is discussed in the sections below. Also included in those sections is the survey respondents' assessment of the effectiveness of each type of faculty development activity on five dimensions: (1) increasing their awareness of their own teaching practice and philosophy; (2) increasing their knowledge of teaching and learning principles; (3) improving their level of confidence in their teaching; (4) increasing their enthusiasm or passion for teaching; and (5) making changes in their teaching practices.

> **Thinking exercise**: Make a list of the teaching development activities you employed in the last five years. Assess the effectiveness of each type of development activity on your list according to the five dimensions above.

Self-Assessment, Reflection, and Study

Many faculty members provide their own faculty development through individual assessment, reflection, and study. Three of the most common teaching development activities for respondents to our survey involved thinking about teaching methods before and after class, reviewing teachers' manuals, and reading articles about teaching and learning. For many of us, the most important source of information is our own observations and reflection on our teaching.

Benefits of reflective practice

Self study and reflection can help us to become more aware of our teaching assumptions and behaviors, to articulate a coherent teaching rationale, and to make informed changes in our instructional practices. Most teachers have deeply ingrained assumptions about teaching and learning, which affect teaching behavior. To grow as teachers, we must identify our current assumptions and behavior that may be hindering our effectiveness. Our observations and reflection can reveal patterns of behavior, habitual responses, underlying motivations, and aspects of our teaching that need improvement. Reflective teachers are able to explain the rationale behind their teaching. That rationale can give us confidence and serve as the foundation for our teaching choices. As a result of examining assumptions and developing a rationale, reflective teachers modify their plans, attitudes, and actions in the classroom. We can model critical thinking for our students by openly questioning our assumptions, articulating our rationale for our actions, and explaining to students the changes we make in our pedagogy.

These benefits of reflective practice are supported by empirical research. Our survey respondents concluded that reflection on their teaching before and after class is effective in increasing their awareness of their teaching philosophy and practices, improving their level of confidence, and increasing their enthusiasm and passion for teaching. Further, law teachers rated reflection (thinking about teaching and keeping a journal about teaching) as the faculty development activities most effective in producing changes in their teaching practices.

Self-Assessment

Evaluation forms and inventories can help teachers engage in self-assessment. We can analyze our teaching behaviors by completing the same course evaluation form that the students fill out at the end of the term. The results can be revealing. According to empirical research of university faculty, most teachers' self-assessments of their strengths and weaknesses agree with their students' assessments.

Inventories help teachers assess the presence, absence, and extent of instructional behaviors. Inventories adapted to legal education allow us assess our teaching in the context of seven empirically derived principles for enhancing learning: Encouraging student-faculty contact; fostering cooperation among students; encouraging active learning, giving prompt feedback; emphasizing time on task; communicating high expectations; and respecting diverse talents and ways of learning. Try completing the inventory dealing with cooperation.

Illustration 8-2. Sample Faculty Inventory

Good Practice Encourages Cooperation Among Students

Assess your teaching practices on each item with the following scale:

    1 Very often
    2 Often
    3 Occasionally
    4 Rarely
    5 Never

____ I ask students to tell each other about their interests and backgrounds.

____ I encourage students to prepare together for classes and exams.

____ I structure out-of-class team projects.

____ I ask my students to provide feedback on each other's work.

____ I ask my students to explain difficult ideas to each other, including to other students whose backgrounds and viewpoints are different from their own.

____ I encourage students to join at least one campus organization.

____ I use small group discussions and exercises in class.

____ I model cooperation and collaboration in my dealings with administrators, staff, and faulty members.

____ I help students understand the value of cooperation and collaboration in law practice.

Did you find doing the cooperation inventory helpful? You can access all seven of the inventories in Appendix 8-1.

Teaching portfolio

Teachers in undergraduate, graduate, and legal education have used teaching portfolios to engage in faculty development. A teaching portfolio is an extensive, reflective type of self-evaluation. One aspect of the portfolio is evidence of a teacher's best work, such as syllabi, course materials, assignments, student work, and a videotape of teaching. Additionally, the portfolio should contain student and peer evaluations of teaching. Most important, portfolios should include the teacher's reflections—the teacher's comments on the evidence in the portfolio, a statement of teaching philosophy, and teaching goals for the future. The process of constructing a portfolio of our teaching can improve our effectiveness as we think deeply about our teaching, rethink practices, and plan for continuing development.

Teaching journal

An excellent tool for reflection is a teaching journal. The process of keeping a professional journal promotes reflection. By writing regularly in a journal we can develop the habit of reflection and reap many benefits of reflective practice.

Journals are a useful device for creating a comprehensive account of our experience. The journal is a place to record problems, successes, strategies for improvement, and ideas for subsequent classes. Because journal entries are made close in time to our experiences, they are often more accurate than our recollections months after the events. Journal writing helps us to clarify our assumptions and theories about teaching and learning, to evaluate the effectiveness of instructional practices, and to identify alternative methods to try in the future. Further, teaching journals are tools for setting goals, planning individual class sessions, and restructuring courses. We can use journals to analyze problems and to work through the strong emotions that accompany teaching. Writing in a journal can helps us deal with our disappointments, fears, and failures. Finally, journal writing can be a vehicle for us to integrate our personal and professional selves and to engage in a lifelong, reflective learning process.

Law teachers who keep a teaching journal rated it as the single most effective faculty development device for prompting actual changes in teaching behavior. Yet, only 9% of the respondents to our survey keep a teaching journal. Why? Keeping a teaching journal is not easy. It takes time, energy, and discipline. And journal writing does not fit the learning style of every teacher; some of us are more comfortable talking about our experiences than writing about them.

Teachers are more likely to engage in journal writing if they find it to be enjoyable rather than a chore. Several practical aspects of the journal writing process can make it more fun and valuable:

- Space. Find a comfortable place to write free of distractions—in the office with the door closed, in a coffee shop, or at home in a comfy chair.
- Time. Schedule time for journal writing; for example, twice a week for thirty minutes or after each class for ten minutes.
- Format. There are many options to fit individual preferences—bound journal books, three ring binders, an artist's sketchbook, a computer.
- Commitment. Put journal time on the calendar and treat it like a professional commitment. But don't let guilt get in the way—if we miss our journal time, so what? Write again later.
- Trust the process. Don't censor. Insight and progress can follow paragraphs of bland, uninspired writing.
- Content. Free-writing in which we describe and explore our experiences is a common form of journaling. An alternative is to write in response to a prompt. Illustration 8-3 contains prompts from Stephen Brookfield's BECOMING A CRITICALLY REFLECTIVE TEACHER (1995). Take a few minutes to respond to the questions in writing.

Was responding in writing to the reflective inventory helpful for you? If so, you can find other reflective prompts in Appendix 8-2.

Print and electronic resources

Numerous print and electronic resources in higher education, including legal education, are available to facilitate self-directed faculty development. Journal articles, books, newsletters, videotapes, and websites address the theory and practice of teaching and learning. Law teachers regularly engage in this type of development—over 80% of our

Illustration 8-3. Reflective Inventory

> What am I proudest of in my work as a teacher?
>
> What would I like my students to say about me when I'm out of the room?
>
> What do I most need to learn about in my teaching?
>
> What do I worry most about in my work as a teacher?
>
> When do I know I've done good work?
>
> What's the mistake I've made that I've learned the most from?

survey respondents reported reading journal articles on teaching and learning and 33% read books on those topics. Reading and viewing these resources can help us improve our teaching in several ways—by causing us to reflect on our instructional practices, by giving us ideas, and by inspiring us to take reasonable risks and exert the effort needed to improve teaching and learning. We react differently to these resources throughout our careers. Each of us has read material on teaching and learning that we found uninspiring and unhelpful yet reread the same material later in light of our new experience and discovered critical insights. The references at the end of this book provide a gateway to the teaching and learning literature.

Formative feedback from students

Feedback from students about our teaching and their learning is an important part of faculty development. Over 90% of our survey respondents engage in two types of activities involving students: reviewing student evaluations after the course and reviewing students' performance on exams, papers, and assignments. In addition, about 50% of the respondents gather feedback from students about teaching effectiveness during the course.

Student evaluations

The most common method of assessing teaching in legal education, and higher education in general, is written student evaluations at the end of the course. Our focus here is not the use of student evaluations of teaching for purposes of making retention, tenure, promotion, and salary decisions. Instead, we address the role that student evaluations can play in teaching development.

Extensive empirical research in higher education demonstrates the value of student evaluations for faculty development. Approximately 80% of college teachers report that student evaluations provide useful feedback that leads to improvements in teaching. Analysis of dozens of studies reveals a persistent positive effect of written feedback from students on subsequent teaching effectiveness. Written student comments provide us with formative feedback and helpful suggestions for improvement in areas such as our clarity, delivery, organization, punctuality, fairness, demeanor, empathy, and availability outside of class.

Despite the potential benefits of end-of-the-term student evaluations for faculty development, some law teachers are reluctant to use them for development purposes. Their reluctance may come from a lack of confidence in the value of student evaluations and the pain that comes from reviewing negative comments. The following ideas may help maximize the usefulness of student evaluations and minimize the discomfort from negative comments.

- Look at the numerical evaluations and read quickly though the comments to get an overall sense of the students' reaction to the course. The first time though the evaluations, many teachers focus on the lower scores and negative comments.
- Review the numerical evaluations a second time to analyze the results. Compare the scores on each item to scores from the previous time or two that you taught the course. Create a chart with these scores and pay attention to the trend in the scores.
- Review the comments a second time to identify themes. Articulate in writing several categories of positive comments. Identify in writing one or two areas in which the students made negative comments or suggested improvement. Compare the positive and negative themes to comments in previous student evaluations.
- Choose an area or two to address the next time you teach the course. Make incremental, not wholesale, changes.
- Try to ignore isolated mean comments, such as "I leaned nothing in this course" or "Professor X should be fired." These types of comments are a reflection on the commentator's problems, not our teaching.
- Read your evaluations with a trusted colleague or two who are reading their evaluations at the same time. Share mean comments. Laugh about them. There is power in camaraderie.
- Have a colleague or consultant review your student evaluations. Another set of eyes can help us see the positive aspects of the evaluations and can assist us in identifying trends, themes, and appropriate adjustments to make in the future.

> **Thinking exercise**: How do you currently use your students' end of the course evaluations of your teaching? How could you make more effective use of those evaluations to improve your teaching?

Feedback from students during the course

Many devices for gathering formative feedback from students during the course are excellent faculty development tools. Our survey respondents rated "gathering and reviewing feedback from students about own teaching during a course" as an effective means of improving teaching in three ways: improving their level of confidence in their teaching, increasing their enthusiasm and passion for teaching, and making changes in teaching practices. The classroom assessment methods described in Chapter 7 help teachers gather feedback from students about their learning and make reasonable adjustments in teaching methods during the rest of the course to maximize students' learning. Additional means of gathering formative feedback including written questionnaires and student advisory teams.

Teacher-Designed Questionnaires. Teachers can design short written questionnaires to obtain detailed feedback from students during the course for the purpose of improving teaching. The questionnaire can focus on a specific aspect of teaching, such as instructional technology, simulation exercises, or course materials.

Illustration 8-4. Teacher Designed Questionnaires

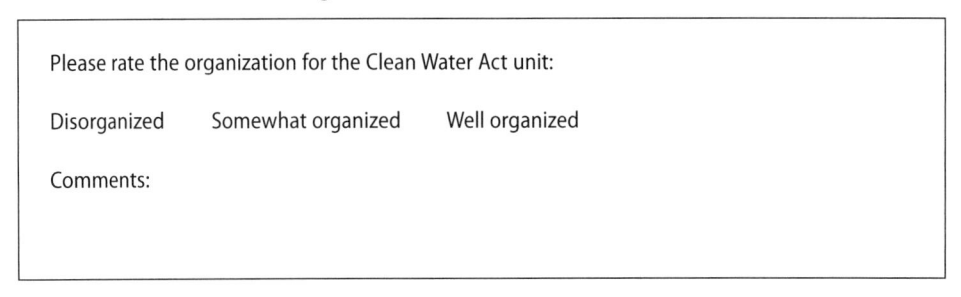

Please rate the organization for the Clean Water Act unit:

Disorganized   Somewhat organized   Well organized

Comments:

Or the questions could address the teaching and learning in the course as a whole and seek suggestions from students.

---

1. What teaching/learning methods have been <u>most</u> effective for you in this course?

2. What teaching/learning methods have been <u>least</u> effective for you in this course?

3. What other teaching/learning methods should we try in this course?

The questionnaire process should be simple. Design a one-page form with three to five questions. Explain to students the purpose of the questionnaire—to gather feedback to make your teaching and their learning more effective. Distribute the form in class. Have your students respond anonymously. Collect and review the responses, looking for prevalent themes. Within a week, report briefly to the class about the common responses to each of the questions. Inform students of at least one suggestion that you intend to implement.

Teachers who use questionnaires during the course can experience several types of benefits. First, students' responses should provide specific feedback and suggestions to improve teaching and learning. Further, the process of seeking feedback from students and implementing reasonable suggestions shows our deep respect for students. Many students will respond by working hard to achieve the goals of the course. Finally, the questionnaire process demonstrates a critical life-long, professional skill—welcoming and profiting from constructive feedback.

Student Advisory Teams. We can get formative feedback by talking with our students informally about their reactions to our teaching methods. A more structured way to gather feedback from our students is through a student advisory team (SAT)—a group of students who meet periodically with the teacher. The students' role is to provide feedback to the teacher about their learning, comment on the effectiveness of particular instructional methods, and offer suggestions to improve the course. The teacher's role is to listen to students' feedback and to implement reasonable suggestions when appropriate.

Illustration 8-5. Student Advisory Team Memo

> I would like to use a Student Advisory Team (SAT) in this course. The purpose of the SAT is to help me improve my teaching and make the course more effective for all students. The SAT will consist of a group of four to eight students. The team will meet weekly throughout the semester for about one hour. I will attend the meeting every other week. The team members will have the responsibility to monitor the course through their own experience, to receive comments from the rest of the class, and to work with other team members to make recommendations to me about how this course, my teaching, and your learning could be improved.
>
> I used SATs in this course last year. As a result of SAT recommendations, I made numerous changes during the year. For example, I made an extra effort to help students see the "big picture," invited outside speakers to class, added more small group work, used more handouts, used more ungraded written assignments, and added litigation documents to illustrate the content and skills we cover. I hope we can use a SAT effectively in this course this semester as well.
>
> If you would like to be a member of the SAT, please let me know by...

The first step in the SAT process is to find student team members. During the first or second week of class, solicit student volunteers via a memo or email message describing the SAT purpose and format. Illustration 8-5 is an example of the body of the memo.

The first meeting with the SAT is important to provide organization, to help the students feel comfortable in their role, and for us to begin receiving feedback. This meeting typically occurs in the fourth week of class or so. To facilitate student preparation for the first meeting, ask them to prepare to respond to three questions:

(1) Why did you volunteer to be a member of the SAT?
(2) Where and when would you like to meet in the future?
(3) What feedback do you have about the course so far — What has been especially helpful for your learning? Not helpful? What suggestions do you have?

Have each student respond to the first and third items, so that, by the end of the first meeting, each student has spoken at least twice. You should listen more than talk.

At subsequent meetings, the students should set the agenda. During those meetings, students provide ongoing feedback and suggestions. Our role is to ask questions to clarify student' comments and explore students' suggestions for the course.

We must decide how to respond to the feedback. Several types of responses are appropriate: (1) implement reasonable suggestions during the course; (2) explore with the team alternatives that we are more comfortable implementing; (3) explain why we will not act on a particular student recommendation; and (4) decide to make changes the next time we teach the course. It is common for some team members to be skeptical about the SAT process until we respond to their suggestions. The best way to motivate team members is for the teacher to immediately implement a suggestion from the team.

Empirical research supports the value of SATs in legal education. Most team members report that their participation improved their attitude toward the course (98%), the teacher (94%), themselves as learners (82%), and law school in general (82%). In addition, most team members believe that the SAT process improved the course (94%), their learning (84%), and the teacher's effectiveness (92%).

Despite the data confirming the benefits of SATs in law school, they are not appropriate for every teacher. Success of the SAT process depends in part on the teacher's belief that students should share responsibility for course design and delivery with the teacher, that students can give accurate feedback on their learning and the effectiveness of teaching methods, and that they can provide useful suggestions for improvement. Even for teachers who hold these beliefs, SATs present significant challenges. The feedback is raw and honest—sometimes it is hard for the teacher to hear. The SAT is unlikely to succeed if the teacher is unwilling to implement reasonable student suggestions. The teacher must be willing to share control of the course with the students.

Collaborating with colleagues

Our colleagues are valuable teaching development resources. Over 90% of our survey respondents talk with colleagues about teaching as one form of faculty development. Around 50% have observed a colleague's classes to provide feedback or had fellow teachers observe their classes for development purposes. Team teaching can be a significant development tool as well. Finally, small group instructional diagnosis combines the benefits of gathering feedback from students and collaborating with a colleague.

Discussions with colleagues

Talking with colleagues about teaching and learning is a common and effective type of development activity. In our survey, law teachers rated this activity as effective on every dimension of teaching development:

- Increasing their awareness of their own teaching practice and philosophy;
- Increasing their knowledge of teaching and learning principles;
- Improving their level of confidence in their teaching;
- Increasing their enthusiasm or passion for teaching; and
- Making changes in their teaching practices.

Discussions among colleagues about teaching and learning can take place in a variety of circumstances. Private conversations between two teachers in a faculty office are commonplace. These conversations between trusted colleagues can uncover common fears and problems, bolster our morale, and motivate appropriate changes in teaching practices. It is especially important for junior faculty members to feel comfortable having these conversations with more senior colleagues. Some of us find colleagues at other institutions that share our passion for educational excellence and engage in monthly phone calls about teaching and learning. Productive interchanges about pedagogy can occur in small groups, for example, at a lunch brown bag discussion. Discussion groups are more likely to lead to instructional improvement if they focus on a particular topic, such as ways to facilitate active student participation in class or how to motivate students to make use of the course website.

Peer observations and feedback

We can help one another improve teaching through class observations and feedback. Peer observations can be especially valuable if pairs of colleagues agree to observe one another's classes. The reciprocal nature of the observations creates mutual vulnerability and shared responsibility. The colleagues can follow a three-step process.

First, the colleagues meet for a pre-observation conference. They discuss their approaches to teaching, goals for the course as a whole and class to be observed, material for the class, expectations for student preparation, what students will do during the class, and the teaching methods to be used. Most importantly, they tell one another the specific types of feedback they would like to receive. Areas for feedback could include organization, clarity, use of visual aids, types of questions, handling student responses, teacher's verbal and nonverbal communication, level of student engagement during class, number of women and men speaking in class, etc.

Second, the pairs visit each other's classes and gather the requested feedback. For example, if the teacher requests feedback on questioning, the observer could write out every question the teacher asks during the class; if the teacher wants feedback on student engagement, the observer could note what the students are doing at one minute intervals during the class.

Third, the colleagues meet for a post-observation conference. Those discussions should include the specific feedback requested in the pre-observation conference, both teachers' positive and negative reactions, the extent to which the goals for the class were accomplished, and an exploration of alternative methods to achieve course objectives.

To maximize the benefits of reciprocal peer classroom observations, the colleagues should work together for a semester. They can sample two or more of each other's classes to get a better picture of one another's strengths and weaknesses. Over the course of a semester, the pairs can develop trust and an ethic of mutual support.

Based on their review of successful peer observation programs at ten colleges and universities, Keig and Waggoner synthesized the following common elements in their book COLLABORATIVE PEER REVIEW (1994):

1. Programs should be built on the premise that "good teachers can become better;" programs should not be considered remedial.
2. Faculty participation should be voluntary.
3. The observed teacher and the observer should be trusted and respected by each other.
4. Classroom visits should be reciprocal (a faculty member should be, in turn, observed and observer)....
5. Observations should occur by invitation only (there should be no surprise visits).
6. Participants should determine in advance what aspects of teaching are to be assessed.
7. Participants should also decide in advance what other procedures, if any, are to be employed in assessing the performance.
8. The lines of communication between the observed faculty member and the observer should be open (feedback should be both candid and tactful).
9. A balance between praise and constructive criticism should guide the feedback process.
10. Results should be kept strictly confidential and apart from summative evaluation [the process of evaluating teachers for retention, tenure, or promotion].

In addition to classroom visits, colleagues are ideally situated to help one another with course design, materials, and evaluation instruments. Peers can provide formative feedback on syllabi, course web pages, readings, and other assignments. Colleagues can be especially helpful in reviewing the materials related to evaluation of student work: quizzes and tests (both graded and ungraded); paper and presentation assignments; student responses to quizzes, tests, and assignments; and the teacher's feedback to students on their performance. Reciprocal review of syllabi, materials, assignments, and tests should have the same supportive dynamic as reciprocal classroom observations.

Checklists can facilitate all aspects of collaborative peer review. Keig and Waggoner include helpful checklists for pre-observation conferences, classroom observations, post-observation conferences, and materials.

> **Thinking exercise**: Identify a colleague with whom you would like to collaborate for a semester in reciprocal classroom visits. Do you feel comfortable committing to observing this colleague and being observed two or three times next semester? If so, give it a try.

Team teaching

Team teaching, in which two or more teachers collaborate in designing or delivering a course, can contribute significantly to faculty development. The extent of the collaboration in team teaching falls within a spectrum. The least collaborative form is guest lecturing in a colleague's course where the colleagues discuss the goals for the class and the methods the guest will use. A more collaborative model involves colleagues in the design of the course but divides the responsibility for delivering class sessions among the teachers. Fully collaborative team teaching involves colleagues in designing the course, planning each class, and teaching together in the classroom.

Team teaching can produce significant benefits. Faculty members report that team teaching produces their most meaningful interactions with colleagues, intellectual stimulation, a closer connection to the university community, and development of teaching skills. Those benefits come from the extensive and ongoing interaction that collaborative team teaching demands, through which colleagues develop trust in one another, discuss their teaching concerns, and generate new approaches to foster student learning. In the classroom, team members have the opportunity to watch closely as their fellow teacher interacts with students day after day, using a style different from their own, and employing different teaching techniques.

Team teaching presents challenges as well. Collaborative design and planning takes lots of time and often involves compromise. Sometimes it is difficult to mesh the team members' teaching philosophies and styles. It may take a while for the team to function smoothly together in the classroom. And there is a danger that two teachers in the classroom will result in more "teacher talk" and less student discussion and active engagement.

Small group instructional diagnosis

Colleagues can help one another gather formative feedback from students. One such technique, Small Group Instructional Diagnosis, receives a strong endorsement from law teacher Gregory S. Munro, in his book OUTCOMES ASSESSMENT FOR LAW SCHOOLS (2000).

An excellent example of a classroom assessment technique for improving teaching is the Small Group Instructional Diagnosis (SGID).... In SGID, feedback about the course and instructor is gathered by breaking the class into small discussion groups to which an outside facilitator [such as a colleague] puts two questions: "(1) What helps you learn in this course?" and "(2) What improvements would you like, and how would you suggest they be made?" Students in each small group discuss and arrive at a consensus in answer to the first question. The facilitator then engages the reporters from each of the small groups in a dialog to arrive at a consensus from the class as to what helps the class learn in the course. The same process is followed in regard to the second question, producing a written set of answers that the facilitator can share with the teacher.

. . . .

Note that the SGID process subjects all student comments or criticisms to peer review while the use of the facilitator maintains anonymity. This increases the validity, reliability, and fairness of the feedback. From the author's experience, peer review screens student comments that would be overly solicitous or particularly hurtful while ensuring that shared objective observations, no matter how harsh, are stated.

Small group instructional diagnosis is a three-step process, similar to the collaborative peer review process discussed above. First, you and a colleague meet to discuss the SGID process, your instructional concerns, and the types of feedback you would like to receive. In that discussion, you and your colleague generate the two or three questions that will be posed to your students. Second, you leave class thirty minutes early to allow your colleague to meet with the students. The colleague collects the feedback from your students and prepares a summary written for you. Third, you and colleague discuss the feedback and suggestions for improvement in the course.

Consultants

Teaching development consultants can be national "experts" from outside of the institution, members of a college or university teaching excellence center, or faculty members from within the law school with expertise in teaching and learning. The roles of consultants and colleagues in faculty development can overlap quite a bit. Consultants can conduct classroom observations, review course materials, lead discussions about pedagogy among colleagues, and act as the facilitator in SGID, all of which are appropriate roles for colleagues as well. Colleagues or consultants could engage in individual coaching and work with peers who videotape their teaching.

Individual coaching

Consultants can coach an individual teacher through a four-phase instructional improvement process.

- Data collection. The consultant interviews the teacher about the teacher's course goals, methods, and materials. They discuss the teacher's concerns about teaching and objectives for the consultation. The consultant gathers information through a self-assessment completed by the teacher, classroom observation, review of materials, student evaluations of teaching, and formative feedback from students.

- Data analysis. The consultant organizes and summaries the data. The teacher and consultant examine the data summary to determine the teacher's strengths and weaknesses. They identify specific areas of the teacher's instruction to address.

- Improvement strategy. The teacher and consultant agree on an objective for change in the teacher's behavior or attitude. The consultant acts as a resource to help the teacher choose an improvement strategy, select new methods to try, or identify appropriate training.

- Feedback. The consultant observes the teacher's instructional changes and provides feedback on their effectiveness. The consultant helps the teacher make appropriate refinements in the improvement strategies.

Empirical research in colleges and law schools establish the effectiveness of individual coaching. For college teachers, the four-stage consultation process resulted in better teaching performance according to student evaluations. Those improvements persisted over time. Although only 5% of the law teachers who responded to our survey reported working with a consultant, they concluded that the consultation was a very effective faculty development activity. The consultation increased teachers' awareness of their teaching practice and philosophy, increased their knowledge of teaching and learning principles, and resulted in changes in teaching practices.

Videotape

Videotape can be a particularly powerful device for assessing and improving our classroom communication skills. A videotape of a class provides accurate, reliable, audio and visual feedback of several areas of our classroom performance:

- Verbal communication—clarity of speech, volume, verbal tics;
- Visual aids—legibility of board work, visual impact of computer presentations;
- Nonverbal behavior—eye contact, movement, gestures;
- Questioning—types of questions we ask and how we handle student responses; and
- Other presentation skills, including organization, flow, pacing, and variety in methods.

Despite the value of videotape in faculty development, many teachers are reluctant to be taped. Only 17% of our survey respondents report viewing a videotape of their own teaching. Their reluctance may be due to anxiety about the taping and review, which can reveal communication glitches and dramatically illustrate to teachers the disparity between their self-image and the behavior they see on the tape.

Several techniques can minimize the anxiety and maximize the value of videotaping and review.

1. Select a "typical" class to be taped. Explain to students that the purpose of the video is to provide feedback on your teaching, not to record their performance. Ask the video operator to try to focus on both you and the students if possible.

2. View the video soon after the class while the class is fresh in your mind. View the tape once to get used to seeing yourself on video and to get over the natural tendency to focus on minor distractions—Do I really sound like that? Look like that? Have those mannerisms?

3. View the tape a second time with a supportive colleague or consultant who can provide perspective and can help you focus on specific strengths and weaknesses rather than the minor distractions (voice, appearance) that have little to do with effective teaching.

4. Use a checklist to help you assess significant components of teaching, such as organization, visual aids, clarity of presentation, questioning, student participation, and classroom climate.

5. Use the video to generate detailed data on specific aspects of your teaching. For example, record every question you ask and analyze the clarity and depth of each question. Or keep track of what is happening at minute intervals—teacher talk? Student question? Student comment? Exercise?

6. With the assistance of a colleague or consultant, choose one or two aspects of your teaching to address in response to the feedback from your review of the tape.

7. Keep control of the tape. It is yours. Save it to review in the future and compare to subsequent videos of your teaching. Or destroy it if that makes you more comfortable.

Here's a link to a checklist for videotape review developed by Barbara Gross Davis in her book TOOLS FOR TEACHING (1993): http://teaching.berkeley.edu/bgd/videotape.html.

Teaching workshops and conferences

Teaching effectiveness workshops rank among the most popular faculty development efforts in higher education and are common in legal education as well. Approximately half of law teachers responding to our faculty development survey report attending a workshop on pedagogy at their own institution or a session on teaching and learning at the Association of American Law Schools' annual meeting. About one quarter of the respondents attended a national or regional teaching conference, sponsored by Association of American Law Schools, CALI, the Legal Writing Institute, the Society of American Law Teachers, or the Institute for Law School Teaching.

Among the twenty-two activities assessed in the faculty development survey, attending a national or regional conference or workshop was among the most effective. Attending these conferences was rated as the most effective in three dimensions: (1) increasing a teacher's knowledge of teaching and learning principles; (2) improving a teacher's confidence in teaching; and (3) increasing a teacher's enthusiasm and passion for teaching. In the two other dimensions—increasing awareness of a teacher's own teaching practice and philosophy, and making changes in a teacher's own teaching practice—attending teaching conferences was rated among the top five most effective teaching development activities. Attending workshops on teaching and learning at their own institutions or sessions on pedagogy at an AALS annual meeting were rated a bit lower than national conferences, but fall in the top half in all five dimensions.

The value of attending national or regional conferences is further supported by a survey that we conducted five years after an AALS teaching and learning conference held in 2001. Most of the respondents reported that their attendance at the conference increased their reflection on teaching methods (97%), knowledge of teaching and learning principles (96%), awareness of their own teaching philosophy (95%), confidence (71%), and enthusiasm for teaching (70%). In addition, 93% of the respondents implemented changes in their teaching practices as a result of the conference. Attending conferences benefited the institution, not just the individual professor. Respondents reported increases in talking with colleagues about teaching and learning (79%), influencing colleagues to implement changes in their teaching practices (53%), making presentations about teaching and learning (43%), influencing the school to emphasize improving teaching and learning (41%), and writing articles and essays about teaching and learning (33%).

Illustration 8-6 presents the complete results on the effects of the conference on attendees.

Illustration 8-6: Teaching Conference Survey — Effects of Conference on Attendees

Effects	Increased Greatly	Increased Somewhat	No Effect	Decreased Somewhat
Thinking about effective teaching methods before and after class	29%	69%	2%	0%
Knowledge of teaching and learning principles	29%	67%	5%	0%
Awareness of own teaching practice and philosophy	24%	71%	5%	0%
Implementing changes in your teaching practices	14%	79%	7%	0%
Talking with colleagues about teaching and learning	17%	62%	21%	0%
Enthusiasm or passion for teaching	18%	52%	30%	0%
Level of confidence in own teaching	7%	64%	24%	5%
Gathering feedback from students about teaching and learning during the course	10%	50%	38%	2%
Influencing colleagues to implement changes in their teaching practices	5%	48%	48%	0%
Reading books, articles, newsletters, or websites on teaching and learning	2%	50%	48%	0%
Making presentations about teaching and learning	10%	33%	57%	0%
Influencing school to emphasize the improvement of teaching and learning	0%	41%	59%	0%
Attending national, regional, or local conferences or workshops on teaching and learning	5%	33%	60%	2%
Observing colleagues' teaching or having colleagues observe your teaching	10%	26%	64%	0%
Writing articles and essays about teaching and learning	0%	33%	67%	0%
Reviewing videotapes of your teaching or your colleagues' teaching	0%	7%	93%	0%

Fostering a culture of teaching

How can a law school create and maintain a culture of teaching and learning? It can employ the same methods that institutions use to foster a culture of scholarship: criteria for appointment, tenure, and promotion; separation between development and evaluation; administrative support; faculty leadership and motivation; institutional reward structure; community, collegiality, and collaboration; scholarship redefined; and continuous process.

> **Thinking exercise**: To what extent does a culture of teaching and learning exist at your institution? As you read this section of the chapter, identify elements of a supportive teaching culture that currently exist at your institution. What would need to happen to enrich that culture? What role would you be willing to play?

Criteria for appointment, tenure, and promotion

Most universities and law schools define the faculty role to include at least three elements—scholarship, teaching, and service. At most institutions, service is subsidiary to teaching and scholarship. The relative weight that an institution gives to teaching and scholarship in appointment, tenure, and promotion decisions demonstrates its commitment to quality in those two areas. If teaching and scholarship have equal weight, faculty will be motivated to excel at both. Schools that value teaching make candidate's aptitude for and experience in teaching a significant element in hiring decisions. Likewise, institutions communicate their commitment to teaching excellence by rigorously assessing teaching through both peer and student evaluations as part of the reappointment, tenure, and promotion process.

Separation between development and evaluation

Law schools evaluate faculty members' performance for purposes of retention, promotion, tenure, and compensation. That summative evaluation process usually assesses performance in all portions of a faculty member's role, including teaching. Rigorous, summative evaluation of teaching can help ensure that personnel decisions are made fairly. However, there is general agreement among researchers that the summative evaluation process has little positive effect on teaching.

Unlike summative teaching assessment, the purpose of which is to judge performance, teaching development activities are designed to improve teaching through formative assessment. At its best, the formative assessment process gathers data and diagnostic feedback, which suggest changes in pedagogical policies and practices to enhance teaching and students' learning. Although the summative and formative processes may gather data from the same sources, including the teacher, peers, and students, the processes should proceed independently. Nearly all faculty development scholars and researchers agree that it is unwise to use the information collected for formative assessment when making personnel decisions. Teaching improvement requires data, feedback, practice, and readjustment, free from the fear that the information will be used against the teacher in the reappointment, tenure, and promotion process.

Administrative support

Successful teaching development requires the clear commitment and support of senior administrators. The law school dean and associate deans should communicate to the faculty, students, and alumni that teaching excellence is a core value of the institution. The dean should give teaching improvement activities the same high visibility that accompanies scholarly achievement. The administration needs to provide financial support for teaching development. Even a modest annual investment can fund significant activities and resources:

- Books, videos, journals on teaching and learning;
- Workshops on pedagogy led by educators from outside of the institution (faculty are often willing to learn new techniques from an outside "expert" even when they reject similar ideas from colleagues);
- Travel and registration fees for faculty to attend national and regional teaching conferences; and
- Consultants to provide coaching, especially for junior faculty as they encounter the steep learning curve and anxiety that can accompany their pre-tenure years.

Many law schools have an associate dean for faculty development. To foster a culture of teaching and learning, the responsibilities of this position should encompass both scholarship and teaching. One role of the associate dean is to work with faculty members to plan teaching development activities. An excellent way to start the planning process is to survey the faculty to determine the activities that would most interest and engage the faculty in a given year. Depending on their interests and level of experience, faculty members' development needs can vary considerably. For example, new teachers may need print resources on basic principles of teaching and learning, workshops on effective questioning, and individual mentoring. Senior faculty may need to rekindle their passion for teaching by attending a national conference on pedagogy or to sharpen advanced teaching techniques, such as methods to develop students' independent learning skills.

Faculty leadership and motivation

Although administrative support is an important part of a teaching culture, faculty development activities that are designed and imposed by the administration may meet with a cold faculty response. Instead, teachers should play leadership roles in all phases of the faculty development effort: planning, design, delivery, and assessment. Faculty involvement in program design, delivery, and guidance increases faculty commitment to the program's success. High levels of faculty input and ownership in faculty development programs correlate with greater faculty participation, satisfaction with the program, and changes in faculty attitudes about teaching.

Faculty participation in teaching development activities should be voluntary. Requiring faculty members to engage in teaching improvement activities will likely lead to resistance and resentment. When teachers are motivated to participate in teaching development, their commitment to implementing instructional changes and to continued improvement are stronger.

Faculty members should be in control of their own faculty development. Teachers not only should decide whether to participate in teaching development activities, but, also, they should choose the extent and nature of their participation:

- Which teaching development activities will be most valuable for them—workshops, discussions with peers, individual reflection?
- What aspects of their teaching should they address—active learning methods, evaluation of students, instructional technology?
- What sources should provide feedback about their current teaching practices—students, peers, videotape, consultants?
- What changes should they make in their teaching—cooperative learning, variety in methods, systematic course and class design?

In her book IMPROVING COLLEGE TEACHING (1990), Maryellen Weimer makes an insightful comparison between teaching development and student learning:

> Improving teaching is very much like teaching students. We do our best to make the content understandable, to make students see its value and importance, to create a climate in which students can experience the content safely. When all is said and done, however, it is the student and the student alone who does the learning. Similarly, it is the teacher alone who changes the teaching.

Institutional reward structure

Law schools support and encourage scholarship with summer stipends, course reductions, release time, and preferential scheduling. The same rewards can support teaching development and increase faculty members' incentives to work on improving their teaching. Institutions should support faculty members who choose to devote their sabbaticals to course development and teaching improvement. Schools that are serious about teaching excellence as a significant factor in tenure and promotion decisions will use the teaching development process and institutional reward structure to help faculty members succeed.

Community, collegiality, and collaboration

A central goal of a faculty development program should be to create and maintain a sense of community around issues of teaching and learning. A critical first step in establishing effective teaching development programs is to help faculty members listen to and respect one another. One of the most important characteristics of a positive teaching culture is collegial interaction and collaboration. Many universities suffer from a lack of collegiality among faculty members. Teaching development programs can open lines of communication among faculty members as they discuss teaching, provide feedback for one another, and support their instructional innovations. Increased communication and collaboration can improve faculty morale and, consequently, faculty commitment to effective teaching and learning.

Most law schools build a culture of scholarship by hosting brown-bag discussions where faculty present scholarly works-in-progress. The same simple process can help law schools establish a culture of teaching and learning. Law schools can host teaching and learning discussion sessions on a biweekly or monthly basis. As with scholarly presentations, faculty could volunteer to lead sessions on topics such as active learning, discussion techniques, instructional technology, student motivation and engagement, course design, and testing and grading. A portion of a videotape of a faculty member's class could be the spark for a lively brownbag session. Faculty should be encouraged to try new techniques and debrief their instructional innovation efforts with their colleagues.

The participation of good and excellent teachers in faculty development activities helps foster a positive teaching culture. Their involvement sends the message that effective teaching is not innate, but is instead a set of knowledge, skills, and attitudes that must be developed through ongoing effort. The participation of passionate, effective teachers can make the discussions about teaching, learning, and students more positive, rather than focusing on the negative comments sometimes expressed by struggling, disengaged teachers. If excellent teachers are enthused with the development activities, it counters the perception that teaching development is "remedial" and encourages less confident teachers to participate.

Scholarship redefined

Faculty productivity in publishing doctrinal law review articles and making presentations on substantive topics is highly valued at most law schools. To foster a teaching culture, presentations and journal articles on pedagogy deserve the same value. Scholarly activities should be evaluated on the same set of criteria (depth of research, quality of writing, originality of ideas, etc.) regardless of the topic.

Presentations and publications on teaching and learning are effective faculty development activities. In our faculty development survey, respondents rated both activities as effective on all five dimensions. Making presentations on teaching and learning was especially effective in improving teachers' confidence and increasing their enthusiasm for teaching. Writing a journal or newsletter article on teaching and learning was especially effective in increasing respondents' passion for teaching and their awareness of their own teaching philosophy and practices.

Continuous process

Teaching development should be an ongoing process, not a one-time event. By offering a flexible mix of development activities throughout the year, the law school helps faculty members maintain collaborative relationships, share new ideas on teaching and learning, and build a teaching community. Improving law professors' teaching skills involves substantial time and effort from teachers, not quick fixes. Empirical research demonstrates that teaching development programs are more likely to have lasting effects if they continue for more than a semester and include follow-up activities, such as refresher training, reports to colleagues on instructional changes implemented, or assessment of the effects of new teaching techniques on student learning.

Illustration 8-7 is a checklist you can use to guide your continued development as a teacher.

Illustration 8-7: Teaching Development Checklist

Teaching Development Activities

- **Self assessment, reflection, and study**
  - Thinking about effective teaching methods before and after class
  - Reading books and articles on teaching and learning
  - Completing inventories on teaching practices
  - Constructing a teaching portfolio
  - Writing an article on teaching and learning
  - Keeping a teaching journal

- **Formative feedback from students**
  - Reviewing student evaluations of your teaching after the course
  - Gathering feedback from students on your teaching during the course (questionnaires, student advisory teams)

- **Collaborating with colleagues**
  - Talking with colleagues about teaching and learning
  - Observing a colleague's class and providing feedback
  - Having a colleague observe your class and provide feedback
  - Engaging in team teaching

- **Working with a consultant**
  - Receiving individual coaching on teaching strengths and weaknesses
  - Reviewing video of your teaching

- **Teaching workshops and conferences**
  - Attending a national or regional conference on teaching and learning
  - Attending a workshop at your institution on teaching and learning
  - Making presentations on teaching and learning at conferences or workshops

Evaluation criteria for teaching development activities

- **Increasing your awareness of your own teaching practice and philosophy**
- **Increasing your knowledge of teaching and learning principles**
- **Improving your level of confidence in your teaching**
- **Increasing your enthusiasm or passion for teaching**
- **Making changes in your teaching practices**

Appendices

The following pages provide examples of how we have implemented the various principles discussed in the book. We have organized this Appendix in the same way we have organized the book. (Note: There are no appendices for Chapters 1 and 2.)

Appendix 3-1: Course Goals

Course Goals for Civil Procedure I Course

A. Affective—Students and teacher will have a challenging and enjoyable learning experience.
B. Values. Students will:
   1. Demonstrate respect for students, staff, and faculty.
   2. Develop an attitude of cooperation with students, faculty, lawyers, judges.
   3. Understand the multiple roles of a lawyer in civil dispute resolution.
   4. Identify ethical issues involved in civil dispute resolution.
   5. Begin to formulate his or her version of the moral lawyer.
   6. Demonstrate honesty, reliability, responsibility, judgment, self-motivation, hard work, and critical self-reflection.
C. Skills.
   1. Case Analysis. Students will master the following skills:
      a. Identification of the elements of a reported opinion: procedural facts, issue, holding, rationale, legal rules, policy.
      b. Synthesis of a line of related opinions.
   2. Statutory Analysis. Students will master the elements of statutory analysis:
      a. Close reading of the words of the statute.
      b. Identifying the purpose of the statute.
      c. Fitting the statute into the broader statutory scheme.
      d. Using legislative history.
      e. Using cases interpreting the statute.
   3. Legal Problem Solving. Students will master these problem-solving skills:
      a. Identifying legal issues in simple and complex fact situations.
      b. Identifying the relevant legal authority and policy.
      c. Identifying potential alternatives to achieve the client's goals.
   4. Legal Argument. Students will be able to make effective legal arguments:
      a. Identifying the legal issues.
      b. Identifying the relevant facts, authority, and policy.
      c. Supporting the client's position with facts, authority, and policy.
      d. Distinguishing unfavorable facts, authority, and policy.
   5. Legal Drafting. Students will draft legal documents that communicate clearly, are persuasive, and comply with applicable rules.
   6. Critical Thinking. Students will:
      a. Evaluate cases, statutes, arguments, documents, and attorneys' actions on their effects on (1) clients, (2) the civil litigation system, and (3) society.
      b. Challenge assumptions made by judges, legislators, attorneys, students, professors, and themselves.
   7. Lawyering Skills. Students will experience basic lawyering skills, such as fact investigation and oral argument.
D. Content. Students will be able to identify:
   1. Alternatives to civil litigation to resolve disputes.
   2. The basic law and policy of civil procedure: Jurisdiction, venue, pleading, pretrial motions, and discovery.

Course Goals for Torts Class

My goal is to have you develop solid skills that will help you as lawyers. Accordingly, I have high expectations for your performance in class and on assignments. I have these expectations because I believe you can do the work, and I will coach you through the process. I demand a lot from you because I seek to prepare you as professionals. I seek to work hard, have fun and have you learn as much about understanding, applying and analyzing the law of torts.

At the end of the course, you should be able to show me in writing and orally how lawyers solve problems in the area of torts—what laws they use, how they apply them to new facts, and how they use those facts to make arguments to judges or juries.

Specific goals include the following:

A. **Affective.** Students and teacher will have a challenging and enjoyable learning experience.
B. **Values.** Students will:
   1. Demonstrate respect for students, staff, and faculty.
   2. Develop an attitude of cooperation with students, faculty, lawyers, and judges.
   3. Develop on-going investment and monitoring of professional development.
   4. Identify ethical issues involved in tort issues.
   5. Demonstrate honesty, reliability, responsibility, judgment, self-motivation, hard work, and critical self-reflection.
C. **Skills.**
   1. **Case Analysis.** Students will master the following skills:
      a. Identifying the elements of a reported opinion: procedural facts, legally relevant facts, issue(s), holding(s), reasons and policies, legal rules, and disposition.
      b. Synthesizing a line of related opinions.
   2. **Legal Problem Solving.** Students will master these problem-solving skills:
      a. Identifying legal issues in simple and complex fact situations.
      b. Identifying the relevant legal authority and policy.
      c. Identifying potential alternatives to achieve the client's goals.
   3. **Legal Argument.** Students will be able to make an effective legal argument by:
      a. Identifying the legal issues.
      b. Identifying the relevant facts, authority, and policy.
      c. Supporting the client's position with facts, authority, and policy.
      d. Distinguishing unfavorable facts, authority, and policy.
   4. **Legal Drafting.** Students will draft legal documents that communicate clearly, are persuasive, and comply with applicable rules.
   5. **Critical Thinking.** Students will:
      a. Evaluate cases, statutes, arguments, documents, and attorneys' actions on their effects on (1) clients, (2) the tort system, and (3) society.
      b. Evaluate the strategy and ethics of applying different torts causes of action.
      c. Challenge assumptions made by judges, legislators, attorneys, students, professors, and themselves.
   6. **Lawyering Skills.** Students will experience basic lawyering skills, such as fact investigation and oral argument.

D. **Content.** Students will learn:
   1. The basic law and policy of torts: negligence, intentional torts and products liability.
   2. Which tort issues are decided by judges, which by juries (or judges sitting as fact finders.)
   3. The interrelationship of different torts causes of actions.

Appendix 3-2: Lesson Objectives

Objectives for a Lesson on Express Conditions

By the end of this lesson, you will be able to:

a. Distinguish contract terms that unmistakably are promises from contract terms that raise an issue as to whether they are express conditions;

b. Analyze whether possible express conditions are, in fact, express conditions;

c. Analyze whether an express condition has occurred;

d. Articulate the rules dealing with the legal significance of the occurrence or non-occurrence of a condition;

e. Apply the rules dealing with the legal significance of the occurrence or non-occurrence of a condition to the facts of a case;

f. Draft a contract term that unmistakably would be treated as an express condition;

g. Draft a contract term that unmistakably would be treated as a promise.

Appendix 3-3: Syllabi

Torts Syllabus

I. GENERAL INFORMATION

Class Meetings: Room __, Tuesday and Thursday 3:00-4:30 p.m.
Office: Room 214
Phone:
Work:
Home:
Mobile:
Email: _____
Office Hours:

Tuesday 10:00-12:00 - and 1:00-2:30 pm (can modify if these times don't work for you) Anytime by appointment

During the Tuesday times, unless I have notified you otherwise, I will be in my office with free time; I strongly encourage you to come see me if you have any questions about the class.

You should feel free to come by at other times. If I am not busy I will be happy to talk with you. You can also email me or talk to me after class to arrange an appointment. For questions about course material, I encourage you to post them to the Torts TWEN discussion board—you can do so anonymously. I will answer them if one of your classmates doesn't do so first. Chances are that if you have questions, your classmates do too.

Preferred contact: Drop by or email

II. MATERIALS

Course Materials:

Required: Best & Barnes, Basic Tort Law, 2nd ed. (Aspen 2007).

Recommended:

Joseph W. Glannon, The Law Of Torts: Examples And Explanations (Examples & Explanations) (2005)

A Concise Restatement of Torts, (ALI 2000)

There will be some oral and written exercises during the class—some in teams and some individual. These are required. I will do my best to schedule all exercises and written assignments to avoid conflict with Legal Skills deadlines.

Teaching Assistants:

- _____ 2L, _____ 2L, _____ 2L, _____ 2L
- Will hold weekly sessions at times to be announced
- You can also seek assistance from the TAs by contacting them via piercelaw email

Course website - TWEN -

- Please sign up by September 2
- Please use your piercelaw.edu email when signing up
- All electronic written course materials will be on TWEN
- Please post questions to TWEN—you may post anonymously

Mass Media - articles, clips, web pages - materials we find related to torts

Class handouts

During the semester, I will hand out assignment sheets, exercises and supplementary material in class. Whenever possible, copies will also be available online, on the Torts TWEN site. These become part of your course materials. I will provide you with one hard copy; you are responsible for other copies.

CALI - on-line computer exercises and tutorials - I will let you know when you may find these useful.

III. COURSE GOALS

My goal is to have you develop solid skills that will help you as lawyers. Accordingly, I have high expectations for your performance in class and on assignments. I have these expectations because I believe you can do the work, and I will coach you through the process. I demand a lot from you because I seek to prepare you as professionals. I seek to work hard, have fun and have you learn as much about understanding, applying and analyzing the law of torts.

At the end of the course, you should be able to show me in writing and orally how lawyers solve problems in the area of torts - what laws they use, how they apply them to new facts, and how they use those facts to make arguments to judges or juries.

Specific goals include the following:

A. **Affective.** Students and teacher will have a challenging and enjoyable learning experience.

B. **Values.** Students will:
   1. Demonstrate respect for students, staff, and faculty.
   2. Develop an attitude of cooperation with students, faculty, lawyers, and judges.
   3. Develop on-going investment and monitoring of professional development.
   4. Identify ethical issues involved in tort issues.
   5. Demonstrate honesty, reliability, responsibility, judgment, self-motivation, hard work, and critical self-reflection.

C. **Skills.**
   1. **Case Analysis.** Students will master the following skills:
      a. Identifying the elements of a reported opinion: procedural facts, legally relevant facts, issue(s), holding(s), reasons and policies, legal rules, and disposition.
      b. Synthesizing a line of related opinions.
   2. **Legal Problem Solving.** Students will master these problem-solving skills:
      a. Identifying legal issues in simple and complex fact situations.
      b. Identifying the relevant legal authority and policy.
      c. Identifying potential alternatives to achieve the client's goals.
   3. **Legal Argument.** Students will be able to make an effective legal argument by:
      a. Identifying the legal issues.
      b. Identifying the relevant facts, authority, and policy.
      c. Supporting the client's position with facts, authority, and policy.
      d. Distinguishing unfavorable facts, authority, and policy.
   4. **Legal Drafting.** Students will draft legal documents that communicate clearly, are persuasive, and comply with applicable rules.

5. **Critical Thinking.** Students will:
    a. Evaluate cases, statutes, arguments, documents, and attorneys' actions on their effects on (1) clients, (2) the tort system, and (3) society.
    b. Evaluate the strategy and ethics of applying different torts causes of action.
    c. Challenge assumptions made by judges, legislators, attorneys, students, professors, and themselves.
6. **Lawyering Skills.** Students will experience basic lawyering skills, such as fact investigation and oral argument.

D. **Content.** Students will learn:
   1. The basic law and policy of torts: negligence, intentional torts and products liability.
   2. Which tort issues are decided by judges, which by juries (or judges sitting as fact finders.)
   3. The interrelationship of different torts causes of actions.

IV. TEACHING AND LEARNING METHODS

Tell me,
I forget.
Show me,
I may remember.
Involve me,
And I'll understand.

—Confucius

We will use a variety of teaching/learning methods to achieve the goals of this course, to keep things interesting, and to accommodate various learning styles. I ask for your forbearance when I am using a style that works for others, but not for you.

The methods include:

A. Teacher and student presentation
B. Whole class, small group and team discussion and problem solving
C. Simulations - preparation of legal documents and participation in legal proceedings
D. CALI
E. Practice exams and quizzes
F. Writing assignments
G. Other

V. ROLES

A. **Teacher**
   1. Work hard to help students succeed in the course
   2. Share knowledge
   3. Model skills and values
   4. Provide feedback to students
   5. Lead in course and class design
   6. Lead in maintaining a positive, challenging learning environment
   7. Provide feedback to students
   8. Grade student performance
   9. Other

B. Students
   1. Work hard to achieve the goals of the course
   2. Assist in course and class design
   3. Actively contribute to maintaining a positive, respectful, challenging learning environment
   4. Share knowledge
   5. Provide feedback to teacher and other students
   6. Cooperate and collaborate with other students working in teams
   7. Other

VI. PROFESSIONAL ENGAGEMENT IN LAW SCHOOL

As you may know, you are creating your professional reputation in the law. Accordingly, please behave as the best attorneys do. This includes paying attention and responding to what others say as well as working with others to collectively learn the material. Please be prepared for class and to be ready to work. Please listen to others, avoid dominating discussion, take the initiative to improve your skills, take risks and be resourceful. Please seek help when you realize you need it or when recommended. Please show up every day on time and stay in class the whole time. If you have questions about this, please contact me.

You will all be working in teams of 6-7 students. I will assign you to your teams on the first day of class. Everyone in the team has the responsibility of making sure that the team works together effectively and efficiently.

If you are unable to attend a class due to illness or other good reason, please notify me and your team in writing **before class,** if at all possible. You may receive an excused absence if you notify me **in writing** why you need to miss class and provide me with sufficient information for me to excuse you. You will automatically be excused for an absence due to religious observation **if you have provided advanced written notice.** Such absence will not count toward your maximum absence total for the semester. If you are not comfortable explaining your reason to me, please contact the Assistant Dean for Student Affairs. Providing notice in writing may be done through email.

If you accumulate 4 or more unexcused absences, you will fail the course and you will be given an "F" in the class.

You are responsible for learning information and getting the handouts provided in class or made available online. If you missed class, talk to classmates to learn what happened and get notes. After talking to classmates, if you have additional questions, talk to TAs and me.

When you are in class, please be *prepared* **to participate in the discussion—and** *to engage.* Being "prepared" does not mean you have become an expert on the material; it does mean that you will have read (generally more than once for court opinions) and thought about the assigned materials, completed assigned work, and be ready to engage and discuss this work with others. You will not be penalized for asking what you might think are "stupid questions" or letting me know when you are confused. You are responsible, however, for asking questions when you do not understand material.

In class, you are each responsible for participating to an appropriate extent, i.e., neither being silent nor dominating the discussion, but doing your share of the talking.

If you cannot prepare for a class, please notify me that you are unprepared at the beginning of class. Being unprepared counts as an unexcused absence. If you are not prepared for some classes, I may ask you to leave. This would be because we will be discussing material specific to a graded assignment, and it is only appropriate to have the discussion with students who have already completed the assignment.

Professional engagement includes:

- *Resourcefulness.* If you have a problem, first try to figure out a way to solve it.
- *Taking risks.* For some of you, this means volunteering to speak in a class. For others, it is the risk of being silent and not leading a small group discussion. It may mean admitting that you are off track or that you need help with an aspect of the course.
- *Behavior in class.* Interrupting others, talking while whole class instruction or discussion is going on, or making disparaging remarks about other students is unacceptable. If you have been assigned an in-class exercise and find that you have finished it before others, ask for feedback or work on other aspects of the course. Encouraging and allowing others to talk is as important as your talking. Listening skills are an enormous aspect of effective lawyering.
- *Computer usage.* Because of computer abuses, using a computer in a way that does not support your learning — checking email, surfing the internet, IMing, etc. — will be considered an absence from class.
- *Attitude.* Having a positive approach to working with others is important. You are welcome to voice your questions, concerns, and complaints about the course. You are asked to do so directly to me, in person. If you have a complaint, be prepared to offer a solution.
- *Depth and thoughtfulness of your work.* This includes in-class contributions and written assignments.
- *Investing in your learning and growing from your mistakes.* If you have received feedback on an assignment, try to understand it and use it. If one learning approach has not worked effectively, try another, and reflect on what works. Ask questions about material you don't understand, and struggle with analyzing a problem before giving up. If you sense you are falling behind, based on exercises and class assignments, please ask for help.
- *Effort and perseverance.* This overlaps with some of the other categories but bears repeating. A student who does not give up, but keeps working to develop his or her skills, regardless of where he or she is, is acting professionally.
- *Timeliness.* Completing all assignments on time.

VI. EVALUATION AND GRADES
  A. **Principles (not negotiable)**
   1. Multiple (more than one evaluation)
   2. Varied (different methods of evaluation)
   3. Fair (opportunity for practice and feedback; clear directions and criteria)
  B. **System (negotiable)**
   Your grade in the course will be based on the total number of points you earn each semester. Points will be awarded for a variety of written assignments (documents, short essays, quizzes) and exams (part essay, part multiple choice). In addition, there may be in-class writing throughout the semester.
  C. **Graded Performances**
   There will be up to six short, multiple choice Readiness Assessment Quizzes (RAQs) given during the course — one ***toward the beginning*** of each unit. (The

same RAQs will be given to individuals and to teams.) There will be one final take home open book exam, and two team open book application assessments.

D. **Grading Criteria:**
Scores in three major performance areas will determine the grades in this class: Individual performance, team performance, and team contribution.

Grade weights*	Within Area	% of Total
1. Individual performance		<u>45%</u>*
Individual Readiness Assessment Quizzes (0–50%)	**50%***	
Individual Final Exam Open Book (50–100%)	**50%***	
2. Team Performance		<u>40%</u>*
Team Readiness Assessment Quizzes	34%	
Team Assessment I	33%	
Team Assessment II	33%	
3. Team Contribution (Evaluated by Peers)		<u>15%</u>*

*As decided by Torts students, Class 1, Tuesday, August 26, 2008

Environmental Law Syllabus

I. **GENERAL INFORMATION**

Office: Faculty Suite 427

Phone: _____

Office Hours:

   Tuesday   11:00-4:00

   Thursday   10:00-11:00

   Anytime by appointment

Email: _____

Faculty Assistant

   _____

   Faculty Suite

   _____ (assistant's phone number)

   _____ (assistant's e-mail address)

II. **MATERIALS**
  A. Course Books
   1. Percival, Schroeder, Miller, Leape, Environmental Regulation: Law, Science, and Policy (5th. ed. 2006)
   2. Environmental Law Statutory and Case Supplement with Internet Guide (Aspen, 2008-2009)
   3. Hess, Environmental Law - Spring 2009 Supplement (available on TWEN)
  B. Mass Media
  C. Documents
  D. TWEN
  F. Internet
  G. Video
  H. CALI

III. **GOALS**
  A. Teacher and students will have an enjoyable and challenging learning experience.
  B. Content. Students will learn the overview and most important details of the following:
   1. Environmental Law Perspectives (personal, ecological, economic, philosophical, historical, risk)
   2. Administrative agency actions and judicial review
   3. National Environmental Policy Act
   4. Clean Water Act
   5. Endangered Species Act
   6. Clean Air Act
  C. Skills. Students will:
   1. Refine statutory analysis skills through standard of review, statutory language, statutory purpose and policy, overall statutory scheme, legislative history, regulations applying the statute, cases interpreting the statute.

2. Analyze problems involving environmental law in real life.
3. Develop presentation skills relevant to working with environmental law issues in real life.

IV. COURSE DESIGN

We will spend part of the first class session engaging in course design. We will make collaborative decisions regarding course goals, methods, roles, responsibilities, and evaluation. In particular, we will address the following design issues.

Goals (What do you hope to get out of the course? What content and skills do you hope to learn?)

Teaching and Learning Methods (What methods should we use to achieve the goals of the course?)

Student Role and Responsibility (What do you expect of yourself and your fellow students?)

Teacher Role and Responsibility (What do you expect of me?)

Evaluation. (See the next page for a proposed evaluation system. Do you have suggestions for changes in the proposal?)

V. EVALUATION
A. Principles
1. Multiple
2. Varied
3. Fair (clear directions and criteria)

B. Methods. Your grade will be based on your performance in the following areas:
   1. Paper (30-50%). The purpose of the paper is to assess your ability to critically analyze a real-world situation based on the content and skills you learned in this course. You must choose a subject related to the coverage of this course. The paper cannot exceed 10 pages, double spaced.
   2. Exam (30-50%). The purpose of the exam is to assess your knowledge of the course content and statutory analysis skills. The final will be a three-hour open book exam. The format will be part essay and part multiple-choice.
   3. Participation (20%) Successful completion of all of the following would earn the full 20% for this portion of the grade. Successful completion of less than all of the following would earn a lower percentage, based on my judgment.
      - Prepare for, attend, and be actively involved in all class sessions
      - Complete five short writing/research/presentation assignments. Each project is limited to one page, single-spaced. Brief descriptions of these projects follows:

<u>Web site review.</u> The purpose is to locate and review a Web site related to environmental law covered in this course. For example, there are applicable Web sites maintained by federal and state agencies, public interest groups, and industries. The paper should give the site's URL, describe the site, explain its usefulness, and include your reflection on what you learned from the site.

<u>Public comment.</u> The purpose is to make public comment in a proceeding relating to a portion of environmental law covered in this course; for example, a proposed rule, a permit application, or an EIS. The paper should contain the text of your written or oral comment and your reflection on what you learned from the comment process.

One of these:

<u>NEPA document.</u> The purpose is to locate and describe an environmental assessment, environmental impact statement, finding of no significant impact, or other NEPA document. The paper should describe the document, explain its usefulness or applicability, and include your reflection on what you learned from the document.

<u>ESA recovery plan or guidance.</u> The purpose is to locate and describe a recovery plan, listing decision, USF&WS guidance document, or other comparable ESA document. The paper should describe the document, explain its usefulness or applicability, and include your reflection on what you learned from the document.

One of these:

<u>CAA emission limit, permit, or guidance.</u> The purpose is to locate and describe an emission limit for an industry, a permit for an industry, an EPA guidance document related to the CAA, or a comparable CAA document. The paper should describe the document, explain its applicability or usefulness, and include your reflection on what you learned from the document.

<u>CWA effluent limit, water quality standard, NPDES permit, or guidance.</u> The purpose is to locate and describe an effluent limit for an industry, an NPDES permit for an industry or municipality, a state water quality standard, an EPA guidance document related to the CWA, or other comparable CWA document. The paper should describe the document, explain its applicability or usefulness, and include your reflection on what you learned from the document.

One of these:

Interview. The purpose is to report on an interview with a person involved with some portion of the environmental law covered in this course. For example, the interview could feature an environmental lawyer, a regulator, or a person subject to regulation. The paper should describe the person's views of environmental law in practice and include your reflections on what you learned from the interview.

Field trip. The purpose is to see an industry, business, governmental facility, or site affected by environmental law covered in this course; for example, a wastewater treatment facility, industrial facility, or a farm. The paper should describe how the site or facility is governed by some aspect of the law we covered in this course and your reflection of what you learned from the trip.

SPRING 2009 SCHEDULE

Week	Unit
January 12	1
January 19	2
January 26	3A, B
February 2	doc, 3C, D
February 9	3E, 4A, B
TFebruary 16	4C, D
February 23	4 E, F, G
THMarch 2	4H, I, J
March 9	Spring Break
March 16	5A, B
March 23	5C, D, E
March 30	6A, B
April 6	6C, D
April 13	6E, F, G
April 20	6H
April 27	Papers

Papers due in class on April 24 .

Final Exam on May 11 at 1:30.

Appendix 4-1: Charts, Tables, and Diagrams

Dismissal under FRCP 41 Chart

Type of Dismissal	Subsection of FRCP 41?	Which party uses this type?	When is this type used?	With or without prejudice?
Voluntary Notice of Dismissal				
Voluntary Stipulation for Dismissal				
Voluntary Order for Dismissal				
Involuntary				

APPENDICES

Chart Depicting Restitution in the Context of a Contracts Course

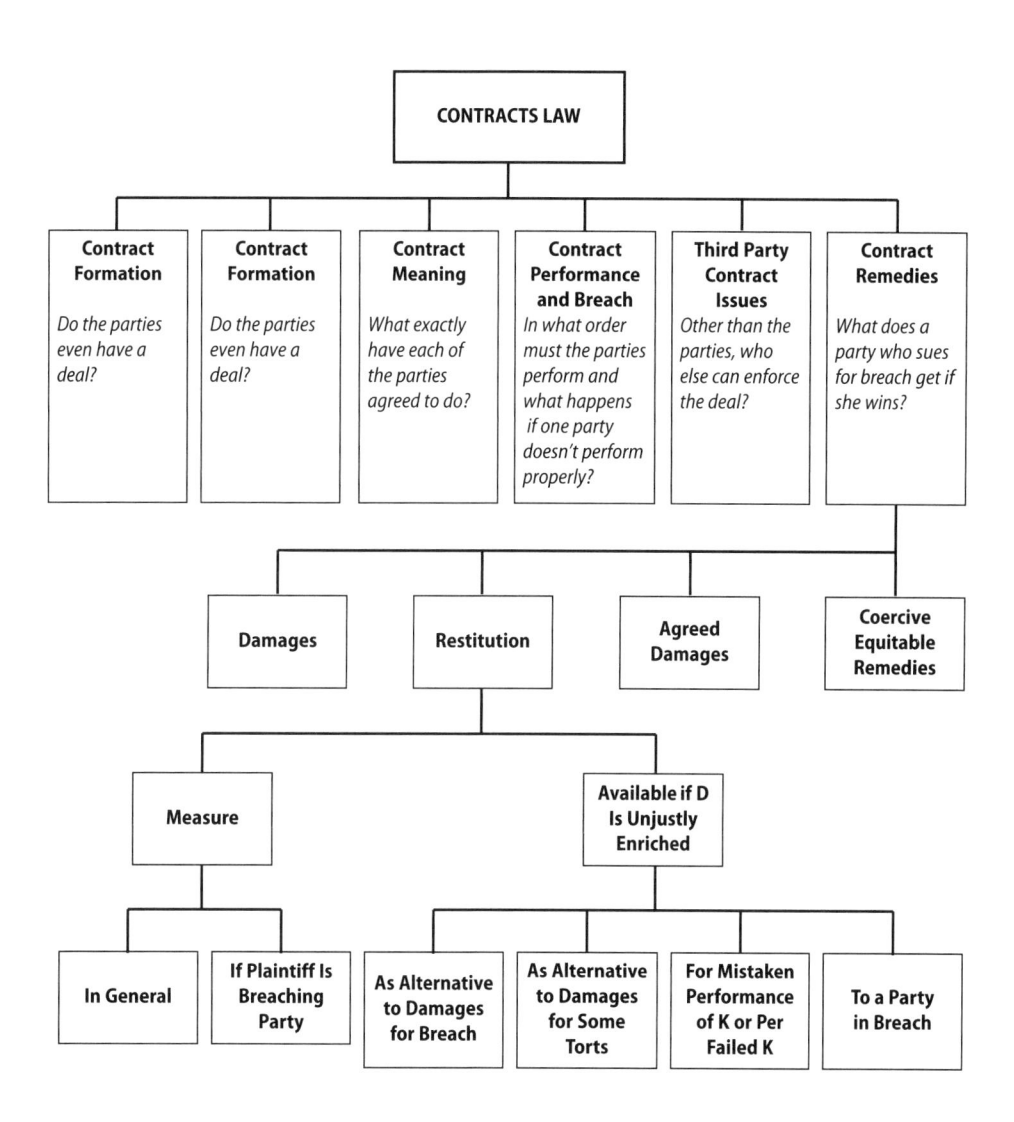

```
                              CONTRACTS LAW
                                    |
   ┌────────────┬────────────┬──────┴──────┬────────────┬────────────┐
Contract     Contract     Contract      Contract    Third Party   Contract
Formation    Formation    Meaning       Performance Contract      Remedies
                                        and Breach  Issues
Do the       Do the       What exactly  In what     Other than    What does a
parties      parties      have each of  order must  the parties,  party who sues
even have a  even have a  the parties   the parties who else can  for breach get if
deal?        deal?        agreed to do? perform and enforce the   she wins?
                                        what happens deal?
                                        if one party
                                        doesn't perform
                                        properly?
                                                                     |
                          ┌──────────────┬─────────────┬─────────────┤
                       Damages       Restitution    Agreed        Coercive
                                                    Damages       Equitable
                                                                  Remedies
                                          |
                              ┌───────────┴────────────┐
                          Measure                  Available if D
                                                   Is Unjustly
                                                   Enriched
                              |                        |
                     ┌────────┴────────┐  ┌────────┬───┴────┬─────────┐
                 In General    If Plaintiff Is  As Alt.  As Alt.  For Mistaken  To a Party
                               Breaching       to Damages to Damages Performance in Breach
                               Party           for Breach for Some   of K or Per
                                                          Torts      Failed K
```

Common Contract Terms Chart

Name of Clause	Goal of Clause
Covenants not to compete	*Communicates that an employee or a seller of a business cannot compete (for a specified period of time and within a specified locale) with the employer or buyer.*
Liquidated damages	*States an amount one or both parties should be awarded by a court if the other party breaches the contract.*
Merger	*Communicates that the written document contains all of the terms to which the parties have agreed and that, therefore, prior agreements that are not reflected in the written document are not part of the parties' contract.*
No oral modification	*Indicates the parties only can modify the contract in writing and not orally.*
Force majeure	*Lists circumstances, usually natural disasters and wars, under which a party can avoid having to perform the contract without penalty.*
Time is of the essence	*Uses the words "time is of the essence" to communicate an expectation about timely performance of the parties' contract promises.*
Choice of law	*States the body of law that will govern any dispute between the parties. May also limit the state or city in which either party may file suit. (Lawyers may refer to this latter provision as a jurisdiction clause.)*
Arbitration	*States an agreement that disputes under the contract will not be decided by a court but, rather, by an arbitrator. Usually includes details about the selection process for arbitrators.*
Indemnification	*Communicates that, if one party is sued for a matter relating to the contract, the other party will pay for the costs of defending the suit and will pay any award of damages ordered by the court.*
No assignments	*States that the rights conferred under the contract (and, in some instances, the duties imposed under the contract) cannot be transferred to someone else.*
Savings	*Indicates the parties have agreed that, if a court invalidates a particular term of the parties' contract, the rest of the contract will remain enforceable.*

Personal Jurisdiction Analytical Framework

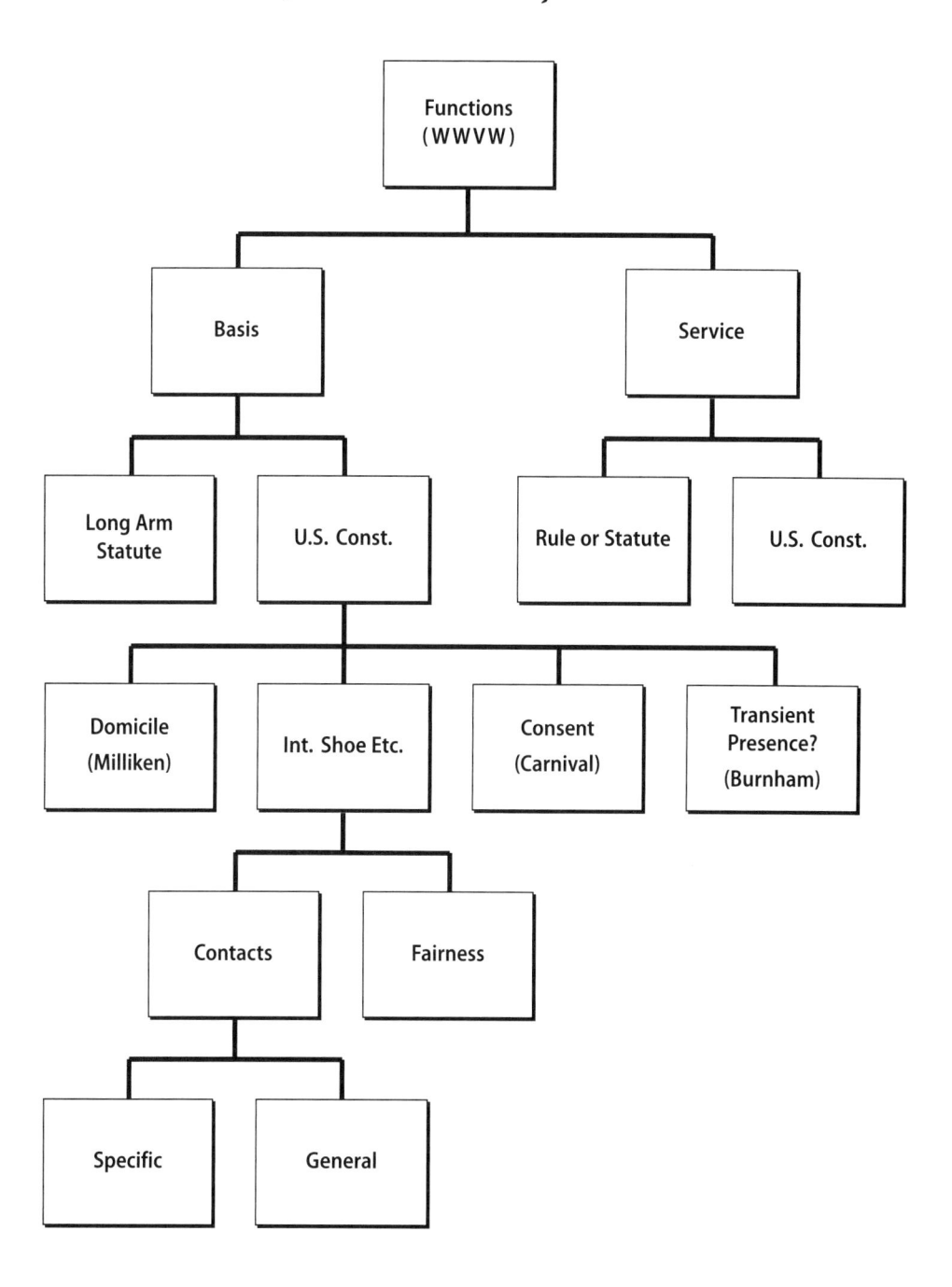

- **Functions (WWVW)**
  - **Basis**
    - Long Arm Statute
    - U.S. Const.
      - Domicile (Milliken)
      - Int. Shoe Etc.
        - Contacts
          - Specific
          - General
        - Fairness
      - Consent (Carnival)
      - Transient Presence? (Burnham)
  - **Service**
    - Rule or Statute
    - U.S. Const.

Partially Completed Graphic Organizer Synthesizing Contract Interpretation Principles

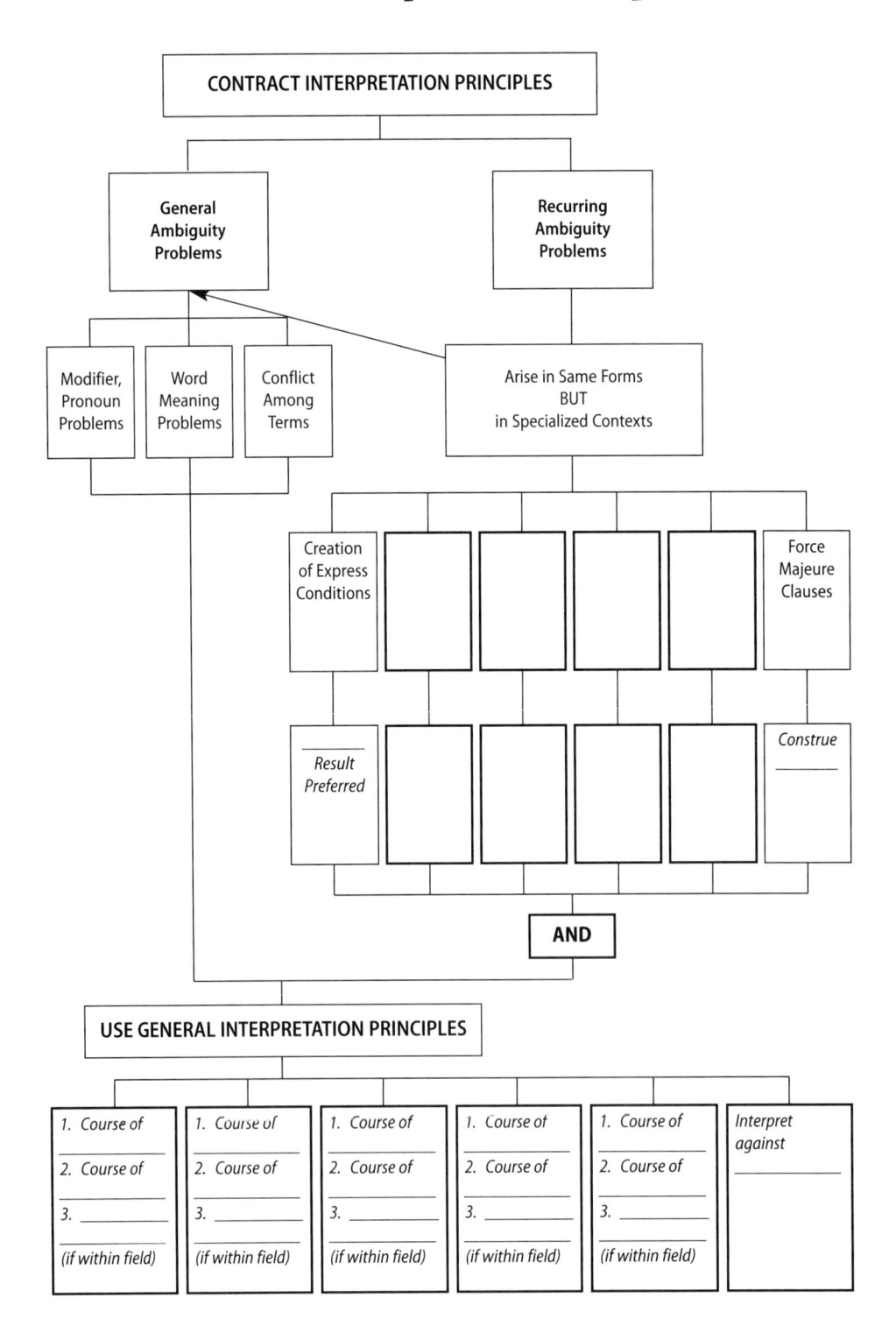

```
                    ┌─────────────────────────────────────┐
                    │  CONTRACT INTERPRETATION PRINCIPLES │
                    └─────────────────────────────────────┘
                           │                    │
              ┌────────────┘                    └─────────────┐
              ▼                                               ▼
       ┌─────────────┐                                 ┌─────────────┐
       │   General   │                                 │  Recurring  │
       │  Ambiguity  │                                 │  Ambiguity  │
       │  Problems   │                                 │  Problems   │
       └─────────────┘                                 └─────────────┘
```

- General Ambiguity Problems:
  - Modifier, Pronoun Problems
  - Word Meaning Problems
  - Conflict Among Terms

- Recurring Ambiguity Problems: Arise in Same Forms BUT in Specialized Contexts

Top row boxes:
- Creation of Express Conditions
- [ ]
- [ ]
- [ ]
- [ ]
- Force Majeure Clauses

Bottom row boxes:
- *Result Preferred*
- [ ]
- [ ]
- [ ]
- [ ]
- *Construe* ____

AND

USE GENERAL INTERPRETATION PRINCIPLES

1. *Course of* _____	1. *Course of* _____	1. *Course of* _____	1. *Course of* _____	1. *Course of* _____	*Interpret against* _____
2. *Course of* _____	2. *Course of* _____	2. *Course of* _____	2. *Course of* _____	2. *Course of* _____	
3. _____	3. _____	3. _____	3. _____	3. _____	
(if within field)	*(if within field)*	*(if within field)*	*(if within field)*	*(if within field)*	

Appendix 5-1: Role Plays

Civil Procedure I Oral Argument Role Play

The arguments will be based on the problem on the next page.

With a partner, prepare a short oral argument. You and your partner will have a total of 10 minutes for your arguments (5 minutes each). Limit your argument to specific jurisdiction. One partner should argue the contacts analysis and the other partner should argue the convenience/fairness analysis. Your arguments should focus on the applicable U.S. Supreme Court cases/analysis/policy. You may address the Fifth Circuit's opinion in *Revell* if you think it is appropriate.

You and your partner will be opposed by two other students. Defendant's lawyers argue first. Neither side gets rebuttal time.

Do not spend your time doing any research for this argument. All the law you will need is contained in the cases we covered in Unit 2B. To prepare for your argument, I recommend the following:

- Review the handout "Playing to the Bench" at pages 33-36 of the Fall, 2008 Civil Procedure I Hess Supplement.
- Review the oral argument rubric (see page three).
- Take notes and ask questions on my short lecture on oral argument.
- Observe the demonstration arguments in class on September 18 and 19.
- Outline, but don't memorize, your argument.

Four students will argue in class on September 18 and four more on September 19. If you (or you and a partner) would like to volunteer for the in-class arguments, please email me. All other arguments will take place outside of class from September 20-23. The signup sheets for the arguments are posted on the glass case outside of classroom 143 beginning Tuesday, September 16. Be sure to sign up on the sheet for your section (2 or 3).

After you complete your argument, fill out a self-assessment on the rubric. The rubric is posted in the Handouts section of our TWEN site. Address each of the four major categories (Structure/Substance, Communication, Responding to Questions, and Overall Reflections). You do not need to address every sub-point in each category. Your assessment/reflections must not exceed the one page rubric form. Your response is due in class on Tuesday, September 30. Put your midterm exam number at the top of the rubric.

This assignment is worth ten points. You will receive ten points if you complete the argument and the rubric, including your correct midterm exam number.

Good luck!

Oral Argument Problem - Fall 2008

Defendant, Timothy Dent, is a resident of Syracuse, New York, who does business as "mrlister." Dent operates a warehouse in Syracuse, New York. Dent sells items through internet auctions on the website www.eBay.com ("eBay"). Dent uses the Syracuse warehouse as part of the online business and lists the warehouse address as the location of his store.

Plaintiff, Maria Paz, is a resident of Portland, Oregon. Paz is an art collector, who specializes in 19th century Spanish sculpture. Paz successfully bid for sculptures in two auctions that Dent conducted through eBay. These two auctions involved the sculptures "Suzanne" and "Iguana" by artist Pedro Menna. Paz alleges that she believed she was bidding on the original artwork because the online auctions identified the sculptures as "Menna sculptures" and included close-up photographs of what appears to be the artist's signature. The auctions in question took place over several weeks, and during the auctions, Paz regularly received updates via email regarding the bidding, Paz regularly logged onto the website to monitor the progress of the auctions, and regularly participated in the auction by raising her bid. After winning both auctions, Paz and Dent exchanged several emails, to verify payment terms and shipping arrangements. Paz's emails to Dent contained her Portland, Oregon address and she arranged for Dent to ship the sculptures to that address. Paz sent a check for $7,000 to Dent's listed address in Syracuse, New York. Dent accepted this payment and cashed Paz's check.

Dent informed Paz via email that the sculptures were copies authorized by Menna, not Menna originals. Dent never shipped the sculptures, but offered, via email, Paz an apology for the misunderstanding and a full refund. Paz refused this refund and demanded the original sculptures or the fair market value of the originals, which Paz alleged to be $40,000. Paz filed this action in state court in Portland, Oregon on June 10, 2008 alleging Breach of Contract and Fraud. Paz requested compensatory damages of $40,000 and punitive damages of $500,000.

Paz provided printed copies of the computer screen displays from the two auctions in question. The auction screen displays information about the item up for bid, the status and progress of the auction, other bidders, the seller, the seller's rating on eBay, and the seller's shipping terms. Under the heading "Seller Information," these screen printouts identify the seller as "mrlister" and display a "Feedback Score" showing "Positive Feedback" of 99.5%, and indicating that "mrlister" has been a "Member since Sep-10-00 in United States." In addition, "mrlister" is identified as an eBay "Power Seller." This information appears to come from eBay. The "Seller Information" includes a promotion to "Visit this seller's eBay Store!" and provides a link to an "eBay store" identified as "MrLister." The "eBay store" for "MrLister" provides headings and links for "Antiques & Collectibles," "Jewelry & Watches," "Clothing Other & SPECIALS," "Computers & Electronics," and "Other." Just below this listing, the site prominently displays a "Mr. Lister" logo that includes the phrase "100% Satisfaction Guaranteed."

Dent provided an affidavit regarding his business. Over the past eight years, he has auctioned over $4,000,000 worth of merchandise on eBay via thousands of auctions. He has made "modest" profits. He has two employees; both work at the warehouse in Syracuse, NY. Dent does not advertise his business. Successful bidders have come from over 40 states, including Oregon. Dent has never been to Oregon for business or pleasure.

Dent responded to the complaint with a motion to dismiss for lack of personal jurisdiction. Neither side is arguing about subject matter jurisdiction, venue, the long-arm statute, or service of process, so do not address those issues in your oral argument.

Civil Procedure Oral Argument Rubric - Fall 2008

Midterm Exam # _____

Structure and Substance
 	
Introduction - roadmap
 	
Substance
    Law - elements
    Policy
    Application of facts
 	
Conclusion - relief requested	

Communication
 	
Verbal
    Clarity
    Pace
    Passion
    Respectful tone
Nonverbal
    Eye contact
    Posture
    Gestures	

Responding to Questions Listen to question Answer directly Transition to argument	
Overall Reflections What you learned Assessment of performance Value of assignment Other	

Client Counseling and Insurance Policy Analysis Exercise

For the purposes of this assignment, assume you are an associate attorney with the law firm of Smith & Smith. Attached to this instruction sheet is a memorandum from the senior partner in the law firm asking you to write a letter to the firm's biggest client.

Below, I describe the rules and standards applicable to this assignment. The purposes of this assignment are twofold and reflect the course objectives: (1) to enhance your client counseling and legal writing skills; and (2) to continue your development of the skill of reading and analyzing insurance policies.

1. **Points available on the assignment.** The assignment is worth 25% of your course grade. There will be 100 points available on this assignment.

2. **Deadline.** The assignment is due at 5:30 pm on the last regular day of class, which is Wednesday, April 21, 2006.

3. **Draft feedback.** You may turn in a draft of your paper one time for feedback no later than 5:30 pm on Wednesday, April 5, 2006. I will need one week to complete such feedback. Please submit your draft electronically and in Microsoft WORD to my secretary, Jessica Johnson at _____.

4. **Format of paper.** The attached memorandum asks you to write a letter to a client. I expect you to use a formal letter format for your paper. You therefore must include the date, the name of the recipient, the name of the company client and your law firm, the job title of the recipient and the business addresses of both the law firm and the client. Also include a line indicating the subject of the letter (i.e., "Re: ..."). Fully justify your letter left. Do not indent paragraphs but do skip a line between paragraphs. You must type your paper, use one inch (1") margins, and use Times New Roman, 12 point size font. Your paper also must be single-spaced and no more than six pages long. I will deduct points (up to a maximum of 10) from your score for each failure to comply with any of these instructions.

5. **Use Your Exam Number, Not Your Name.** Do not place your name anywhere on your paper. Use your exam number. Sign your letter,
   Associate # _____ (insert your exam number).

6. **Standards to be applied in grading the assignment.** I plan to assign the following weights to what I regard as the three aspects of this assignment: Analysis of the Policy - 50%, Client letter-writing skill - 20%, Grammar, usage, Word Choice, Organization, etc. - 30%. I describe each of these categories in more detail below.

   <u>Analysis of the policy</u>. I will evaluate your analysis in terms of the sophistication of your reading and explanation of the policy and degree to which your analysis reflects an understanding of the policy and the legal authorities we have discussed in class. The letter from your client asks you to explain the policy and to address three issues. I will assign points to each of these four tasks based on each task's difficulty.

   <u>Client letter-writing skill</u>. I will evaluate your client letter-writing skills in terms of the standards set forth in the PowerPoint slideshow posted to the course webpage.

<u>Grammar, usage, etc</u>. I expect to find no errors in your papers that could be caught by using the grammar and spell check features on most word processing software. Students who fail to correct such errors will receive especially heavy point deductions from their scores. I also will deduct significant points for other grammar, usage, word choice and organization errors.

7. **Work alone.** <u>YOU CANNOT WORK WITH ANY OTHER PERSON ON THIS ASSIGNMENT IN ANY WAY</u>. Do not discuss this assignment or your paper with anyone, including, but not limited to, any student, tutor, law professor, proofreader, attorney, friend, relative, spouse, significant other or child.

8. **Library for assignment.** This assignment is a closed library assignment. You may rely only on cases actually reprinted in your casebook. This assignment takes place in the fictional state of Columbia. Columbia is a new state that has not yet decided any insurance law cases. Consequently, all of the cases in your casebook are, at most, persuasive authority.

9. **Examples.** Attached to this document you also will find examples of the various possible sections of a client letter to an attorney based on the *Atwater Creamery Company v. Western National Insurance Company* case on page 55 of the Abraham <u>Insurance Law and Regulation</u> text.

10. **Questions about assignment.** Please post all questions about this assignment to the course webpage forum designated for such questions. I will only answer questions that would be appropriate for a junior associate to ask a senior associate.

SMITH & SMITH, ATTORNEYS AT LAW

MEMORANDUM

Date: February 27, 2006

To: Associate Exam # _____

From: Senior Partner Samantha Leigh Smith

RE: Client Request for Advice Letter

I attach to this memorandum a copy of a letter from Kendra Lynn, vice president and in-house counsel to All Medical Testing Laboratories, Inc. ("AMTLI"), the largest medical testing laboratory in Columbia City, Columbia.

Ms. Lynn has asked us to evaluate the policy form AMTLI received from RA&MCO, the largest insurer doing business in the state of Columbia. Although Lynn is an attorney, she has served in a business role with AMTLI for the past fifteen (15) years, and she has no background whatsoever in insurance law. She also may show this letter to Stacey Hunter, the president of AMTLI. Consequently, while you can assume Ms. Lynn is a sophisticated reader, you need to be careful to respond to her queries in plain and, mostly, non-legal language.

Please prepare a detailed response to Lynn's letter. Please keep in mind that AMTLI is a new client and already is the firm's largest client. I trust you will make a good impression.

ALL MEDICAL TESTING LABORATORIES, INC.

11111 SOUTH STATE UNIVERSITY AVENUE, COLUMBIA CITY, COLUMBIA 11111-1111

February 27, 2006

Samantha Leigh Smith, Esq.
Smith & Smith, Attorneys at Law
22222 Peter, Paul & Mary Street, Suite 1000
Columbia City, Columbia 11111-1111

Re: RA&MCO's Testing Laboratories Professional Liability Insurance Policy

Dear Ms. Smith:

I enclose a copy of the above-referenced insurance policy. As I mentioned to you last week, we are in the process of switching insurance companies. RA&MCO has submitted the lowest bid of all the insurers we contacted. The policy, however, seems very different from our prior policy from a different insurer. To assist our evaluation of the policy, please address the issues described below.

First, please explain the coverage provided by the policy. I am not particularly familiar with "claims" policies. What is the significance to us of this policy's focus on "claims" as opposed to "occurrences" as a basis for insurance liability?

Second, detail what we should do if someone complains about our services. We have a regular business practice of redoing for free any test about which there is any question. Our referral sources (doctors, clinics and hospitals) appreciate this "customer is always right" policy.

Third, the first exclusion worries us. Our contracts with medical providers include indemnification clauses requiring us to indemnify the providers and hold them harmless for claims alleging negligent testing. Does this exclusion wipe out our coverage?

Thank you for your assistance. We look forward to your prompt reply.

Very truly yours,

Kendra Lynn, Esq., Vice President and General Counsel

encl.

Example Sections of a Client Letter

(Assuming client was the owner of the creamery warehouse in the *Atwater* case in our text and had asked outside counsel to evaluate its coverage claim and assuming the state had neither adopted nor rejected the reasonable expectations rule)

Introduction:

Thank you for referring this matter to us. I enjoyed our lunch last week and believe we will work well together.

You have asked us to assess Atwater Creamery Company's chances of prevailing in a lawsuit against Western National Mutual Insurance Company seeking insurance coverage for the recent burglary of Atwater's warehouse.

Issue:

To assess Atwater's likelihood of success in a coverage suit, we have analyzed the following legal question, which is the key issue in your dispute with Western National and the only stated basis for its denial of your claim:

Under a policy providing coverage for burglary if the burglar leaves "evidence of forcible entry," does the policy cover a burglary where the only evidence of the burglary was missing property, two open doors, both of which are usually locked, and two missing padlocks but where the police have concluded that the burglary was not an "inside job"?

Short Answer:

The question is a close one, but you are likely to prevail. On the one hand, the absence of damage to the doors or to the padlocks presents a potential barrier to coverage. The requirement of "evidence of forcible entry" seems to suggest that the policy does not cover situations, like Atwater's, where the burglar did not damage the windows, doors or walls and the locks are simply missing, as opposed to being broken. On the other hand, most courts have found coverage under similar circumstances. Some courts have held that the "evidence of forcible entry" requirement is met in cases like this one because the problems the requirement was designed to address, "inside jobs" and failures to use due care to secure the premises, are not implicated; the police determined that Atwater's loss was not an inside job and Atwater did secure the warehouse. Other courts have found evidence of forcible entry in the fact that locks are missing or opened. Still other courts have applied a fairly new concept of insurance law in which courts find coverage if a reasonable insured would have expected it. In this context, a court applying reasonable expectations law would find coverage by reasoning that a reasonable company would be shocked to discover that the burglary insurance it had purchased provided no coverage simply because the burglar broke in without damaging the building and successfully disposed of the locks. Accordingly, based on one or more of the above theories, a court probably would find coverage for Atwater's loss in this case.

Statement of Facts:

Prior to April 1977, Atwater had purchased $20,000 in burglary insurance from Western National. The policy defined burglaries to include only those burglaries in which the burglar leaves "evidence of forcible entry." According to Western National, the purpose of this clause is to discourage Atwater from burglarizing itself just to get the insurance proceeds and to encourage Atwater adequately to secure the premises.

Sometime between April 9 and April 11, 1977, one or more persons entered your warehouse without permission and stole chemicals worth $15,587.40. You discovered the theft on the 11th. You found two unlocked doors that you had left locked and discovered that the padlocks on those doors and the chemicals had disappeared. There was no other evidence other than the evidence described above. The police who investigated the crime determined that no one affiliated with Atwater was involved in any way.

Atwater filed a burglary claim with Western National. Western National denied the claim, citing the "evidence of forcible entry" clause as the basis for its decision.

Discussion:

[The discussion would use many of the ideas addressed in the case and in our class discussion of the case but would translate those ideas into simpler language, would delete citations and the long policy discussion and would be shorter.]

Conclusion:

Although the question is a close one and Atwater will lose its lawsuit if the court narrowly interprets Western National's policy, Atwater is likely to prevail in its claim. The fees and costs of bringing the lawsuit and pursuing it to final judgment, however, almost certainly will exceed the approximately $15,600 loss Atwater has have sustained. The trickiness of the policy language at issue means the losing party may even choose to appeal, thereby increasing the expense of pursuing a claim. We therefore suggest that Atwater communicate an analysis of the merits of this claim in a demand letter to Western National and work towards a compromise. We propose drafting such a letter. If Western National continues to deny coverage, we can discuss whether filing suit makes sense, but we suspect Western National can be made to recognize that it may lose if Atwater sues and, even if Western National were to win, it would spend more money defending the suit than Atwater is claiming.

I look forward to hearing from you regarding this letter and our suggested next steps.

Environmental Law Role Play — Philosophical Perspectives

Read pages 8-18 and 53-57 in the text. Those pages describe a variety of perspectives on environmental law and provide a factual background for a current environmental dispute - whether to open the Arctic National Wildlife Refuge to oil exploration and drilling.

Assume that a Senate Committee is holding hearings on whether to open 1.5 million acres of ANWR for oil exploration and drilling. For one of the following groups, you will be assigned to create a single slide with an image and text (one to three points) to support 60 seconds of testimony the group would give to the Senate Committee regarding ANWR:

- Thoughtful Use of Tundra (human-centered)
- Tundra First! (Leopoldian ecologists)
- Dino Oil (sensible economic development)
- Catholic Church ("Peace with All Creation")
- Wilderness Society (preservationists)
- Alaska Governor's Office (state sovereignty)
- Arctic Village (environmental justice)
- Inupiat Eskimos (economic opportunity)
- Caribou Caretakers (animal rights)

Appendix 5-2: Experiential Professionalism Instruction

Lucy Lockett Professionalism Problem

You are two years out of law school, practicing in a small law firm not far from where we are now. The firm does general litigation.

It is now evening. You are at home, enjoying a relaxed dinner. The telephone rings. The distraught voice on the other end belongs to your friend Carl Lockett.

Carl is calling about a disaster that has just befallen his 23-year-old daughter Lucy. According to Mr. Lockett, Lucy had been working part-time at Tropics North Inc., an exotic pet store on Sherrill Avenue in Bethesda, Maryland. Last Saturday, she was bitten on the wrist by a poisonous snake. The accident occurred as she was trying to remove the snake from its case to sell it to a customer.

The store manager, Mr. McConnell, assured her that the snake was not poisonous; indeed, Lucy knew that the store did not carry any poisonous animals. The customer, a Mr. Adams, wanted to buy the snake despite its having bitten her, and she completed the sale. Her wrist hurt a little, but the pain diminished rapidly.

About an hour later, however, her arm began to hurt. After another hour, it had begun to swell. Mr. McConnell drove her to the emergency room at Community Hospital.

The emergency room resident observed her for several hours. Her arm continued to swell and to become more painful. Treatment of the arm with benadryl did not help. By late Sunday morning, the arm had swelled to twice its normal diameter. Lucy was in excruciating pain. After X-raying the arm and discovering that the swelling was threatening to kill the muscle tissue, the doctors decided that the snake must have been poisonous and that they needed to operate to save Lucy's arm. They operated the same day, cutting her arm open from wrist to elbow to drain fluids from it. They say that a further operation will be necessary in a day or two and that plastic surgery to reduce the scar will be desirable in several months. They hope that there will be no long-term damage, but they can't be sure.

Just before he called you, Mr. Lockett spoke again with Mr. McConnell. McConnell reported that he had just called Mr. Adams and told him what had happened to Lucy. He'd offered Mr. Adams his money back, an offer Adams had accepted. Adams said that he would call his local police department and ask them to take the snake away and kill it.

McConnell says that he doesn't have any insurance but he feels terrible about what happened and would like to pay half of Lucy's hospital bill, which is expected to be about $4,000.

What questions do you have for Mr. McConnell?

[This problem is adapted from an extensive set of simulation materials developed by Professor Philip G. Schrag of Georgetown. Gerry uses this problem on the first day of Civil Procedure for first semester, first year law students. He ends the class with a 10-15 minute discussion of this problem. As students volunteer questions, he writes them on the board and asks each volunteer to explain why the question is important. With two minute to go in class, he tells the students that they have generated an impressive list of "lawyer questions." However, they have omitted the first question that he would ask Mr. McConnell. He then writes on the board in huge letters "HOW'S LUCY?"

Gerry uses this problem for on the first day of Civil procedure for several reasons. First, it gets many students to participate on the first day of class, which begins a course-long dynamic of active engagement in class. Second, it sends the message that students will apply what they learn in this course to real-life problems. Most importantly, it allows Gerry to make a dramatic point about professionalism. After writing "HOW'S LUCY?" on the board, he comments that when we are in our role as lawyers, lawsuits do not walk into our offices. People do. It is easy for students to lose sight of that as they begin law school. But our effectiveness as lawyers depends in large part on our humanity. That ends day one in Civil Procedure.]

Handout for Small Group Public Service Experiential Learning Exercise

As you know, you have been placed in a small, six-person group led by an upper-division student.

You need to do the following to complete your small group public service experiential learning obligation:

1. On Friday, you will be attending a luncheon to welcome you to the law school. The guest speak, Judge _____, will discuss your obligations, as a lawyer to your community. Afterwards, you will have the opportunity to hear from and talk to the various student organizations at this law school that have, as at least part of their mission, providing service to the community.

2. You will then have 30 minutes to begin to work in your small group to decide on a group public service project. Try to pick something that is personally meaningful to the members of your group.

3. Your project must be selected by September 15. In 200 words or less, describe your project and post it to the public service TWEN course webpage set up by Dean _____. To honor your choice, the law school will be publicizing all of the projects.

4. After you complete your group project, each member of the group must write at least a 250-word essay describing what he or she learned from this experience.

Professionalism/Values Exercise Arising out of a Class Incident

<u>Introduction to four stories</u>. My goal: focus on professional values.

Cluster of three stories and then tell fourth story and connect it to an issue in this class.

<u>First three stories</u>.

<u>Story 1</u>: Produced privileged document. Mistakes in law practice.

<u>Story 2</u>: Story of anesthesiologists. History of malpractice. Policed themselves, learned value of apologies and paying for patients' out-of-pocket losses.

<u>Story 3</u>: Client who said, "What should I say happened?" when asked what facts led to his lawsuit against a former partner.

<u>Fourth Story</u>.

When I was in law school, I never told anyone my grades. One day, a group of four people grilled my then-girlfriend for 30 minutes to try to get her to tell them my grades.

<u>Relationship of stories to this class</u>.

I have been told that a few students in this class have violated the privacy of other students by looking at how the students did on the midterm I handed back this week. Part of the problem was my mistake—I should have placed the exams in sealed envelopes. I am sorry. Those who looked let law school competitiveness overwhelm their sense of what they know is right—respecting others. They made a mistake. I believe those whose privacy rights were violated would appreciate an apology.

<u>Exercise</u>. Take out a blank sheet of paper. Write down what you want lawyers to say about you when you retire from law practice. Place it in the envelope I have given you. Seal the envelope. I will arrange for this envelope to be mailed to you when you graduate from this law school.

<u>Questions?</u>

Identifying Criteria for Successful and Positive Interactions with Classmates

Background and goals:

At the beginning of the semester, you were all clustered in diverse teams of 5-7 people. The goal was to have each of you learn from each other and develop the attributes and skills of working with others, skills and attributes essential to practicing law.

Each team identified the written criteria upon which you would evaluate each other's participation and contribution to the team's success. These criteria may overlap but are individual for each team and will be used to evaluate your classmates at the end of the course.

Many of you identified criteria that included points like the ones below:

Criteria for evaluating team contributions:
- Listening to team members
- Being receptive to and respectful of others' thoughts/input
- Being patient with others' process and learning
- Being prepared - good faith effort
- Contributing to discussions
- Communicating with teammates about absences and other team-related tasks
- Having a sense of humor
- Being on time

Now you have been working with your team for several weeks, including taking team quizzes, brainstorming problems in class, and completing a team assessment. The goal here is to honestly and professionally check in with your teammates and determine if there things you can do to enhance your team's effectiveness in contributing to each students' learning, and, if so, how you might accomplish them.

Please take the next 10 minutes to:

1. Review the initial criteria your team developed;
2. Discuss among your teammates whether you want to revise your criteria;
3. Check-in and discuss with your teammates how well the team is succeeding in meeting the criteria; and
4. Discuss any additional points about working together as a team. (One effective team-building technique is to have each person identify one positive thing about the team.)

[Before students engage in this exercise, Sophie spends a few minutes reminding students about the need to provide honest and respectful feedback, the difficulty of acting with civility when under stress, the power of positive social emotional interactions, and the connection between effective interactions and professional performance.]

Appendix 5-3: Time Management/ Self-Monitoring Log

Concept/ Skill to be Studied	Learning Goal(s)	Strategy(ies) for Learning	Time and Place for Studying and for Breaks		Ability to Focus	Steps Used to Study	Effectiveness of Studying
			Plan	Actual			

Appendix 5-4: Post-Assessment Reflection Exercises

General Post-Assessment Reflection Exercise

Select an exam, legal writing paper or exercise on which you have received feedback and then answer the following questions. Keep in mind that the key to learning in general and to learning from examinations in particular is being open to feedback and to change.

1. How well did you think you had learned the material before you took the test/quiz/exercise/paper? (check the item that best describes your perception of the degree to which you achieved mastery)

   ❏ Excellence ❏ Mastery ❏ Competence

   ❏ Approaching competence ❏ Poor

2. How well did you do on the test/quiz/exercise/paper? (check the description that best describes your outcome)

   ❏ Excellence ❏ Mastery ❏ Competence

   ❏ Approaching Competence ❏ Poor

3. Given your results on the test/quiz/exercise/paper, how accurately did you self-assess your learning? (check the description that best describes your outcome)

   ❏ Very accurately ❏ OK ❏ Poorly

   If you did not check "very accurately" in response to the above question or if you "very accurately" predicted a poor outcome, discuss why your self-assessment was inaccurate or why you predicted a poor outcome.

   _____
   _____
   _____
   _____
   _____
   _____
   _____

4. Given your results, discuss how efficient and effective your learning strategies were.

   _____
   _____
   _____
   _____
   _____
   _____
   _____

5. If you did not perform as well as you would have liked to have performed or if you believe that your learning process, while effective, was inefficient, identify the cause of your performance issue. Below is a checklist of possible causes. Check all that apply.

   Possible problems in the forethought phase

   ____ Failure to set appropriate goal (you set no goal or set an improper one)

   ____ Incorrect assessment of the learning task (you erroneously classified the task)

   ____ Failure to invoke self-efficacy (you failed to identify past success in similar learning enterprises)

   ____ Failure to develop intrinsic interest in the learning task (you did not determine why you needed to learn the material)

   ____ Poor motivational strategy choices (you could not stay motivated)

   ____ Poor environmental choices (you made bad location, timing, rest sequence choices)

   ____ Poor cognitive strategy choices (the strategy choices proved unsuited to the learning task or you also should have used additional strategies)

   Possible problems in the performance phase

   ____ Incorrect implementation of strategy choices (you incorrectly used the strategies)

   ____ Failure to maintain focused attention (you were unable to focus during implementation)

   ____ Failure to self-monitor (you failed to recognize a breakdown in the learning process while it was ongoing)

   ____ Insufficient persistence (learning task simply requires multiple learning cycles)

   Possible problem in the reflection phase

   ____ Failure to pursue opportunities for self-assessment (you did not take advantage of or create opportunities for practice and feedback)

6. How did you do on this test / quiz / exercise / paper in comparison to tests / quizzes / exercises / papers you took before law school?

   How did you do on this test / quiz / exercise / paper in comparison to other tests / quizzes / exercises / papers you have taken in law school? Why did you do better or worse on this test / quiz / exercise / paper?

   _____

   _____

   _____

   _____

   _____

   _____

   _____

7. What were the most common comments your professor made on your answer to this test/quiz/exercise/paper (or on all my law school tests/quizzes/exercises/papers)?

_____
_____
_____
_____
_____

What did the professor(s) mean by these comments?

_____
_____
_____
_____
_____
_____

8. Based on your outcome and your response to the above questions, how do you feel about yourself and your law studies and why do you feel that way?

_____
_____
_____
_____
_____
_____

9. Based on your outcome and your response to the above questions, how will you change your approach to studying similar material in the future?

_____
_____
_____
_____
_____
_____

Cognitive Protocol

At the end of this course, you will have completed at least 6 assignments in which you have read, analyzed, selected, and cited to authorities, applied facts to law, and organized complex material:

- Memo 1 - Is an advertisement an offer?
- Memo 2 - Was Rienzo a licensee or invitee? Who decides? What duty of care did Montshire Law owe her? (draft and final)
- Memo 3 - Was the Corrow/Michaud Prenuptial agreement enforceable? How could it be validated?
- Memo 4 - Does South Dakota have personal jurisdiction over PPR? (draft and final)

Altogether, this constitutes a significant body of work—between 25-30 pages of written legal analysis. Congratulations!

Take a few minutes to skim through Memo 1.

If you wish, skim over Memos 2 and 3.

Reviewing your portfolio, over this semester, what have you learned about researching, analyzing, and writing about legal issues?

_____
_____
_____
_____
_____
_____
_____
_____

Appendix 6-1: Discovery Sequence Exercises

Duty to Disclose Discovery Sequence Exercise

Instructions:

The general rule is that contracting parties do not have a duty to speak regarding the subject of a contract; in other words, there is no general duty to disclose material facts to the other party. Below you will find 17 hypotheticals. For each one, I have stated whether the seller would have a duty to disclose. Your task is to determine the four principles governing when a seller does have a duty to disclose based on reviewing the hypotheticals and conclusions and then deriving the principles. Write your four principles in the space provided.

Exercise:

1. Sophie Seller entered into negotiations with Betty Buyer to sell Seller's house to Buyer. If Seller knows a murder was committed in the house five years ago, must Seller disclose that fact to Buyer? (**Answer:** *No*, **Seller would not have a duty to disclose under these circumstances**).

2. Assume the facts are the same as in hypothetical #1 except Seller also is Buyer's regular lawyer. Must Seller disclose the fact to Buyer? (**Answer:** *Yes*, **Seller would have a duty to disclose under these circumstances**).

3. Assume the facts are the same as in hypothetical #1 except Seller also is Buyer's mother. Must Seller disclose the fact to Buyer? (**Answer:** *Yes*, **Seller would have a duty to disclose under these circumstances**).

4. Assume the facts are the same as in hypothetical #1 except Seller had raised Buyer since she was a child and had been Buyer's chief advisor with respect to all matters since Buyer was fifteen years-old. Must Seller disclose the fact to Buyer? (**Answer:** *Yes*, **Seller would have a duty to disclose under these circumstances**).

5. Assume the facts are the same as in hypothetical #1 except Seller also is a friend of Buyer, although Seller never has rendered any advice or help to Buyer. Must Seller disclose the fact to Buyer? (**Answer:** *No*, **Seller would not have a duty to disclose under these circumstances**).

6. Assume the facts are the same as in hypothetical #1 except Seller also is Buyer's employee, although Seller never has rendered any advice or help to Buyer. Must Seller disclose the fact to Buyer? (**Answer:** *No*, **Seller would not have a duty to disclose under these circumstances**).

7. Sophie Seller entered into negotiations with Betty Buyer to sell Seller's house to Buyer. If Seller knows that Buyer does not know the house is riddled with termites, must Seller disclose that fact to Buyer? (**Answer:** *Yes*, **Seller would have a duty to disclose under these circumstances**).

8. Sophie Seller entered into negotiations with Betty Buyer to sell Seller's house to Buyer. If Seller knows the neighbors are noisy on Saturday nights, must Seller disclose this fact to buyer? (**Answer:** *No*, **Seller would not have a duty to disclose under these circumstances**).

9. Sophie Seller entered into negotiations with Betty Buyer to sell Seller's house to Buyer for $350,000. If Seller knows that the building and safety department has issued a

warning to Seller that Seller must enclose Seller's septic tank (at a cost of $2,000) or face substantial fines (as much as $500 per day), must Seller disclose that fact to Buyer? (**Answer:** *No*, **Seller would not have a duty to disclose under these circumstances**).

10. Sophie Seller entered into negotiations with Betty Buyer to sell Seller's restaurant to Buyer for $75,000. If Seller knows that the health department has issued repeated warnings to Seller that Seller must make expensive improvements to the restaurant (at a cost of as much as $50,000) or the health department will close the restaurant, must Seller disclose that fact to Buyer? (**Answer:** *Yes*, **Seller would have a duty to disclose under these circumstances**).

11. Sophie Seller entered into negotiations with Betty Buyer to sell Seller's house to Buyer for $350,000. If Seller knows that the house has a well-established reputation for being inhabited by ghosts, must Seller disclose that fact to Buyer? (**Answer:** *No*, **Seller would not have a duty to disclose under these circumstances**).

12. Sophie Seller, seeking to induce Betty Buyer to purchase Seller's house and land, tells Buyer that the house "has no problems." Unknown to Seller, all of the electrical wiring in the house is a fire hazard and needs to be replaced. If Seller then learns of the electrical wiring problem, must Seller disclose that fact to Buyer? (**Answer:** *Yes*, **Seller would have a duty to disclose under these circumstances**).

13. Sophie Seller, seeking to induce Betty Buyer to purchase Seller's house and land, tells Buyer that Gary Frank, a world-renowned architect, designed Seller's house. After escrow closes and Buyer takes possession, Seller learns that Frank's daughter actually designed the house after Frank died. Must Seller disclose that fact to Buyer? (**Answer:** *No*, **Seller would not have a duty to disclose under these circumstances**).

14. Sophie Seller, seeking to induce Betty Buyer to purchase Seller's house and land, tells Buyer that the house "has only a few problems" and gives Buyer a list labeled "Problems With Betty's House." If Seller knows that, in addition to the problems she listed, the house needs a new roof, must Seller disclose that fact to Buyer? (**Answer:** *Yes*, **Seller would have a duty to disclose under these circumstances**).

15. Assume the facts are the same as in hypothetical # 14 except Seller did not tell Buyer that the house had any problems at all. If Seller knows that the house needs a new roof, must Seller disclose that fact to Buyer? (**Answer:** *No*, **Seller would not have a duty to disclose under these circumstances**).

16. Sadie Spouse entered into negotiations with Crafty Creditor to pay off her husband's debts. If Creditor knows that Creditor, without expressly saying so, has given Spouse the incorrect impression that Spouse's husband will be arrested imminently if Spouse does not agree to Creditor's demands, must Creditor disclose the true facts to Spouse? (**Answer:** *Yes*, **Seller would have a duty to disclose under these circumstances**).

17. Assume the facts are the same as in hypothetical # 16 except Creditor did nothing to give Spouse the impression that Spouse's husband would be arrested imminently. Must Creditor disclose the true facts to Spouse? (**Answer:** *No*, **Seller would not have a duty to disclose under these circumstances**).

The Four Circumstances in Which Parties Have a Duty to Disclose

1. _____

2. _____

3. _____

4. _____

Binding vs. Persuasive Authority Discovery Sequence Exercise

Instructions:

Review each of the hypothetical questions and answers below. Each hypothetical question involves a question of whether, assuming both courts were addressing the same legal question based on facts that were identical in every non-trivial way, the first court decision would be binding on the second court decision. The answers are in parentheses. After you have reviewed all the questions and answers, try to derive the legal rules that explain all of the questions and answers.

Exercise:

Hypo 1: A decision of the Kansas Supreme Court on a decision of a trial court sitting in the Kansas 7th Judicial District (located in Douglass County). (**binding**)

Hypo 2: A decision of a trial court sitting in the Kansas 3rd Judicial District (located in Shawnee County) on a decision of the Kansas Court of Appeals. (**not binding**)

Hypo 3: A decision of the United States Tenth Circuit Court of Appeals made by judges sitting in Denver, Colorado on a decision of a United States District Court, District of Kansas court. (**binding**)

Hypo 4: A decision of the United States Tenth Circuit Court of Appeals on another decision of the United States Tenth Circuit Court of Appeals. (**binding**)

Hypo 5: A decision of the United States Ninth Circuit Court of Appeals on a decision of the United States Tenth Circuit Court of Appeals. (**not binding**)

Hypo 6: A decision of a trial court sitting in the Kansas 7th Judicial District on a decision of another trial court sitting in the Kansas 7th Judicial District. (**not binding**)

Hypo 7: A decision of a court sitting in the Jefferson City, Missouri location of the United States District Court, Western District of Missouri on another decision of a court sitting in the Jefferson City, Missouri location of the United States District Court, Western District of Missouri. (**not binding**)

Hypo 8: A decision of the Kansas Court of Appeals on a decision of a trial court sitting in the Kansas 3rd Judicial District. (**binding**)

Hypo 9: A decision of the United States Ninth Circuit Court of Appeals on a decision of a United States District Court, District of Kansas court. (**not binding**)

Hypo 10: A decision of the Kansas Supreme Court on a decision of the United States Supreme Court as to a question of whether a provision of the Kansas Constitution violates the United States Constitution. (**not binding**)

Hypo 11: A decision of the United States Supreme Court on a decision of the Kansas Court of Appeal as to whether a contract for the sale of land located in Kansas must be in writing to be valid. (**not binding**)

Appendix 7-1: Assessment Instruments

Peer Feedback Formative Assessment Exercise

Observations and details about conducting a peer feedback class on writing client letters.
- Students found writing a client letter was harder to do than they thought.
- It was hard **not** to just cut and paste their memo.
- Very helpful to read and apply the rubric to classmate's letter.
- It was hard for them to keep their client audience in mind.
- They realized that they had learned more than they thought.
- Writing a letter after a memo was like writing an executive summary.
- It is hard but ok to give the client bad news.
- At the end of the day, almost everyone said, "I have to rewrite the whole letter."
- Got some requests for more assignments like this, including having letters to opposing counsel.

Here is how class went today:
- Each student picked a card from a group of 8 - they matched up with corresponding card- sat together.
- Took out their client letters.
- Gave them a blank client letter rubric - had them put their name, followed by "consultant" or "senior analyst" or any other term they liked that was similar.

Ask them to put themselves in the context of the busy smart client:
- You are a dental surgeon.
- Picked up your mail after a long day at the office fixing people's teeth.
- In the mail are some catalogs, bills, requests for donations, and this letter from your attorney.
- You still have to do laundry, make a meal, etc.
- You are tired and hungry.
- You don't have a legal background.
- This is who you are when you read this draft.
- Pay attention: what confused you? What made sense?

Give "reader-based feedback"—the reader, like the customer, is always right.
- If the reader is confused, the letter needs clarity.
- If the reader can't follow the information, the letter needs clearer organization.
- This letter should be at the level of writing the directions for the game of Monopoly: Steven Stark says, "9 year olds can mortgage real estate by following those directions." And they don't need to know about fixed and variable rates of interest.

Write on the rubric and the partner's letter—these will be returned to your classmates. **10 minutes: read each other's complete rubric.**

I circulated after the first 10 minutes to answer questions or pose my own.

Put on the board: as they read each other's

- Salutation - Dear ___: [should be Dr. Rienzo]
- What is the likely outcome of her claim- known or unknown? [unknown; likely need more legal research and factual investigation]
- What is the status regarding settlement? [Montshire unlikely to settle without filing a complaint]
- Who decides whether to pursue this claim? [the client]
- Legalese? [discussed whether client needs to know the terms "licensee" or "invitee" or "matter of law" - my view: probably not]
- Further action - discussed the need to gather more evidence and do more research - probably want her to come in and have a follow-up conversation.

Midterm/Peer Feedback, Reflection Assessment

Guidelines for Mockterm Phase II (Review of Peer Essay) and Phase III (Reflection)

Introduction

In the last class session (Phase I of this midterm experience), you wrote an essay in response to a hypothetical question. As I announced in class, the process for this midterm has two additional phases. In Phase II, you anonymously will be providing feedback to one of your peers in the class. In Phase III, you will be reviewing your own essay, and the feedback from your peer and from me and then reflecting on what you have learned from the entire process. I will be evaluating all three phases in assigning you a grade for this midterm. Please review the syllabus for the relative weight and grading criteria I will be using in evaluating your work and assigning you a grade.

Guidelines for Phase II: Review of Peer Essay:

General Guidelines.

- ✓ *Note: There is no reason for you to hold back on any critique you feel is appropriate because I intend to exercise my own, independent judgment in evaluating your peer's work.*
- ✓ Be sure to mix positive and negative comments.
- ✓ Be concrete and specific. Rather than saying "too conclusory," say, "this failed to explain why fact X was important in resolving the issue."
- ✓ Pay attention to details. Did the student identify *all* of the relevant facts? Did the student explain the significance of each fact the student stated? Did the student quote or paraphrase the rule correctly (either is fine) or did the student paraphrase the rule in a way that changed its meaning?
- ✓ Provide feedback on the student's time management. Did the student devote more time (more bluebook space) to the major issues and less time to the minor issues? Did the student state unnecessary law? Did the student address non-issues?
- ✓ If you encounter a paper that addresses a matter or argument not addressed below, acknowledge that fact and use your common sense in evaluating whether the issue is really an issue and how well the student did in analyzing it.

Guidelines re issues on exam.

- ✓ There was no parol evidence issue (PER) on the exam. In fact, there was no even possible basis for thinking there was a PER issue.
- ✓ There was no statute of frauds issue—the contract was written and signed.
- ✓ The first issue was a pure ambiguity/interpretation issue. Here's what students should have been discussing regarding this issue:
  - ○ Students MUST have explained, in depth, what aspect of the contract is ambiguous and what the parties' arguments were about that ambiguity: Here, the ambiguous word was "ethically." Students needed to explain that the word could *only* refer to the ethical standards stated in the state's applicable statute, which seems to require only disclosure or could refer to compliance with statutes and a broader concept of moral behavior so that refusing to meet with persons for whom the SCAM deals would be foolish is not a breach of contract.

- Excellent papers also would attempt to resort to an English dictionary and quote from it. My dictionary, however, cuts both ways. On the one hand, it states that ethically refers to "conforming to accepted and especially professional standards of conduct" but also "of or relating to ethics" which it defines as "a discipline dealing with moral duty..., moral principles or practice."
- Students then must apply the contract interpretation principles to try to resolve the ambiguity. Principles students could have discussed were:
  - Trade usage — Whether the statute created a trade usage was debatable at best — I don't think it really was a trade usage because there were no facts indicating the trade had adopted the statute as a usage or was otherwise using it (many students will recognize this fact and simply not address trade usage — I wouldn't have addressed trade usage)
  - Interpret the contract to be consistent with itself (i.e., reconcile the various provisions) (Note: I did not expect every student to see every argument below):
    - The provision re making the contract consistent with all applicable statutes
      - D may argue that this statute suggests the parties intended ethical to have its technical, statutory meaning.
      - P may argue that the clause really isn't on point because the interpretation that ethical includes moral obligations and *not just* statutory obligations is entirely consistent.
      - P's best argument in the whole case is that the word "ethically" would be unnecessary, given the comply with law clause, if it only referred to technical rules of professional behavior.
    - The provision re SCAM advertising "encouraging all GREEDS residents to consider SCAM deals" probably does help a little because it suggests SCAM was not permitted to decide which residents with which to meet. There was a decent counter-argument here — the clause really only addresses who hears about SCAM's services, not who must receive them
  - Interpret to be reasonable (this argument goes both ways):
    - Could argue that it is reasonable to not take a paternalistic approach because some residents would want the comfort of secure lifelong care, even if it is a poor investment decision and SCAM cannot know for certain how long each resident will live, how much each resident values security or whether each resident has any relatives worthy of giving an inheritance
    - Could argue it is reasonable to save residents and SCAM time and effort where a SCAM deal would be a terrible decision
  - Contra proferentem was not a viable argument because we cannot charge either party with being the drafter.
- ✓ The second issue was a pure specific performance issue.
  - There really wasn't a 13th Amendment issue because the parties are corporations and therefore the fact that services were being rendered by individuals doesn't matter (I wouldn't deduct points from students if they raised the issue as long as they immediately dismissed it).

- Inadequacy
  - Ability to collect really was not an issue
  - Inability to calculate: Can find what another company would charge to work with the people SCAM is not seeing but cannot know how many such residents would have signed up, what those residents' assets would have been upon death and how much their care would have cost GREEDS so cannot estimate at all GREEDS' damages
  - Inability to replace (D will argue that they are not the only company that provides such services and the fact that SCAM is the largest and most highly-respected firm doing this work doesn't make it difficult to find another company to do it; P will argue that, with D already advising most residents, having someone else come in will be seen as an obvious scam against the wealthy residents and the length of the contract (10 years) and the benefit to D of using the most highly-respected company doing these services, which may increase sign-ups with SCAM deals, cannot be replaced)
- Discretionary considerations
  - Undue burden on the D—given that the contract required this per the call, there is NO extra burden at all so this really is not an issue
  - Undue burden on the court: Excessive supervision because complicated interactions between SCAM employees and residents may generate complaints about how SCAM< employees are counseling the residents at issue [e.g., are they using body language cues and negative phrasing of the options to discourage such residents] plus long-term length of contract
  - Unfair K is NOT an issue
  - Public interest (some students may make other arguments):
    - Pro: Enforce contracts
    - Con: SCAM deals are usually unfair and SCAM was working to minimize the most egregious abuses so ordering specific performance would make the most abusive contracts more possible and encouraging professionals to think about ethics as meaning more than just doing what is legal is a good thing!

Guidelines for Phase III: Reflection

Part I: Complete Exercise 16-2 from EXPERT LEARNING FOR LAW STUDENTS WORKBOOK (below):

This exercise focuses in on the recommended approach to learning from examinations addressed both in Chapter 16 and in Chapter 8. Select an exam, legal writing paper or exercise on which you have received feedback and then answer the following questions. Keep in mind that the key to learning in general and to learning from examinations in particular is being open to feedback and to change.

1. How well did you think you had learned the material before you took the test/quiz/exercise/paper? (check the item that best describes your perception of the degree to which you achieved mastery)

    ❏ Excellence   ❏ Mastery   ❏ Competence

    ❏ Approaching competence   ❏ Poor

2. How well did you do on the test/quiz/exercise/paper? (check the description that best describes your outcome)

    ❏ Excellence   ❏ Mastery   ❏ Competence

    ❏ Approaching competence   ❏ Poor

3. Given your results on the test/quiz/exercise/paper, how accurately did you self-assess your learning? (check the description that best describes your outcome)

    ❏ Very accurately   ❏ OK   ❏ Poorly

    If you did not check "very accurately" in response to the above question or if you "very accurately" predicted a poor outcome, discuss why your self-assessment was inaccurate or why you predicted a poor outcome.

    _____
    _____
    _____
    _____
    _____

4. Given your results, discuss how efficient and effective your learning strategies were.

    _____
    _____
    _____
    _____
    _____
    _____
    _____
    _____

5. If you did not perform as well as you would have liked to have performed or if you believe that your learning process, while effective, was inefficient, identify the cause of your performance issue. Below is a checklist of possible causes. Check all that apply.

   Possible problems in the forethought phase

   ____ Failure to set appropriate goal (you set no goal or set an improper one)

   ____ Incorrect assessment of the learning task (you erroneously classified the task)

   ____ Failure to invoke self-efficacy (you failed to identify past success in similar learning enterprises)

   ____ Failure to develop intrinsic interest in the learning task (you did not determine why you needed to learn the material)

   ____ Poor motivational strategy choices (you could not stay motivated)

   ____ Poor environmental choices (you made bad location, timing, rest sequence choices)

   ____ Poor cognitive strategy choices (the strategy choices proved unsuited to the learning task or you also should have used additional strategies)

   Possible problems in the performance phase

   ____ Incorrect implementation of strategy choices (you incorrectly used the strategies)

   ____ Failure to maintain focused attention (you were unable to focus during implementation)

   ____ Failure to self-monitor (you failed to recognize a breakdown in the learning process while it was ongoing)

   ____ Insufficient persistence (learning task simply requires multiple learning cycles)

   Possible problem in the reflection phase

   ____ Failure to pursue opportunities for self-assessment (you did not take advantage of or create opportunities for practice and feedback)

6. How did I do on this test / quiz / exercise / paper in comparison to tests / quizzes / exercises / papers I took before law school?

   How did I do on this test / quiz / exercise / paper in comparison to other tests / quizzes / exercises / papers I have taken in law school? Why did I do better or worse on this test / quiz / exercise / paper?

   _____
   _____
   _____
   _____
   _____
   _____

7. What were the most common aspects of feedback you received from your peer and from your professor on this test / quiz / exercise / paper?

What did they mean by these comments?

8. Based on your outcome and your response to the above questions, how do you feel about yourself and your law studies and why do you feel that way?

9. Based on your outcome and your response to the above questions, how will you change your approach to studying similar material in the future?

Part 2: Reflective Essay

On separate sheets you attached hereto, reflect thoughtfully on what you have learned from grading your peer's paper and what you have learned about exam-taking strategies from the entire process of taking this midterm, reviewing your peer's essay, and reviewing your peer's and my feedback on your essay. Use two pages *at most*.

International Environmental Law Quiz

Treaties (True/False) (Explain why and/or your support for your answer)

1. Treaties create specific legal obligations on parties through their express consent.
2. The United States is not a party to and does not comply with the Vienna Convention on the Law of Treaties.
3. Treaties governed by the Vienna Convention on the Law of Treaties must be between states and in writing.
4. Adoption of the treaty by 2/3 of the states present at an international conference makes the treaty provisions binding on all states that participate in the conference.
5. Ratification of treaties by the U.S. requires either the signature of the president or the 2/3 vote of the Senate.
6. Accession allows states that were not involved in treaty negotiation to be bound by the treaty by their consent.
7. A state may agree to be bound by only part of a treaty, unless the treaty prohibits reservations.
8. The U.S. is not bound by a treaty until the treaty enters into force and the U.S. ratifies the treaty.
9. Treaties can be updated by amendments, protocols, and technical annexes, all of which require unanimous consent of the parties to the treaty.
10. A treaty should be interpreted beginning with the ordinary meaning of the treaty terms in context and in light of the treaty's purpose.

Treaties (short answer)

Explain the roles the following play in treaty development, negotiation, and/or administration.

Secretariats

Conference of the parties

IGOs (such as UNEP)

NGOs (such as public interest groups or corporations)

Custom, General Principles, and Judicial Opinions (short answer)

1. Identify the two elements to establish customary international law.

2. On what states is customary international law binding?

3. How can treaties contribute to the creation of customary international law?

4. Identify potential sources of general principles of international law.

5. On what states are general principles of international law binding?

6. In the Gaabcikovo-Nagymaros Project case, the ICJ characterizes sustainable development as a "concept" that the parties must consider in their negotiations. Identify at least three ways Judge Weeramantry characterizes sustainable development in his separate opinion.

7. Compare and contrast the ICJ opinion in the Gaabcikovo-Nagymaros Project case to a typical opinion from the U.S. Supreme Court.

Soft Law

1. What is it?

2. Identify sources of "soft law."

3. How does "soft law" contribute to the development of binding IEL?

4. Give examples of "soft law" principles of IEL.

Civil Procedure – Reflections on Civil Litigation

Court Field Trip and *A Civil Action*

The purpose of this document is to describe two activities and the Litigation Perspectives Assignment that take place after Spring Break.

Court Field Trip

Between Monday, March 8 and Friday, March 19, please review a civil file and observe a hearing at the United States District Court for the Eastern District of Washington, the Spokane County Superior Court, or both. For either court, leave cell phones, laptops, and cameras at home. Bring a picture ID. No hats in court. Please be quiet entering and leaving the courtroom.

United States District Court for the Eastern District of Washington

The court is located at 920 West Riverside. The Clerk's office is in room 840.

File Review. The Clerk has selected five closed files. To review one, go to the Clerk's office, identify yourself as a student in my class, and request a file. The clerk will select one for you to review. The files will be available during business hours (8:00-5:00); the Clerk requests that you arrive before 4:00.

Hearing. Trials and motion hearings will take place throughout the week. Check the schedule in the Clerk's office or the court's Web site – www.waed.uscourts.gov. Please do not call the Clerk to check on scheduling for hearings.

Spokane County Superior Court

The court is located at 1116 West Broadway. The Clerk's office is on the third floor.

File Review. You can review civil files at any time during normal business hours (8:00-5:00). To review a file, go to the Clerk's office, identify yourself as a student in my class, and ask to see one of the files the clerk has selected for you to review. If the person at the desk appears not to know what you are talking about, ask to speak with Tom Fallquist, the Clerk of the Court, or one of the supervisors. They will direct you to a table and to files they have selected for you to review.

Hearing. At any time, there are motions and trials going on at the Superior Court. In the Clerk's office you will see signs that tell which case each judge is hearing that day. Pick one!

A Civil Action

The week of March 15 will be devoted to Unit 12, which explores civil litigation in the context of *A Civil Action*. Please finish reading the book by the beginning of the week. There is a movie based on the book. The movie is so-so. The book is not only a gripping story it is an outstanding device for understanding civil procedure in real life. Do not cheat yourself by seeing the movie instead of reading the book.

Litigation Perspectives Paper

The court field trip and *A Civil Action* are designed to give you some experience with civil litigation in real life. One important element of experiential learning is for the learner to reflect on the experience. Consequently, reflection is the focus of this assignment.

Court Field Trip.

- What did your observations of the file and hearing teach you about civil litigation?

- About the practice of law?
- About law school?
- About yourself as a future lawyer?

A Civil Action.

- What did you learn about the process of civil litigation (pleading, motions, discovery, trial, appeal) from the book?
- What did you learn about ethics that you believe may be important for you as an attorney?
- *A Civil Action* paints quite a picture of the practice of law. What are your personal views and feelings about the implications the book has for your future as an attorney?

Your assignment is to write an essay reflecting on your field trip and your reading of A Civil Action. Your essay must include your reflections on both the field trip and A Civil Action. You need not address all of the questions above—they are intended merely to start your thinking. Your essay is due in class on Tuesday, March 23. Your response is limited to no more than one page, single-spaced, on 8.5"x11" paper, with one-inch margins on all four sides, and type size no smaller and no more compressed than the type on this page. Please put your exam number at the top of the first page. You will receive 10 points for your response if you hand in a good-faith effort that complies with all of the directions on this page and your exam number is correct. I encourage you to discuss this assignment with your classmates. Your written work, however, must be your own.

Appendix 7-2: Rubrics

Torts Rubric

Given to students before they take the assessment.

	Exemplary	Competent	Developing
Law 25%	Accurately identifies all elements/factors and sub-issues.	Accurately identifies all elements – 1 factor or sub-issue missing.	Accurately identifies all elements – 2 factors or sub-issues missing.
Facts – applying facts to the law 65%	Thoroughly applies specific facts and makes reasonable inferences from facts to legal elements, factors and sub-issues.	Applies facts and reasonable inferences from facts to legal elements, factors and sub-issues – a few minor areas are not thorough.	Applies facts and reasonable inferences from facts to legal elements, factors and sub-issues – 2 or more areas are not are thorough.
Writing and format 10%	Writing is clear, concise, and precise. Paragraphing and sentence structure coherent. Follows requested format. Uses headings.	Writing has minimal minor errors. Or may have minor organization or format errors.	Has a few minor errors or 1-2 major errors with formatting, organization or writing.

Rubric/Scoring Sheet

Completed and given to students as feedback after they complete the assignment.

Damien's Duty to Patrick - 20

- ❏ **Conclusion** – Damien's definitely owes a duty to Patrick as either a business or public invitee. Exact status as invitee unknown without more facts.
- ❏ **Business relationship** – Patrick could be a business invitee because he is a customer or potential customer of Damien's skating rink. Assumes that Damien's is a privately owned business.
- ❏ Statute § 343 and § 343(a) refers to public places, with skating rinks being a kind of public place. Patrick's status would then be a public invitee. In addition, Damien's could be an enterprise that public officials lease to provide recreation.
- ❏ Accurate facts, e.g. unknown if Patrick paid fee, if Damien's private

Standard of Care Damien's owed Patrick – as invitee - 10

- ❏ Damien's had duty to exercise ordinary care to protect Patrick from
- ❏ Risks that Damien's knew of if not open and obvious
- ❏ Risks Damien's should have known of
- ❏ Duty to use reasonable care to discover risks
- ❏ Duty to warn Patrick of risks if not open and obvious

Damien's breach of care - 45

Conclusion

- ❏ Statute has been violated by Damien's but not relevant so not proof of breach

May be other ways to prove breach – would need additional evidence

- ❏ **Relevance of statutory breach** – ID statute and language—Montshire Criminal Code § 343(a)—prohibits children under 16 years to be unaccompanied by a parent or adult at public places—including skating rinks.
- ❏ **Damien's violated** statute by allowing Patrick, age 15, into skating rink without adult supervision.

  Apply 2 part test:
  - ❏ **Is Patrick in the group of people meant to be protected by the statute?** Group identified in § 343(a) is children under 16
    - ❏ Yes, Patrick, a 15 year-old is in the group meant to be protected
  - ❏ **Is Patrick's broken ankle's kind of harm the kind of harm that was meant to be prevented by § 343 and § 343(a)?**
    - ❏ NO. § 343 and § 343(a) are focused on "protecting children's morals and good habits" and engaging in certain "public activities at late hours" because it of its potential harm to children's school work.
    - ❏ While the statute relates to harm to children as a result of being out late, Patrick has a broken ankle, which is unrelated to his school work, morals or good habits.

- ❏ **Other ways to prove breach**

    No evidence present that Damien's breached its duty of care – would need to further investigate basis for Patrick's claim of breach of care

Damien's breach being the factual cause of Patrick's injury - 10

Conclusion

- ❏ Need additional evidence of breach to determine whether Patrick has a valid claim for causation.
- ❏ Assuming some kind of breach—liquid on the floor or other dangerous condition—Patrick would have to prove that Damien's factually caused Patrick's broken ankle – Patrick would have to prove that "but for" the dangerous condition on Damien's premises Patrick would not have broken his ankle, or that Damien's breach otherwise contributed to Patrick breaking his ankle

Policy - 5

- ❏ Can be woven into the analysis in different places

Writing and organization - 10

- ❏ Organization overall – separates headings or uses signposts to convey different areas
- ❏ Concise – very few extra words
- ❏ Precise – accurate grammar, punctuation and word choice
- ❏ Paragraph structure – coherent and organized
- ❏ Format – follows all directions

Score: _____

Remedies Peer Review Rubric

Please focus on categories 1-3 first	Practice ready performance	Comments
1. Identifies basic legal issues and ambiguities in legal issues – 25%	❑ Identifies major kinds of remedies available ❑ Identifies which remedies definitely available ❑ Identifies which remedies *may* be available ❑ Accurately uses terms recognized by legal sources	
2. Uses law and reasoning – 25%	❑ For major kinds of remedies available, identifies and analyzes tests, rules and authorities ❑ Explains basics about designing or measuring remedies ❑ Explains other considerations in designing remedies, such as identifies weaknesses in the analysis	
3. Applies facts from problem – 40%	❑ Identifies and applies key facts ❑ Draws reasonable inferences from facts ❑ Names assumed facts	
4. Responsiveness to questions asked and organization – 10%	❑ Responds to assigned task ❑ Organizes writing so easy to follow ❑ In beginning of memo, provides a coherent and accurate summary ❑ Uses headings and subheadings to help the reader follow content ❑ Virtually error free grammar and spelling	

Client Letter Rubric

Levels of Quality			
	Exemplary Advanced work for first year law student in LS I at this time in the course – on a job, the work would need very little revision for a supervising attorney to use.	**Competent** Proficient work for a first year law student in LS I at this time in the course – on a job, the work would need to be revised with input from supervising attorney.	**Developing** Work needs additional content or skills to be competent – on a job, the work would not be helpful and supervising attorney would need to start over.
SUMMARY PARAGRAPH The purpose of the summary is to let the client know the most essential points of the analysis. This is what you might want the client to read as the client is waiting to meet with you.	❏ **Clearly communicates** most important legal analysis in layperson's terms. ❏ Includes recommended course of action. ❏ Applies law to facts to show support for the recommended course of action.	❏ Analysis is generally clear; may contain portions where there is too much legalese or where the language is too formal. ❏ Includes somewhat clear recommended course of action. ❏ Somewhat applies law to facts to show support for the recommended course of action but may lack clear connections.	❏ Analysis is unclear because of legalese or language or writing mechanics and grammar make it too difficult to follow. ❏ Refers to course of action but client would be confused about what she is being counseled to do. ❏ Minimally applies law to client facts OR relies too much on law OR relies entirely on facts to summarize the explanation.
FACTS Facts should be stated specifically in letters to avoid confusion by the client. Facts that are unknown, but critical to the case, are often identified.	❏ **Clearly states** dispositive facts in an organized way, notes absence of necessary facts (if applicable). ❏ States that opinion was formed based on facts in letter. ❏ Asks client to review closely and report any discrepancies. ❏ Clearly identifies additional facts that might be helpful or facts that need further development.	❏ **Facts** are identified but may include minimal irrelevant facts or omit a couple dispositive facts. ❏ States that opinion was formed based on facts in letter. ❏ Asks client to review facts. ❏ Some reference to developing facts additional facts.	❏ **Facts** are identified but include several irrelevant facts or omit several dispositive facts or overly general. ❏ Omits that opinion was formed based on facts in letter. ❏ Does not ask client to review facts closely and report any discrepancies. ❏ Little reference to developing facts additional facts.

	Exemplary	Competent	Developing
LEGAL ANALYSIS (EXPLANATION) Client letters must include the relevant legal analysis necessary to answer the client's question.	❏ **Identifies** all relevant steps in legal analysis in a way that the client can easily understand. ❏ **Clearly articulates** applicable rule. ❏ **Client's facts** are woven into analysis so that client can clearly understand how lawyer made prediction. ❏ **Notes** any uncertainty or unsettled aspects of the law, weaknesses, and resolves them.	❏ **Identifies** the most relevant steps in legal analysis in a way that the client can understand. ❏ **Articulates** applicable rule somewhat clearly. ❏ **Client's facts** are woven into analysis but may have one area where relationship between law and fact is unclear. ❏ **Notes** some uncertainty or unsettled aspects of the law, as well as weaknesses, but may not resolve them.	❏ **Identifies** some of the legal analysis but omits important points. ❏ **Rules** and/or tests are unclear or inaccurate. ❏ **Client's facts** are woven into analysis but relationship between law and fact is unclear or client's facts not woven into analysis. ❏ **Lacks** noting uncertainty or unsettled aspects of the law, as well as weaknesses or notes them but ineffectively resolves them.
ORGANIZATION Like all legal writing, client letters require organization around central points of analysis.	❏ **Large-scale** organization is evident in clearly written, plain English, concise topic sentences. ❏ **Organization** within paragraphs is evident in clear, concise sentences logically ordered. ❏ **Headings** are effective.	❏ **Large-scale** organization is somewhat evident in clearly written, plain English, concise topic sentences. ❏ **Organization** within paragraphs is mostly evident but some sentences' sequence may be difficult to follow. ❏ **Headings** somewhat effective.	❏ **Large-scale** organization is hard to follow; topic sentences mostly lacking. ❏ **Organization** within paragraphs is confusing. ❏ **Headings** mostly ineffective.
WRITING MECHANICS	❏ Uses correct grammar, punctuation, and spelling.	❏ There are some errors to fix, but generally uses correct conventions.	❏ Errors distract the reader and make letter difficult to read.

Clinical Rubric – Performance Competencies

	LEVELS OF QUALITY		
	Exemplary – Practice Ready Excellent work for a law student – on a job, this student could perform well with minimal supervision. Score 2 for each exemplary criterion met	Competent Proficient work for a law student – on a job, the student would need some input from a supervising attorney before the student was ready to represent clients. Score 1 for each competent criterion met	Developing Work needs additional content or skills to be competent – on a job, the work would not be helpful and a supervising attorney would need to start over or fix mistakes. Score 0 for each developing criterion met
PROFESSIONAL RELATIONSHIPS (8 criteria)			
Clients Adversaries Staff Classmates Supervisor	❏ Keeps clients advised of case developments ❏ Helps clients make well-informed decisions ❏ Communicates effectively and respectfully with clients without using legalese ❏ Interacts effectively and respectfully with adversaries ❏ Interacts effectively and respectfully with clinic, court and other staff ❏ Interacts effectively and respectfully with classmates ❏ On time and prepared for all meetings with supervisor ❏ Open and honest with supervisor; keeps supervisor informed of all pertinent case developments	❏ Usually keeps clients advised of case developments ❏ Usually helps clients make well-informed decisions ❏ Mostly communicates effectively and respectfully with clients without using legalese ❏ Usually interacts effectively and respectfully with adversaries ❏ Usually interacts effectively and respectfully with clinic, court and other staff ❏ Usually interacts effectively and respectfully with classmates ❏ Almost always on time and prepared for all meetings with supervisor ❏ Open and honest with supervisor; keeps supervisor informed of all pertinent case developments	❏ Sometimes keeps clients advised of case developments ❏ Sometimes helps clients make well-informed decisions ❏ Sometimes communicates effectively and respectfully with clients without using legalese ❏ Sometimes interacts effectively and respectfully with adversaries ❏ Sometimes interacts effectively and respectfully with clinic, court and other staff ❏ Sometimes interacts effectively and respectfully with classmates ❏ Sometimes on time and prepared for all meetings with supervisor ❏ Not always open and honest with supervisor; does not keep supervisor informed of all pertinent case developments

PROBLEM SOLVING (6 criteria)				
Issue Spotting **Generating alternatives** **Planning** **Executing**	❏ Identifies and diagnoses legal problems ❏ Generates alternative solutions and strategies ❏ Thoroughly assesses alternative strategies ❏ Develops a detailed plan of action ❏ Reliably implements a plan of action ❏ Regularly seeks out and keeps the planning process open to new information and ideas	❏ Identifies and diagnoses legal problems ❏ Generates some alternative solutions and strategies ❏ Assesses alternative strategies ❏ Develops a coherent plan of action ❏ Implements a plan of action ❏ Keeps the planning process open to new information and ideas	❏ Identifies and diagnoses some legal problems ❏ Generates few alternative solutions and strategies ❏ Somewhat assesses alternative strategies ❏ Somewhat develops a plan of action ❏ Somewhat implements a plan of action ❏ Somewhat keeps the planning process open to new information and ideas
DEVELOPING PROFESSIONAL IDENTITY AND INDEPENDENT LEARNING (6 criteria)			
Taking initiative **Learning from experience** **Contributing to others' growth** **Self-reflection and evaluation** **Developing independence**	❏ Takes the initiative to be resourceful, raise issues, strategize ❏ Takes responsibility for actions and consequences ❏ Learns from feedback, critique, observations and experience ❏ Reflects critically and honestly about own performance ❏ Helps classmates improve their performance ❏ Experiments and tries new ways of doing things – willing to take risks	❏ Sometimes takes the initiative to be resourceful, raise issues, strategize ❏ Usually takes responsibility for actions and consequences ❏ Usually learns from feedback, critique, observations and experience ❏ Usually reflects critically and honestly about own performance ❏ Usually helps classmates improve their performance ❏ Sometimes experiments and tries new ways of doing things – willing to take risks	❏ Infrequently takes the initiative to be resourceful, raise issues, strategize ❏ Sometimes takes responsibility for actions and consequences ❏ Sometimes learns from feedback, critique, observations and experience ❏ Sometimes reflects critically and honestly about own performance ❏ Occasionally helps classmates improve their performance ❏ Rarely experiments and tries new ways of doing things – willing to take risks

ETHICAL PRACTICE (4 criteria)		
Issues Rules Communication Performance	❏ Identifies and analyzes ethical issues ❏ Observes client confidentiality ❏ Informs supervisor about ethical issues as they arise ❏ Follows ethical rules	❏ Usually identifies and analyzes ethical issues ❏ Observes client confidentiality ❏ Usually informs supervisor about ethical issues as they arise ❏ Follows ethical rules	❏ Sometimes identifies and analyzes ethical issues ❏ Usually observes client confidentiality ❏ Sometimes informs supervisor about ethical issues as they arise ❏ Sometimes follows ethical rules

ORGANIZING AND MANAGING LEGAL WORK (5 criteria)		
Case monitoring Files Office Procedures Time management	❏ Tracks case developments and meets all deadlines ❏ Follows office procedures ❏ Keeps files organized and updated ❏ Asks for guidance about unsettled case management issues ❏ Manages time effectively	❏ Tracks case developments and meets deadlines but needs reminders ❏ Generally follows office procedures ❏ Usually keeps files organized and updated ❏ Usually asks for guidance about unsettled case management issues ❏ Usually manages time effectively	❏ Ineffectively tracks case developments and deadlines ❏ Does not follow office procedures ❏ Sometimes keeps files organized and updated ❏ Sometimes asks for guidance about unsettled case management issues ❏ Sometimes manages time effectively

Appendix 8-1: Principles for Enhancing Student Learning – Faculty Inventory

Principles for enhancing student learning in law school include:

    Promote Student-Faculty Contact
    Articulate Clear, High Expectations
    Use Time Effectively
    Respect Differences Among Students
    Foster Cooperation Among Students
    Provide Prompt Feedback
    Encourage Active Learning

The following inventories assess the extent to which your teaching incorporates these principles. These inventories are based in part on inventories found at 49 J. OF LEGAL EDUC. 462-466 (1999).

Asses your teaching by responding to each of the statements in the following inventories with:

    (1) very often, (2) often, (3) occasionally, (4) rarely, or (5) never.

Promote Student-Faculty Contact

____ I advise my students about career opportunities.

____ I invite students to drop by my office to ask questions or to talk.

____ I share my past experiences, attitudes, and values with students.

____ I attend events sponsored by student groups.

____ I know my students by name.

____ I serve as a mentor or informal adviser to students.

____ I employ one or more research assistants each year.

____ I create opportunities for students to get to know me and other faculty.

____ I am an advisor to student groups or organizations.

____ I learn about my students' backgrounds, experience, and professional aspirations.

Identify one aspect of promoting student-faculty contact that you commit to improve during this academic year.

Articulate Clear, High Expectations

    (1) very often, (2) often (3) occasionally, (4) rarely, or (5) never.

____ I articulate specific goals (content, skills, values) for each class and my course as a whole.

____ I clearly communicate my expectations to students for each class, each graded event, and the course as a whole.

____ I involve students in setting expectations for themselves and the course.

____ My expectations for students are reasonable and achievable.

____ I provide feedback on students' performance so that they understand the expectations.

____ I make myself available to help students achieve my expectations.

____ I publicly and privately call attention to student success.

____ I provide clear, specific evaluation criteria to students before a graded performance, paper, or exam.

____ I model for students by setting and achieving high expectations for my own performance.

____ I elicit from students their expectations of me and I try to meet reasonable student expectations.

____ I provide examples of diverse legal professionals who establish and meet high expectations.

Identify one aspect of articulating clear, high expectations you commit to improve this year.

Use Time Effectively

    (1) very often, (2) often, (3) occasionally, (4) rarely, or (5) never.

____ I expect my students to complete their assignments promptly.

____ I facilitate student preparation for class by providing questions, hypotheticals, and problems to consider before class.

____ I underscore the importance of regular work, steady application, sound self-pacing, and scheduling.

____ I monitor student attendance and explain the consequences of nonattendance.

____ I meet with students who are having difficulty to discuss their study habits, schedules, and other commitments.

____ Through midcourse quizzes, examinations, papers, and exercises, I provide students with an opportunity to determine the effectiveness of their course preparation.

____ I spend class time addressing the material and skills upon which students ultimately will be evaluated.

____ I model effective use of time by beginning and end class on time, by keeping appointments with students, and by promptly reviewing/grading student work.

____ I help students understand the importance of time management in law practice.

____ I facilitate effective use of time outside of class through reasonable assignments and clear directions.

Identify one aspect of using time effectively that you commit to improve during this year.

Respect Differences Among Students

(1) very often, (2) often, (3) occasionally, (4) rarely, or (5) never.

____ I learn about my students' backgrounds and motivations at the beginning of each course.

____ I create a safe learning environment by not embarrassing students or tolerating sarcasm or degrading comments.

____ I provide extra materials and exercises for students who lack essential background or skills.

____ I make special efforts to be available to students of a culture or race different from my own.

____ I help students understand the importance of dealing with diverse clients, lawyers, and judges in law practice.

____ I include material and assignments that reflect diverse perspectives.

____ I build on students' prior knowledge and experience to help them learn new concepts and skills.

____ I use a variety of teaching/learning methods (Socratic dialog, lecture, discussion, writing, simulation, experiential, etc.)

____ I assess student achievement more than once in the course through a variety of evaluation methods (essay tests, objective tests, papers, skill performance, etc.)

Identify one aspect of respecting differences among students that you commit to improve this year.

Foster Cooperation Among Students

(1) very often, (2) often, (3) occasionally, (4) rarely, or (5) never.

____ I ask students to tell each other about their interests and backgrounds.

____ I encourage students to prepare together for classes and exams.

____ I structure out-of-class team projects.

____ I ask my students to provide feedback on each other's work.

____ I ask my students to explain difficult ideas to each other, including to other students whose backgrounds and viewpoints are different from their own.

____ I encourage students to join at least one campus organization.

____ I use small group discussions and exercises in class.

____ I model cooperation and collaboration in my dealings with administrators, staff, and faulty members.

____ I help students understand the value of cooperation and collaboration in law practice.

Identify one aspect of fostering cooperation among students that you commit to improve this year.

Provide Prompt Feedback

(1) very often, (2) often, (3) occasionally, (4) rarely, or (5) never.

____ I use quizzes (mock or graded) and practice exams during the course.

____ I give feedback on quizzes by posting answers and reasoning or by discussing them in class.

____ I give feedback on essay questions (mock or graded) by distributing model answers, sample student responses, and score sheets, by discussing them in class, or by writing individual comments.

____ I provide written feedback on draft and final papers.

____ I provide timely, specific, positive, and corrective feedback on student performance of skills.

____ I invite students to sign up for one or more conferences to discuss their performance.

____ I make appropriate adjustments in my teaching during the course according to feedback from students and after the course based on student evaluations.

Identify one aspect of providing prompt feedback that you commit to improve this year.

Encourage Active Learning

(1) very often, (2) often, (3) occasionally, (4) rarely, or (5) never.

____ I design exercises that require students to organize, apply, and synthesize concepts.

____ I involve students in making significant decisions concerning course goals, teaching and learning methods, assignments, evaluation criteria, and classroom procedures.

____ I involve all students in responding to questions during each class.

____ I use discussion to help students discover ideas, use critical thinking, and understand different perspectives.

____ I use writing exercises in and out of class to help students develop thinking skills, apply concepts in new situations, and explore their attitudes.

____ I use simulations and role-playing to help students apply concepts, solve problems, develop skills, and articulate values.

____ I use computer exercises and electronic discussions to help students apply concepts, practice skills, and receive feedback.

____ I provide opportunities for my students to apply course content and skills in real life through clinics, externships, field trips, service learning, etc.

____ I use videos and documents so students can apply their learning to real life in the classroom.

____ I use games that require students to understand and apply concepts and skills.

Identify one aspect of encouraging active learning that you commit to improve this year.

Appendix 8-2: Reflection Prompts

The prompts below all appear in Gerald F. Hess, *Learning to Think Like a Teacher: Reflective Journals for Legal Educators*, 38 Gonz. L. Rev. 1129 (2002-2003) and are based on the work of Stephen Brookfield, Susan Wilcox, and Parker Palmer.

The first set of reflection prompts are from Sephen Brookfield's Becoming a Critically Reflective Teacher (1995).

Questions to spur free-writing:
- What was the moment (or moments) this week when I felt most connected, engaged, or affirmed as a teacher—the moment(s) I said to myself, "This is what being a teacher is really all about"?
- What was the moment (or moments) this week when I felt most disconnected, disengaged, or bored as a teacher—the moments(s) I said to myself, "I'm just going through the motions here"?
- What was the situation that caused me the greatest anxiety or distress—the kind of situation that I kept replaying in my mind as I was dropping off to sleep, or that caused me to say to myself, "I do not want to go through this again for a while"?
- What was the event that most took me by surprise—an event where I saw or did something that shook me up, caught me off guard, knocked me off my stride, gave me a jolt, or made me unexpectedly happy?
- Of everything I did this week in my teaching, what would I do differently if I had the chance to do it again?

Teaching and learning audits: Please think back over the past term/year in your life as a teacher and complete the following sentences as honestly as you can
- Compared with this time last term/year, I now know that ...
- Compared with this time last term/year, I am now able to ...
- Compared with this time last term/year, I could now teach a colleague how to ...
- The most important thing I've learned about my students in the past term/year is ...
- The most important thing I've learned about my teaching in the past term/year is ...
- The most important thing I've learned about myself in the past term/year is ...
- The assumptions I had about teaching and learning that have been most confirmed for me in the past term/year are that ...
- The assumptions I had about teaching and learning that have been most challenged for me in the past term/year are that ...

Role model profiles. This exercise asks you to think about the colleagues with whom you work or have worked, or those you know who work in other institutions and settings. Please answer the following questions about these colleagues:
- As you look back over your career, which colleagues ... best represent what a teacher should be?
- What characteristics have you observed in these people that ... make them so admirable?

- As you think about how these people work, which of their actions most encapsulates and typifies what it is that you find so admirable about them?
- As you think about what these people do well, which of their abilities would you most like to be able to borrow and integrate into your own teaching?
- As you read your responses to these questions, remember that those we regard as heroes and heroines are often people who embody talents and characteristics that we feel are glaringly absent from our own practice and being. Rightly or wrongly, we view as heroic those who can do easily the things with which we struggle the most.

The next set of prompts are from an unpublished manuscript from Susan Wilcox, *Critical Self-Reflection and Self-Evaluation: Learning from Practice.*

EDUCATIONAL GOALS and STRATEGIES

1. What are the chief goals you have for your students? What content knowledge and process skills, including career and lifelong goals, need your students achieve?
2. In your experience, what teaching/learning strategies and experiences BEST help students achieve the above learning goals?
3. What goals do you have for your own development and improvement as a teacher?

CONSIDERING THE LEARNING CLIMATE

1. It's difficult for me to learn when …
2. My students seem to find it difficult to learn when …
3. Things that make it difficult for me to build a positive learning climate:
4. Things students might say about a class or teacher that would make me worry about the learning climate in that course:
5. A personal story (arising from my experience as a teacher or student) about learning climate and the way it affects learning:

ARTICULATING AN EDUCATIONAL PHILOSOPHY

1. What beliefs do you have about [law] students as learners?
2. What do you believe is the overall or primary purpose of [legal] education?
3. What do you believe is the role of content or subject matter in [legal] education?
4. How do you believe [law] students learn best?
5. What do you believe is the primary role of the [law] teacher?

The third set of prompts come from Rachel C. Livsey & Parker J. Palmer's THE COURAGE TO TEACH: A GUIDE FOR REFLECTION AND RENEWAL (1999).

- Think of a moment when you were teaching at your best. Then fill in the blank: "When I am teaching at my best, I am like a _____." [Explain] what [this metaphor] reveals about [your] gifts and limits as a teacher.
- What are some of your fears in the classroom? In relation to colleagues? In relation to your professional career? How have you dealt with them? What have you learned about yourself and about fear as a result?
- What sorts of fear are healthy for our students? Are those same fears healthy for ourselves? If they are healthy, can they be used more fully in the educational process? Should we do so?

- Draw three columns. In the first column, list some negative images of today's students. In the second column, list some of the fears faced by young people in today's society. In the third column, list the positive attributes that you've observed in today's students. How do these lists relate? How might this profile inform your teaching?

- Name some of your key gifts or strengths as a teacher. Now name a struggle or difficulty you commonly have in teaching. How do you understand the relation between your profile of giftedness and the kind of trouble you typically get into in the classroom?

- Write a personal statement trying to express what is at the heart of your life as a teacher. Consider the following questions: Why did I become a teacher? What do I stand for as a teacher? What do I want my legacy as a teacher to be?

Selected Resources – Books, Articles, Newsletters, Videos, and Websites

The print and electronic literature on teaching and learning in higher education and law school is enormous. Excellent resources addressing both theory and practice abound for teachers who want to know more and to improve their skills. Below we have collected the books, articles, newsletters, videotapes, and websites on which we relied in writing this book (along with a few others that we just couldn't resist including). We encourage you to sample these and other resources as you seek to enhance your teaching and your students' learning. And we apologize to the authors of the many wonderful resources that are not listed here.

Books

Thomas A. Angelo & K. Patricia Cross, Classroom Assessment Techniques: A Handbook for College Teachers 3 (2d ed. 1993).

Ken Bain, What the Best College Teachers Do (2004).

Charles C. Bonwell & James E. Eison, Active Learning: Creating Exciting in the Classroom (1991).

John Bransford et. al., How People Learn: Brain, Mind, Experience, and School (National Academies Press, 2000) (available online at http://www.napedu/books/0309070368/html.).

Stephen Brookfield, Becoming a Critically Reflective Teacher (1995)

Stephen Brookfield, The Skillful Teacher (2d ed. 2006).

Stephen Brookfield & Stephen Preskill, Discussion as a Way of Teaching: Tools and Techniques for Democratic Classrooms (1999).

Patricia Cranton, (ed.) Authenticity in Teaching (2006).

Barbara Gross Davis, Tools for Teaching (1993).

Walter O. Dick, Lou Carey & James O. Carey, The Systematic Design of Instruction (6th ed. 2005).

L. Dee Fink, Creating Significant Learning Experiences (2003).

Donald L. Finkel, Teaching with your Mouth Shut (2000).

Steven Friedland & Gerald F. Hess, Teaching the Law School Curriculum (2004).

Frank Heppner, Teaching the Large College Class (2007).

Gerald F. Hess & Steven Friedland, Techniques for Teaching Law (1999).

Larry Keig & Michael D. Waggoner, Collaborative Peer Review: The Role of Faculty in Improving College Teaching (1994).

Joseph Lowman, Mastering the Techniques of Teaching (2d ed. 1995).

Robert MacCrate, Report of the Task Force on Law Schools and the Profession: Narrowing the Gap, 1992 A.B.A. Sec. Legal Educ. & Prof. Dev.

Peggy L. Maki, Assessing for Learning: Building a Sustainable Commitment Across the Institution (2004).

Wilbert J. McKeachie, Teaching Tips: Strategies, Research and Theory for College and university teachers (12th ed. 2005).

Larry K. Michaelsen, Arletta Bauman Knight and L. Dee Fink, Team-Based Learning (2002).

Gregory S. Munro, Outcomes Assessment for Law Schools 57 (2000).

Linda Nilson, Teaching at its Best (2d ed. 2003).

Michael B. Paulsen & Kenneth A Feldman, Taking Teaching Seriously: Meeting the Challenge of Instructional Improvement (1995).

Michael Hunter Schwartz, Expert Learning for Law Students (2d ed. 2008).

Patricia L. Smith & Tillman J. Ragan, Instructional Design (3d ed. 2005).

Dannelle D. Stevens & Antionia Levi, Introduction to Rubrics (2005).

Roy Stuckey et al., Best Practices in Legal Education (2007).

William M. Sullivan et al., Educating Lawyers: Preparation for the Profession of Law (2007).

Linda Suskie, Assessing Student Learning (2004).

Barbara E. Walvrood, Assessmemt Clear and Simple: A Practical Guide for Institutions, Departments, and General Education (2004).

Barbara E. Walvrood & Virginia Johnson Anderson, Effective Grading: A Tool for Learning and Assessment (1998).

Maryellen Weimer, Improving College Teaching (1990).

Maryellen Weimer, Improving Your Classroom Teaching (1993).

Maryellen Weimer, Learner-Centered Teaching: Five Key Changes to Practice (2002).

Articles

Susan B. Apel et. al., *Seven Principles for Good Practice in Legal Education*, 49 J. Legal Educ. 367 (1999) (eight articles applying the seven principles to legal education).

Gerald F. Hess, *Collaborative Course Design: Not My Course, Not Their Course, But Our Course*, 47 Washburn L. Review 367 (2007).

Gerald F. Hess, *Heads and Hearts: The Teaching and Learning Environment in Law School*, 52 J. Legal Educ. 75 (2002).

Gerald F. Hess, *Improving Teaching and Learning in Law School: Faculty Development Research, Principles, and Programs*, 12 Widener L. Rev. 443 (2006).

Gerald F. Hess, *Learning to Think Like a Teacher: Reflective Journals for Legal Educators*, 38 Gonzaga L. Rev. 129 (2003).

Gerald F. Hess, *Listening to Our Students: Obstructing and Enhancing Learning in Law School*, 31 U.S.F. L.Rev. 941 (1997).

Gerald F. Hess, *Student Involvement in Improving Law Teaching and Learning*, 67 U.M.K.C. L. Rev. 443 (2006).

Gerald F. Hess & Sophie M. Sparrow, *What Helps Law Professors Develop as Teachers?—An Empirical Study*, 14 Widener L. Rev. 149 (2008).

James B. Levy, *As a Last Resort, Ask the Students: What They say Makes Someone an Effective Law Teacher*, 58 Me. L. Rev. 49 (2006).

Michael Hunter Schwartz, *Teaching Law Students to be Self-Regulated Learners*, 2003 Mich. State L. Rev. 447 (2003).

Michael Hunter Schwartz, *Teaching Law by Design: How Learning Theory and Instructional Design Can Inform and Reform Law Teaching*, 38 San Diego L. Rev. 347 (2001).

Sophie Sparrow, *Describing the Ball: Describing the Ball: Improve Teaching by Using Rubrics—Explicit Grading* Criteria, 2004 Mich. St. L. Rev. 1.

Sophie Sparrow, *Practicing Civility in the Legal Writing Course: Helping Law Students Learn Professionalism*, 13 J. Leg. Writing 113 (2007).

Kent D. Syverud, *Taking Students Seriously: A Guide for New Law Teachers*, 43 J. Legal Educ. 247 (1993).

Newsletters

The National Teaching & Learning Forum, James Rhem, Executive Editor; 2203 Regent Street, Madison, WI 53726, jrhem@chorus.net; www.ntlf.com.

The Law Teacher, Institute for Law Teaching and Learning, Gonzaga University School of Law, ghess@lawschool.gonzaga.edu; Washburn University School of Law, Michael.schwartz@washburn.edu.

The Teaching Professor; Maryellen Weimer, Editor; Pennsylvania State University-Berks Campus, P.O. Box 7009, Reading, PA 19610-7009, grg@psu.edu.

Tomorrow's-Professor Mailing List: desk-top faculty development one hundred times a year. Email: <Majordomo@lists.standford.edu>. Subject: leave blank. Body of message: subscribe tomorrows-professor.

Videos

Gerald F. Hess, Paula Lustbader, Laurie Zimet, Principles to Enhance Legal Education (Inst. for L. Sch. Teaching 2001).

Gerald F. Hess, Paula Lustbader, Laurie Zimet, Teach to the Whole Class: Barriers and Pathways to Learning (Inst. for L. Sch. Teaching 1997).

Websites

http://lssse.iub.edu/index.cfm The Law School Survey of Student Engagement is co-sponsored by the American Association of Law Schools (AALS) and the Carnegie Foundation for the Advancement of Teaching and directed by the Indiana School of Education. The Annual Reports for 2003-2007 summarize the survey results for thousands of students at dozens of law schools.

http://bestpracticeslegaled.albanylawblogs.org This blog contains postings on legal education curriculum, teaching, reform, and assessment, providing a web-based source of information on current reforms in legal education arising from the publication of Roy Stuckey's Best Practices for Legal Education and the Carnegie Foundation's Educating Lawyers.

http://idd.elon.edu/blogs/law/ is a blog hosted by Professor Steven Friedland of the Center for Engaged Learning at Elon School of Law. The blog is intended to contribute to the discourse on teaching and learning in law, from the inspirational to the whimsical, to the mechanical. It includes the varying perspectives of teachers, administrators, learners, and practitioners.

www.law.gonzaga.edu/ilst The Institute for Law School Teaching serves as a clearinghouse for ideas to improve the quality of education in law school. It publishes an on-line newsletter and its website contains helpful materials and links to law school and higher education resources.

www.law.umkc.edu/faculty/profiles/glesnerfines/bgf-edu.htm is Professor Barbara Glesner Fines' "Teaching and Learning Law" website which contains helpful materials for law students and teachers.

http://www.washlaw.edu/ This site contains links to over 100 topical sites. The sites – ranging from law schools, to legal books, women in the law, and even every state in the union – are alphabetically organized. The Study Law link, for example, connects the user to links concerning outlines, study aides, other resource guides, and examinations. The Teaching Methods link, on the other hand, connects the user to Web site addresses enabling law school professors to subscribe to educational periodicals.

www.podnetwork.org The Professional and Organizational Development Network in Higher Education (POD) supports a network of nearly 1,800 members - faculty and teaching assistant developers, faculty, administrators, consultants, and others who perform roles that value teaching and learning in higher education. Contains valuable links to university teaching and learning centers.

Index

active learning, 5, 11, 13, 18, 19, 24, 53, 57, 60, 67, 90, 91, 93, 107, 116, 118, 119, 169, 185, 186, 256, 259, 263
  criticisms of, 179
  definition, 12, 13
  examples, 21, 32, 37, 41, 48, 50, 51, 69–72, 77, 80, 83, 99, 102, 125, 132, 138, 142, 143, 159, 160, 189, 195, 215, 244, 257
  methods, 7, 8, 17–20, 24, 28, 29, 36, 37, 47, 55–57, 59, 60, 66, 67, 70, 72–74, 90, 91, 93, 137, 144, 148, 149, 165–169, 171, 173, 174, 176–180, 182–185, 187, 197, 199, 202, 203, 258, 259, 266
    experiential, 18, 19, 23, 221, 223, 245, 258
    large group, 17, 65, 72, 73, 80, 83, 84, 117
    minute papers, 131, 150, 152, 153
    point-counterpoint, 116, 118, 130
    presentations, 6, 18, 30, 77, 139, 142, 158, 180, 182, 186, 187
    problem-solving, 17, 19, 41, 44, 47–49, 51, 54, 64, 69–70, 72–73, 191, 192, 196–197, 254
    role-plays, 91, 93, 116–117, 139, 197, 259
    simulations, 7, 18, 19, 29, 72, 73, 117, 126, 139, 142, 147, 158, 197, 259
    small group, 17, 19, 30–31, 43, 51, 62, 66, 67, 72–75, 83, 99, 103, 112, 116, 117, 119, 125, 127, 130, 132, 142, 152–153, 167, 170, 175, 176, 178, 179, 197, 199, 223, 258
    think-pair-share, 116–117, 123, 125, 130

writing, 5, 6, 14, 18–21, 30, 31, 33, 35, 37, 39, 41, 42, 53, 54, 55, 59, 62, 63, 65, 66, 73–75, 78, 82, 83, 88, 100, 102, 104, 105, 110, 114, 116, 122–124, 126, 129, 131–133, 139, 140, 142, 156, 157, 159, 168, 170, 171, 173, 181, 182, 186, 187, 192, 196–199, 203, 208, 214, 222, 227, 230, 234, 235, 240, 243, 247, 249–252, 258, 259, 260, 263, 265
  value of, 28, 30, 31, 41, 56, 59, 60, 70, 72, 94, 95, 97–99, 101, 102, 126, 133, 137, 144, 147, 165, 170, 172, 173, 175, 180, 182, 184, 186, 212, 213, 224, 258, 266
adult learning theory, 3, 8, 9, 28
  characteristics of adult learners, 8
affect, 14, 66, 67, 95, 97–98, 101, 108, 114, 127, 159, 169, 170, 291, 192, 196, 204, 261
affective learning, 96–97, 191, 192, 196
ambiguity, 132, 156, 196, 210, 237, 238
  need to teach, 5, 12, 42, 148
arguments, 4, 19, 31, 40–42, 46, 49, 69, 77, 92, 95, 96, 113, 114, 118, 126, 139, 140, 147, 191, 192, 196, 197, 211, 237, 239
  assigning, 30, 45, 49, 50, 62, 63, 237
assessment, 7, 16, 21, 37, 38, 42–47, 52, 63, 76, 103, 104, 107, 124, 135–163, 166–169, 173, 178, 179, 180, 183, 184, 186, 187, 199, 200, 203, 211, 213, 225, 227, 228, 235, 237, 240, 241, 247, 263, 264, 266
  characteristics, 8, 9, 21, 24, 42, 66, 68, 75, 96, 102, 143, 148, 155, 185, 260, 261

assessment, *continued*
   checklist, 36, 45, 64, 85, 104, 105, 129, 134, 143, 144, 146–148, 159, 161, 163, 178, 181, 187, 228, 241
   classroom, 5, 6, 12, 13–17, 19–21, 24, 25, 27–29, 32, 33, 35, 44, 50, 52, 55, 57, 59, 61–63, 66, 70–72, 75, 76, 78, 80, 100, 108–110, 112, 118, 123, 124, 126–130, 133, 134, 137, 138, 149, 150, 153, 154, 157, 161, 165, 166, 169, 173, 177–181, 211, 259, 261–264
   course, 5, 6, 8, 12–21, 23, 24, 28, 32–40, 42–70, 72, 73, 76, 77, 82–85, 89, 90, 92, 97, 99, 100–102, 104, 107, 108, 112–115, 123–127, 129, 133, 135–138, 140–142, 144, 146, 147, 149–151, 153, 154, 158–160, 162, 165, 167–170, 171, 172–179, 182, 185–187, 191, 192, 195–199, 201–204, 207, 210, 214, 215, 222, 223, 225, 230, 251, 256–259, 261, 264, 265, 266
   criteria, 20, 21, 40, 69, 77, 91, 143, 144, 155, 158–161, 163, 165, 183, 186, 187, 199, 200, 202, 225, 237, 253–255, 257, 259, 265
   fair, 40, 58, 60, 155, 158, 159, 162, 163, 172, 169, 183, 198, 199, 202, 209, 211, 212, 218, 239
   formative, 13, 21, 76, 124, 137, 141, 144, 150, 159, 166, 167, 172–174, 177, 178, 180, 183, 187, 235
   grading, 20, 24, 55, 58, 60, 114, 135, 136, 154–156, 158, 159, 161–163, 186, 200, 214, 237, 242, 257, 258, 264, 265
   institutional, 136, 165, 168, 183, 185
   instruments, 43, 44, 135, 137–139, 144, 149, 156, 158, 163, 177, 235
   learning objectives, 17, 19, 40, 42–44, 46, 47, 50, 51, 61, 63, 65, 66, 68, 70–72, 80, 82, 85, 93, 107, 108, 112, 113, 115, 118, 122, 126, 128, 130, 131, 134, 136, 138–140, 150, 158, 163
   methods, 7, 8, 17–20, 24, 28, 29, 36, 37, 47, 55–57, 59, 60, 66, 67, 70, 72–74, 90, 91, 93, 137, 144, 148, 149, 165–169, 171, 173, 174, 176–180, 182–185, 187, 197, 199, 202, 203, 258, 259, 266
   multiple, 6, 7, 12, 32, 35, 36, 43, 44, 47–49, 60, 62, 63, 73, 76, 99, 102, 116, 137, 149, 150, 153, 155, 156, 157, 158, 163, 191, 199, 202, 203, 228, 241
   reliable, 51, 58, 155, 158, 180
   rubrics, 58, 76, 78, 80, 91, 93, 143–145, 147, 148, 158, 159, 161, 247, 264, 265
   scoring sheets, 160, 259
   summative, 154, 156, 177, 183
   valid, 14, 15, 23, 26, 66, 140, 145, 155, 179, 208, 230, 234, 249
assignments, 11, 14, 15, 17, 19, 20, 27, 29, 30, 33, 35, 36, 39, 40, 44, 49, 50, 52–60, 64, 67, 114, 117, 140, 147, 149, 150, 157, 159, 168, 170, 172, 175, 178, 192, 195–197, 199, 203, 208, 230, 235, 257–259
   concept maps, 73
   design of, 16, 17, 19, 20, 37–40, 42–45, 47, 49, 52, 61–68, 70–74, 76, 77, 80, 84, 85, 138, 139, 141, 167, 174, 176, 178, 184, 186, 198, 202, 263
   drafting, 6, 18, 39, 48, 50, 51, 53, 66, 67, 73, 74, 77, 84, 126, 132, 137, 155, 191, 192, 196, 219
   graphics, 73, 120, 128, 142
   group, 7, 8, 15, 17, 19, 23, 25, 28, 29, 30, 31, 36, 43, 51, 61, 62, 65–67, 71–75, 80, 82, 83, 84, 85, 92, 96, 99, 103, 111–114, 116–119, 125, 127, 130–133, 142, 144, 152, 153, 167, 170, 174–176, 178, 179, 197, 199, 220, 223, 224, 235, 248, 258
   in-class, 29, 74, 99, 107, 114, 149, 199, 211
   individual, 8, 15, 17, 27, 31, 33, 41, 47, 51, 52, 58, 65, 67, 68, 72–75, 103, 107, 113, 115, 118, 127, 131, 135, 138, 142–144, 148, 149, 150, 160, 169, 171, 179, 180, 182, 184, 185, 187, 195, 200, 203, 225, 238, 256, 259
   out-of-class, 49, 100, 121, 170, 258

variety in, 14, 15, 18, 20, 21, 28, 36, 38, 44, 47, 50, 53, 58, 60, 66, 67, 72, 77, 78, 90, 101, 103, 114–116, 125, 126, 131, 148, 155, 158, 163, 176, 180, 185, 199, 220, 258
    writing, 5, 6, 14, 18–21, 30, 31, 33, 35, 37, 39, 41, 42, 54, 55, 59, 62, 63, 65, 66, 73–75, 78, 82, 83, 88, 100, 102, 104, 105, 110, 114, 116, 122–124, 126, 129, 131–133, 139, 140, 142, 156, 157, 159, 168, 170, 171, 173, 181, 182, 186, 187, 192, 196–199, 203, 208, 214, 222, 227, 230, 234, 235, 240, 243, 247, 249–252, 258, 259, 265
atmosphere *see* classroom environment
attention, 4, 5, 10, 11, 14, 16, 17, 21, 49, 50, 52, 53, 67, 71, 72, 76–80, 90, 92, 101, 102, 111, 119, 120, 123, 125, 133, 135–237, 141, 154, 173, 198, 228, 235, 237, 241, 257
    focusing student, 14, 30, 102
    selective, 4, 78, 141
    student in-class, 99
attitude, 15, 16, 19, 20, 41, 58, 87, 88, 89, 90–99, 149–151, 167, 169, 175, 180, 184, 186, 191, 192, 196, 199, 256, 259
    learning, 41, 94, 98
authentic learning, 7, 8, 43, 60, 90, 93, 118
automaticity, 5
autonomy, and student learning, 91, 93
bar exam, 66, 72, 76
Bloom's taxonomy of educational objectives, 69, 70
body language, 90, 109, 160, 239
    emotional messages, 108
    nonverbal communication in class, 177
CALI (the Center for Computer-Assisted Learning Instruction), 18, 51, 63, 67, 73, 77, 78, 85, 139, 149, 181, 196, 197, 201
    exercises, 51, 63, 77, 139, 149
casebook (textbook), 18, 30, 45–46, 50, 52, 65, 78, 83, 142, 215
    selection, 11, 12, 45–46, 72, 77, 208
cases, 4, 6, 21, 30, 33, 39–41, 45, 46, 49–52, 58, 60, 62, 63, 65, 68, 69, 73, 77–81, 102, 113, 127, 191, 192, 197, 201, 211, 215, 218

analysis, 18, 69, 191, 192, 196
synthesizing, 33, 47, 49, 50, 51, 52, 192, 196, 210
using, 113, 191
challenges, students facing, 67, 114
class design, 17, 19, 20, 39, 47, 49, 64–68, 70–72, 74, 76, 77, 80, 82, 84, 85, 115, 141, 178, 185, 186, 197, 198, 202
    checklist, 36, 45, 64, 85, 104, 105, 129, 134, 143, 144, 146–148, 159, 161, 163, 178, 181, 187, 228, 241
    classroom, 5, 6, 12, 13–17, 19–21, 24, 25, 27–29, 32, 33, 35, 44, 50, 52, 55, 57, 59, 61–63, 66, 70–72, 75, 76, 78, 80, 92, 99, 100, 108–110, 112, 118, 123, 124, 126–130, 133, 134, 137, 138, 149, 150, 153, 154, 157, 165, 166, 169, 173, 177–181, 211, 259, 261–264
    context, 4, 7, 20, 28, 39, 41, 43, 44, 48, 51, 53, 58, 65–70, 72, 77, 82–85, 88, 90, 91, 94, 96, 99, 100, 103, 113, 122, 124, 156, 167, 169, 207, 210, 218, 235, 243, 245
    student, 3, 5, 7, 9–12, 14–21, 23–28, 30–36, 39–42, 44, 45, 47, 48, 50–52, 55–63, 65–68, 70–78, 79, 80, 82, 83, 84, 85, 87–94, 95, 96, 97, 98–105, 107, 108, 109, 110, 112–117, 118, 119, 120, 121, 122–125, 126, 127, 131, 133, 135–163, 165, 167, 168, 170, 172–181, 183, 185–187, 197–199, 202, 215, 223, 235, 237, 238, 245, 251, 253, 256–259, 261, 264–266
    teacher, 3–21, 23, 24, 25, 26, 28, 29, 31, 33–35, 39, 43, 45, 46, 47, 49, 51, 54, 57, 59, 65–68, 69, 71, 75–77, 83–85, 88–90, 92, 93, 94, 96, 100, 101, 107, 108, 110, 112, 113, 115, 116, 119, 120, 122, 126, 129, 130, 131, 133, 134, 136, 137, 142–144, 146, 148, 149, 150, 151, 157, 159, 160, 165–187, 191, 192, 196–198, 201, 202, 260–263, 264, 265, 266

class design, *continued*
  enrollment, 67, 83, 84
  feedback, 8, 9, 13, 14, 17, 19, 21, 24, 30, 32, 34, 36, 49, 60, 62, 65–67, 70, 76–78, 82–85, 90, 94, 95, 97, 101, 103, 104, 119, 120, 124, 125, 131, 137–140, 142–150, 152, 153, 155, 159–161, 163, 165–170, 172–183, 185, 187, 197–199, 214, 225, 227, 228, 235, 237, 240–242, 248, 254, 256–259
  five-step process, 65, 82
  grouping strategies, 72, 82
  instructional activities, 65–67, 70, 71, 73, 77, 78, 82–85, 111, 115, 116, 118, 127, 130, 131, 134, 186
  learning styles, 18, 26, 50, 57, 58, 61, 67, 72, 73, 78, 167, 197
  materials, 78
    characteristics of effective, 24, 96, 143, 148, 155, 185
    focus devices, 79
    functions, 61, 77, 78, 80, 209
    interactive, 4, 78–80
  teacher preparation, 49, 59, 197
class sessions, 17, 37, 39, 47, 49, 59, 65, 67, 69–71, 76, 88, 113, 115, 131, 137, 158, 171, 178, 203
  addressing controversial topics, 111, 126–127, 134, 152
  arriving early, 112
  body of class, 19, 39, 71, 72, 77, 78, 111, 113, 115, 116, 130, 134
  closings, 76, 111, 131, 133, 134
  material, 5, 6, 11, 14, 24, 25, 28–30, 34, 46, 53, 54, 62, 65–68, 77–80, 89, 90, 92, 98, 101, 102, 114, 115, 118–120, 122, 123, 125, 130, 131, 140, 141, 149, 151, 152, 155, 159, 172, 177, 195, 198, 199, 227–231, 240–242, 257, 258
  objectives, 17–20, 38, 40, 42–44, 46, 47, 50, 51, 61, 63, 65–72, 77–80, 82–85, 93, 107, 108, 112, 113, 115, 118, 122, 126, 128, 130–132, 134, 136, 138–140, 150, 158, 163, 177, 180, 194, 214
  openings, 71, 111, 112, 131, 133, 134

clarity, 13, 14, 20, 21, 54, 122, 172, 177, 180, 181, 213, 235
classroom assessment techniques, 21, 52, 76, 99, 137, 149, 150, 153, 154, 263
  analysis charts, 150, 153, 154
  minute papers, 150, 152
  small group instructional diagnosis, 176, 178, 179
  student advisory teams, 173, 174, 187
  student surveys, 150, 152, 153
  teacher-designed feedback forms, 174
classroom environment, 20, 25–26, 108, 128
  addressing controversial issues, 111, 127
  creating positive learning environment, 35, 108, 126
closing, 32, 56, 64, 71, 75–78, 82, 84, 85, 91, 111, 115, 130, 131, 132, 133, 134
  end of class, 20, 21, 28, 66, 75, 76, 102, 107, 115, 130, 131, 133, 151, 153, 158, 159, 257
  end of course, 16, 20, 33–35, 38, 40, 43, 53, 54, 66, 76, 158, 169, 172, 173, 192, 196, 225, 230
  end of unit, 20, 54, 66
closure, 20, 91, 116, 118, 131, 133, 237
coaching, 8, 98, 146, 179, 180, 184, 187
cognitive, 3, 4, 6, 8, 19, 41, 47, 48, 50, 61, 96–98, 100, 108, 121, 158, 228, 230, 241
  learning theory, 3, 4, 6–9, 12, 19, 21, 37, 42, 51, 85, 167, 171, 263–265
  processing, 4, 49–51, 80, 127, 147, 215
  psychology, 88, 118
  strategy, 11, 18, 41, 50, 73, 83, 90, 93, 97, 101, 103, 104, 146, 148, 180, 192, 197, 226, 228, 241
  think-aloud, 48, 121
collaborative course design, 19, 20, 178, 202, 264
communication, 61, 69, 109, 177, 180, 185, 211, 213, 255
competency, 4, 91, 136, 155, 158
computers, 112, 212
concept learning, 41, 49, 50, 51, 66, 102, 103, 226
concept maps, 73
connections, 5, 6, 28, 32, 251

experience and learning, 8, 9, 29, 32, 43, 48, 73
  with law practice, 36, 93, 99
  with student career goals, 8
constructivist learning theory, 3, 7–9
control, 9, 24, 45, 60, 61, 87, 88, 90, 91, 93, 118, 176, 181, 185
  in the classroom, 118, 176
  students' over learning, 5, 9, 23, 45, 87, 93, 101, 135, 172
cooperative learning, 7, 9, 11, 19, 31, 58, 61, 62, 90, 142, 185
course design, 16, 17, 19, 20, 37–40, 43–45, 47, 52, 53, 61–64, 66–68, 72, 73, 76, 82, 84, 85, 114, 138, 141, 174, 176–178, 185, 186, 197, 198, 202, 259, 264
  checklist, 64
  course webpage, 37, 47, 52, 55, 58, 61–64, 90, 101, 113, 124, 127, 214, 215, 223
  feedback, 8, 9, 13, 14, 17, 19, 21, 24, 30, 32, 34, 36, 49, 60, 62, 65–67, 70, 76–78, 82–85, 90, 94, 95, 97, 101, 103, 104, 119, 120, 124, 125, 131, 137–140, 142–150, 152, 153, 155, 159–161, 163, 165–170, 172–183, 185, 187, 197–199, 214, 225, 227, 228, 235, 237, 240–242, 248, 254, 256–259
  goals *see* learning goals
  grading, 20, 24, 55, 58, 60, 114, 135, 136, 154–156, 158, 159, 161–163, 186, 200, 214, 237, 242, 257, 258, 264, 265
  learning, 3–21, 23–63, 65–78, 80, 82, 85, 87–94, 96–105, 107–110, 112–120, 122, 124–128, 130–163, 165–169, 171–176, 178–187, 191, 192, 196–199, 201, 202, 223, 225–228, 240, 241, 245, 254, 256, 258–261, 263–266
    activities, 5, 7, 9–11, 17–21, 28, 29, 39, 47, 49–53, 58, 59, 62, 65–67, 70, 71, 73–78, 82–85, 90, 92–94, 98–100, 111, 115, 116, 118, 119, 125, 127, 130, 131, 134, 165, 167–169, 172, 181, 183–187, 245, 248
  objectives, 17–20, 38, 40, 42–44, 46, 47, 50, 51, 61, 63, 65–72, 77–80, 82–85, 93, 107, 108, 112, 113, 115, 118, 122, 126, 128, 130–132, 134, 136, 138–140, 150, 158, 163, 177, 180, 194, 214
  types, 17–19, 21, 28, 35, 39, 41, 43, 47, 49, 50, 53, 59, 66, 67, 73, 78, 80, 95, 104, 122, 167, 172–175, 177, 179, 180
  units, 47–49, 52, 108
  pacing, 17, 35, 142, 180, 257
  policies, 5, 6, 16, 55–58, 60, 83, 113, 115, 183, 192, 196, 214, 217
  process, 3–7, 9–11, 23, 28, 31, 37, 38, 40, 41, 43–45, 49, 50, 52, 55, 59, 60, 62–65, 67–69, 72, 82, 85, 87–91, 94, 97, 98, 100–102, 107, 114, 115, 120–125, 129, 134, 136, 137, 142, 146, 147, 149, 155, 159, 160, 162, 163, 166, 170, 171, 174, 175, 177, 179, 180, 183–186, 192, 196, 203, 208, 212, 217, 225, 228, 237, 241, 242, 246, 254, 261
  syllabus, 6, 16, 28, 30, 37, 39, 47, 48, 52, 53, 54–61, 63, 64, 114, 140, 195, 201, 237
coverage, 40, 48, 60, 61, 68, 93, 203, 217–219
  course, 5, 6, 8, 12–21, 24, 28, 32–40, 42–70, 72, 73, 76, 77, 82–85, 89, 90, 92, 97, 100–102, 107, 108, 112–115, 123–127, 129, 133, 135–138, 140–142, 144, 146, 147, 149–151, 153, 158–160, 162, 167–170, 172–179, 182, 185–187, 191, 192, 195–199, 201–204, 207, 210, 214, 215, 222, 223, 225, 230, 251, 256–259, 261, 264, 265
  subject matter, 9, 12, 13, 16, 19, 29, 108, 110, 212, 261
declarative knowledge, 41, 52
discovery sequence instruction, 111, 125
discussion techniques, 49, 87, 89, 98, 131, 186, 263
diversity, 94
  in examples, 32, 37, 41, 48, 50, 51, 69, 70, 80, 83, 99, 102, 125, 132, 138, 189, 215

diversity, *continued*
　respecting student, 258
　student backgrounds, 15, 256
drafting, 6, 18, 39, 48, 50, 51, 53, 66, 67, 73, 74, 77, 84, 126, 132, 137, 155, 191, 192, 196, 219
dress, clothing, 129
email, 13, 15, 21, 56, 75, 78, 109, 113, 127, 153, 160, 175, 195, 198, 199, 201, 211, 212, 265
encouragement, 90
enthusiasm, 16, 31, 32, 59, 104, 110, 131, 168, 169, 173, 176, 181, 182, 186, 187
ethics, 83, 192, 197, 239, 246
evaluation of students *see* assessment
evaluation of teachers, 19, 177
examples, using, 21, 32, 37, 41, 48, 50, 51, 69–72, 77, 80, 83, 99, 102, 125, 132, 138, 142, 243, 159, 160, 189, 195, 215, 244, 257
expectations, 13–15, 20, 24, 29, 32, 33, 39, 40, 53–55, 57–60, 64, 102, 111, 112, 114, 118, 159, 160, 169, 177, 192, 196, 218, 256, 257
　students' of teachers, 40, 60, 257
　teachers' of student learning, 13–15, 20, 24, 29, 32, 33, 39, 53, 54, 58, 60, 64, 90, 111, 112, 114, 118, 159, 169, 177, 192, 196, 256, 257
experiential learning, 18, 19, 23, 223, 245, 258
experts, 3, 5, 23, 38, 40, 43, 44, 50, 56, 61, 62, 80, 88, 89, 94, 96, 103, 109, 110, 114, 121, 122, 135, 138, 141, 142
　expert learning *see also* self-regulated learning, 9, 240, 264
　teaching and learning, 89
faculty development *see* teaching development, 167–174, 176, 178–180, 181, 183–186, 265
feedback *see* assessment, 124, 147
　formative, 13, 21, 76, 124, 137, 141, 144, 150, 159, 166, 167, 172–174, 177, 178, 180, 183, 187, 235
　summative, 154, 156, 177, 183
flexibility in teaching, 58
flow, 78, 80, 87, 88, 91, 92, 107, 108, 149, 180
flowcharts, 50, 61, 73, 99, 142

focus questions, 20, 78–80, 83, 94, 108, 121, 122, 140, 151
free writing, 104, 105, 171, 260
fun, 25, 35, 55, 114, 135, 157, 171, 192, 196
goals *see* learning goals
grading *see also* assessment
　challenges/appeals, 21, 67, 84, 90, 93, 97, 114, 126, 165, 176, 178
　discussions with students, 160, 176, 185
　principles, 154–160
graphic organizers, 50, 58, 61, 80, 99
groups, 7–9, 11, 19, 23, 30, 36, 43, 61, 62, 67, 74, 75, 80, 83, 84, 92, 103, 112, 113, 117–119, 132, 142, 152, 153, 176, 179, 203, 220, 243, 256
　accountability, 8
　assignments, 19, 75, 116, 117, 223, 258
　composition, membership, 74, 75
　developing positive interdependence, 8
　formal, 15, 70, 74, 75, 114, 129, 130, 214, 251
　informal, 70, 74, 75, 129, 256
　large groups, 19, 62, 67, 83, 84
　size, 24, 67, 74, 75, 142, 214, 246
　small group learning, 17, 19, 62, 67, 72–74, 99, 116, 119, 125, 223
handouts, 21, 28, 73, 77, 79–81, 85, 112, 121, 153, 158, 175, 196, 198, 211
humanity in teaching, 24, 25, 26, 31, 114, 222
humility, 59
humor, 16, 24, 59, 114, 123, 157, 225
hypotheticals, 34, 47, 48, 50, 51, 73, 77, 80, 231, 257
implementation phase, 10, 11, 228, 241
instructional activities, 65–67, 70, 71, 73, 77, 78, 82–85, 111, 115, 116, 118, 127, 130, 131, 134, 186
instructional design, 3, 9, 47, 64, 65, 70, 71, 73, 77, 164–165, 167, 186, 264, 265
instructional techniques, 49, 91, 111, 116, 118, 126, 134, 186
internet, 20, 66, 85, 120, 199, 201, 212
kinesthetic learning, 73
laptop computers, 55, 102, 109, 118, 140, 245

law practice, 4, 5, 6, 7, 34, 36, 43, 47, 49, 53, 56, 57, 60, 66, 69, 70, 73, 93, 97, 99, 113, 118, 170, 171, 224, 257, 258, 263
Law School Survey of Student Engagement, 36, 266
lawyering skill(s), 12, 19, 41, 69, 70, 114, 131, 137, 191, 192, 197, 199
learner-centered, 19, 68, 85, 264
learning, 3–21, 23–63, 65–78, 80, 82, 85, 87–94, 96–105, 107–110, 112–120, 122, 124–128, 130–163, 165–169, 171–176, 178–187, 191, 192, 196–199, 201, 202, 223, 225–228, 240, 241, 245, 254, 256, 258–261, 263–266
   active *see also* active learning, 5, 7, 9, 11, 15, 18, 19, 29, 32, 36, 73, 76, 80, 89, 110, 115, 116, 120, 123, 176, 178, 198, 203, 222
   deep, 19, 29, 49, 51, 60, 62, 67, 73, 78, 115, 118, 126, 131, 137, 140
   retrieving, 4, 7
   storing, 4, 6
learning goals, 8, 11, 38–42, 91, 93, 103, 104, 108, 112, 117, 128, 131, 138, 140, 141, 142, 144, 150, 157, 159, 226, 261
   active verbs for, 70, 71
   assessment, 37, 43–44, 47, 60, 135–149, 154–161, 163, 266
   class planning, 65, 66, 71, 76
   course planning, 47, 49
   examples of, 41
   institutional, 136
   relationship with syllabus, 55
   subsidiary, 40, 44
   types, 19, 41, 67
      knowledge/doctrine/theory, 68, 85
      skills, 5, 6, 9, 12, 14, 16–21, 26, 30, 32–35, 37–44, 46–49, 51, 53, 54, 59, 61–63, 66–70, 72, 73, 76–80, 85, 92, 95, 98–101, 104, 105, 108, 113, 114, 118, 120, 121, 124, 126, 130, 133, 135–139, 141, 143, 145, 148–150, 152, 153, 163, 165, 175, 178, 180, 184, 186, 191, 192, 195–199, 201–203, 214, 225, 251, 253, 256–259, 261, 263
      values/professionalism, 19, 70, 79, 87, 94, 97, 224

learning objectives (*see also* learning goals), 93
learning theories, 3–12, 37, 167, 265
   adult, 3, 8–9, 19, 60
   cognitive, 3, 4–7, 8
   constructivist, 3, 7–9
   self-regulated, 3, 9–12, 39, 60, 63, 94, 95, 98–104, 105, 133, 137, 265
lectures, 28, 29, 42, 111, 115, 119, 120, 134
levels of intellectual skills, 5, 40, 53, 62
listening, 18, 30, 31, 42, 90, 109, 116, 199, 225, 265
mastery, 4, 10, 11, 44, 59, 91, 92, 93, 94, 100, 103, 104, 227, 240
   goals, 10, 11, 91, 94, 103
memory, 4–7, 9, 69, 73, 102, 129
   long-term, 4–7, 9, 69
   retrieving, 4
   short-term, 6
   storing, 4, 6
   trace, 6
   working, 4, 5
metacognition, 100, 158
mnemonics, 5, 6, 73
models, 14, 15, 51, 94, 95, 96, 97, 98, 99, 103, 105, 110, 121, 126, 127, 134, 146, 169, 178, 197, 257, 258, 259, 260
   student essays, 140, 161, 162
   teachers as, 14, 15, 51, 94, 95, 97, 99, 110, 121, 126, 127, 134, 146, 169, 197, 257, 258
motivation, 9, 14, 15, 18, 19, 20, 66, 70, 72, 74, 76, 87–93, 98, 104, 111, 167, 169, 183, 184–185, 186, 191, 192, 196, 228, 241, 258
   extrinsic, 87–89
   intrinsic, 87–89
multiple choice questions *see* assessment
names, 13, 24, 26, 27, 36, 108–109, 113, 119, 120, 134, 157, 161
   learning students', 13, 108–109
   name tents, 109
   on exams, 157
non-examples, 50, 51, 102, 125
nonverbal behavior, 16, 21, 108, 177, 180, 213
novice learners, 3, 8, 12, 24, 34, 48, 52, 61, 101, 120, 140, 141, 146

organization, 12, 13, 16–17, 20, 21, 28–29, 54, 70, 73, 172, 174, 175, 177, 180, 181, 214, 215, 235, 247, 249, 250, 252
outcomes, 11, 38, 126, 141, 178, 227, 229, 236, 240, 242, 264
   assessment, 178, 264
outlines, student-generated, 11, 33, 61, 69, 77, 103, 115, 117–118, 131, 139, 146, 211
outlines, teacher-generated, 28, 29, 54, 61, 73, 79, 80, 99, 102, 112, 120, 132, 266
overlearning, 5
paraphrasing, 5, 71, 237
passion, 13, 16, 23, 24, 55, 60, 72, 87–90, 93, 104, 112, 168, 169, 173, 176, 181, 182, 184, 186, 187, 213
perspectives, 3, 7, 13–15, 19, 23–36, 84, 87, 89, 91, 93, 107, 127, 137, 143, 181, 201, 220, 245, 258, 259, 266
   lawyers', 91, 147, 155, 191, 196, 204, 208, 211, 222, 223, 224, 246, 258, 266
   students', 13–15, 19, 23–36, 107, 127, 143, 266
planning, 10, 11, 17, 18, 37, 47, 49, 53, 54, 60, 63, 65–67, 71, 73, 74, 76, 93, 101, 107, 118, 135, 171, 178, 184
   assessment, 8, 38, 43, 56, 70, 71, 135–163, 170, 171, 178, 184
   class, 8, 17, 59, 65–85, 107–134, 169, 170, 171, 178, 184
   course, 8, 16, 17, 37–64, 169, 170, 171, 178, 184
   student, 10, 11, 18, 41, 53, 58, 70, 89, 97, 101, 103, 104, 226, 254
pleadings, teaching and using, 6, 48, 50, 51, 73, 78, 92, 125, 191, 246
policies, class and course, 6, 55–60, 113, 160, 183, 191–205, 225
PowerPoint, use of, 6, 52, 80, 122, 128–129, 214
practice, law, 4, 5, 6, 7, 8, 15, 32, 36, 41, 43, 47, 49, 51, 53, 56, 57, 60, 66, 69, 70, 72, 73, 93, 97, 99, 113, 114, 115, 116, 118, 126, 132, 133, 140, 144, 148, 158, 170, 204, 224, 246, 253–255, 257, 258

preconceptions and learning, 23, 91, 149
preferences, learning *see also* learning styles, 11, 18, 23, 27, 28, 42, 43, 49, 50, 57, 58, 60, 67, 72, 91, 103, 104, 114
preparation, students', 9–10, 14, 15, 17, 27, 29–33, 35, 38, 39, 49, 50, 51, 55, 57, 58, 59, 66, 73, 75, 77, 78, 79, 83, 87–105, 115, 119, 121, 131, 150, 152, 157, 159, 160, 170, 175, 177, 192, 196, 197, 198, 199, 203, 211, 216, 225, 253, 257, 258
   teacher, 13, 14, 16–17, 24, 49, 54, 82, 88, 97, 107–134, 138, 139–143, 147, 148, 149, 150, 152, 153, 156, 161, 163, 179
principle learning, 41, 51
problem-solving, engaging students in, 41, 44, 47, 48, 54, 64, 191, 192, 196
procedural learning, 41
professional development, 8, 15, 101, 138, 165–186, 192, 196
professionalism, 12, 17–19, 54, 70, 79, 87, 94, 97, 129, 153, 221–222, 224, 265
questions, in assignments, 14, 15, 17, 20, 34, 41, 46, 47, 56, 63, 77–81, 121, 211, 213, 227–229, 234, 237–242, 245–246
   levels, 46, 69
   on assessments, quizzes, and exams, 5 44, 62, 102, 139, 142, 149–153, 156–157, 237, 243–244
   responding to students', 26, 52, 61, 62, 90, 110, 123, 124, 135, 140, 149, 160, 195, 198, 199, 215
   using in class, 15, 18, 21, 27, 30, 31, 40, 49, 56, 59, 67, 69–85, 93, 99, 102, 113, 116–125, 126, 129, 130–133, 134, 174–176, 178–179, 180, 181, 184, 187, 221–222, 235–236
   wait-time, 121, 123
reading, assignments *see also* student preparation, 20, 49, 50
   length, 29–30, 65, 68, 77–80
real-world experiences, 7, 8, 29, 32, 35, 67, 203
recall *see* memory

reflection, students, 7, 10, 11, 47, 50, 54, 67, 76, 87, 88, 94, 97, 98–105, 114, 116, 118, 123, 126–127, 133, 158, 191, 192, 196, 199, 203, 204, 211, 213, 227–230, 237–242, 245–246, 254
    teachers, 21, 63, 71, 76, 82, 99, 126–127, 133, 134, 136, 148, 166, 169–172, 187, 256–262
rehearsal, 5, 107
reinforcement, of student learning, 16, 34, 58, 66, 67, 90–104, 114, 116, 118, 144, 151
    intermittent, 93
research, teaching and learning, 3–21, 37, 49, 59, 62, 73, 74, 76, 78, 88–89, 94, 96, 97, 101, 107, 109, 121, 123, 126, 137, 142, 144, 145, 154, 155, 165, 169, 172, 175, 180, 183, 186, 263–266
respect, 13–14, 19, 23–27, 31, 36, 45, 56, 60, 70, 90, 91–98, 110, 112, 123, 126, 127, 131, 146, 153, 167,174, 177, 185, 191, 192, 196, 198, 213, 224, 225, 253, 256, 258
roadmap, 20, 29, 112, 213
role-plays, 29, 31, 73, 91–93, 116–117, 133, 139, 146, 211–220
role of teacher *see* teacher's role
rubric, rubrics, 58, 76, 77, 78, 80, 91, 93, 143–145, 147, 148, 158, 159, 160, 161–163, 211, 213, 235–236, 247–255, 264, 265
scaffolding, 61, 141
schema, schemata, 5, 6, 49, 61
scholarship of teaching and learning, 167, 183, 184, 186
self-directed learning *see* self-regulated learning
self-efficacy, 11, 52, 104, 108, 110, 228, 241
self-regulated learning, 3, 9–12, 39, 61, 87–105, 137, 265
    characteristics of learners, 8
    cycle, 10–12, 63
    implementation phase, 10, 11, 228, 241
    phases of, 10, 237
    planning phase, 10, 11
    reflection phase, 10, 11, 228, 237, 240, 241

sequencing, class, and pacing, 17, 35, 111–134, 231
    course, 35, 47–53, 92, 100, 108, 180, 231–234
    learning, 4, 7, 41, 47, 92, 99, 108
simulations, 7, 18, 19, 29, 72, 73, 84, 117, 126, 139, 142, 147, 174, 197, 221, 258, 259
small group instructional diagnosis, 176, 178–179
social intelligence, 7, 8, 30, 225
Socratic dialog/teaching, 7, 11, 17–18, 31, 36, 53, 60, 65, 72, 73, 91–93, 101, 107, 116, 120, 124–125, 272
stress, 24, 27, 44, 92, 112–115, 130, 133, 146, 156, 157, 161, 225, 260
student, advisory teams, 174–176, 187
    backgrounds, 13, 15, 23, 26, 27, 142, 170, 256, 258
    conferences, 15, 30, 259
    evaluations, 6, 168, 172–173, 180, 183, 187, 259
    group instructional diagnosis of teaching, 176, 178–179
    interactions, 7, 54, 101, 115, 140, 178, 225
    perspective, 13–15, 19, 23–36, 107, 127, 143, 266
    self-evaluation *see* self-regulated learning
surveys, 152–153
student engagement *see also* active learning
Law School Survey of Student Engagement, 36, 266
study skills, study strategies, 9–10, 14, 15, 17, 27, 29–33, 35, 38, 39, 49, 50, 51, 55, 57, 58, 59, 66, 73, 75, 77, 78, 79, 83, 87–105, 115, 119, 121, 131, 150, 152, 157, 159, 160, 170, 175, 177, 192, 196, 197, 198, 199, 203, 211, 216, 225, 253, 257, 258
subject expertise, 12–13, 17, 108
summarizing, 20, 28, 29, 63, 71, 75, 77, 111, 116, 118, 119, 130–134, 151, 152, 153, 236
syllabus, 6, 16, 28, 30, 37, 39, 47, 48, 52, 54–61, 63, 64, 115, 140, 195–205
task analysis, 40
teacher's role, 19–20, 24–36, 90, 107–111, 118, 165, 166, 174–175, 197, 202

teacher's role, *continued*
  authenticity, 7, 111, 114, 118, 133, 134, 263
  availability, 16, 24, 89, 117, 124, 127, 172, 257–258
  coaching, 8, 98, 110–112, 123, 146, 179–180, 184, 187, 192, 196
  confidence, 56, 59–60, 89–93, 104, 109–111, 124, 169, 173, 176, 182, 186–187
  enthusiasm *see also* passion, 16, 24, 26, 31, 59, 104, 110, 112, 134, 168, 169, 173, 176, 181, 182, 186, 189
  humility, 59
  humor, using, 16, 24, 59, 114, 123
  mentoring, 93, 184
  modeling, 15, 96–99, 105, 146
  respect, showing, 9, 13–14, 23, 24–27, 36, 52, 57, 60, 90–91, 110, 112, 123, 126, 127, 132, 146, 169, 172, 191, 192, 196, 256, 258
  risks, taking, 16, 35, 110, 134, 156, 172
teaching, 1, 3–9, 12, 13, 15–21, 23–39, 42, 43, 45, 46, 48, 49, 52, 53, 55–63, 65, 69, 72–74, 76, 78, 80, 82, 85, 87–91, 94, 97–99, 102, 104, 105, 107, 108, 110–114, 116–118, 120, 122, 124, 126, 128–130, 132–138, 141, 147, 149, 150, 154, 156, 157, 162, 163, 165–187, 195, 197, 202, 256, 258–266
  collaborative, 19, 20, 57, 74, 101, 177–179, 186, 202, 264
  conferences, 15, 30, 87, 135, 178, 181, 182, 184, 187, 259
  consultant, 168, 173, 179–181, 187
  development, 8, 14, 15, 19, 21, 49, 51, 60, 81, 87, 89, 94, 97, 101, 138, 149, 154, 165–173, 176, 178–181, 183–187, 192, 196, 214, 220, 243, 244, 251, 261, 265, 266
  effective, elements of, 12–14, 24, 96
  feedback, 8, 9, 13, 14, 17, 19, 21, 24, 30, 32, 34, 36, 49, 60, 62, 65–67, 70, 76–78, 82–85, 90, 94, 95, 97, 101, 103, 104, 119, 120, 124, 125, 131, 137–140, 142–150, 152, 153, 155, 159–161, 163, 165–170, 172–183, 185, 187, 197–199, 214, 225, 227, 228, 235, 237, 240–242, 248, 254, 256–259
  fostering a culture of, 183
  individual coaching, 179, 180, 187
  inventories, 169, 170, 187, 256
  journal, 12, 35, 63, 100, 101, 114, 135, 168–172, 186, 187
  observations, 169, 176–179, 235, 245, 254
  peer review, 102, 177–179, 237, 250, 264
  philosophy, 55–57, 165–170, 176, 180–182, 186, 187, 261
  promotion, 165, 172, 177, 183–185, 212
  reflection, 10, 11, 19, 67, 76, 94, 97, 99–104, 114, 118, 123, 127, 166, 169, 170, 173, 182, 185, 203, 204, 227, 228, 237, 240, 241, 245, 260, 261
  resources, 13, 17, 46, 63, 75, 77, 147, 167, 171, 172, 176, 184, 263–266
  scholarship of, 183, 184, 186
  self-assessment, 103, 104, 145, 169, 180, 211, 227, 228, 240, 241
  subject expertise, 12, 13, 17, 108
  support, 7, 13, 15, 17, 18, 49, 78, 80, 107, 124, 133, 177, 183–185, 199, 220, 243, 251
  sustainable practice, 165–167
  team, 19, 170, 174–176, 178, 187, 197, 198, 200, 225, 258
  workshops, 87, 181, 182, 184, 185, 187
technology, 81, 112, 129, 167, 174, 185, 186
  electronic response devices, 144, 148, 150, 153
  graphics, 73, 120, 128, 142
  PowerPoint, 52, 80, 122, 128, 129, 214
tests, testing *see* assessment
thinking, 7, 9, 10, 12, 14, 16, 19, 20, 26, 27, 31, 33, 36, 38–40, 42–44, 47, 50, 52, 59, 67, 69–71, 74, 76, 85, 88, 89, 92, 101, 108, 111, 112, 115–117, 119–123, 135, 138, 144, 150, 168, 169, 173, 178, 182, 183, 187, 191, 192, 197, 237, 246, 259
  classroom time and, 13, 50, 52, 57, 62, 63, 78, 100, 108, 130, 153

critical, 13, 14, 19, 21, 24, 34, 39, 68–70, 75, 77, 108, 118, 120, 166, 169, 172, 185, 191, 192, 196, 197, 251, 259, 261
  exercises, 17–19, 28–31, 44, 51, 52, 63, 74, 77, 90, 93, 100, 104, 105, 107, 114, 118, 125, 126, 139, 140, 149, 155, 170, 174, 195, 196, 199, 227–229, 231, 241, 257–259
  hierarchy of skills, Bloom's taxonomy, 71, 122, 129
  wait-time, 121, 123
think-pair-share, 116, 123, 125, 130
timing, 107, 111, 130, 131, 134, 228, 241
  beginning and ending class, 71–72, 75–76, 85, 112–115, 131–133, 134
  during class, 4, 13, 17, 21, 29, 66, 67, 71, 76–80, 83, 97, 107, 109, 113, 115, 124, 127, 131, 137, 147, 149, 153, 168, 175, 177, 195, 196, 245, 257, 259
  throughout semester, 54, 63, 88, 91, 136, 167, 175, 199
  valuing students,' 13, 57, 313, 257
  waiting, 121, 123
transfer, 4, 48, 74–76, 81, 97
transitions, classes, 72, 89, 113
validating students, 14
values *see also* professionalism
  assessing, 35, 37, 39, 42–44, 56, 63, 77, 88, 113, 135–138, 140, 142, 144, 146, 148–150, 152, 154, 156, 158, 160, 162, 163, 165, 172, 177, 180, 183, 264
  practicing, 5, 49, 51, 68, 99, 116, 125, 137, 147, 221, 225, 265
  teaching, 1, 3–9, 12, 13, 15–21, 23–39, 42, 43, 45, 46, 48, 49, 52, 53, 55–63, 65, 69, 72–74, 76, 78, 80, 82, 85, 87–91, 94, 97–99, 102, 104, 105, 107, 108, 110–114, 116–118, 120, 122, 124, 126, 128–130, 132–138, 141, 147, 149, 150, 154, 156, 157, 162, 163, 165–187, 195, 197, 202, 256, 258–266
variety, 13–15, 17, 18, 20, 21, 28, 36, 38, 44, 47, 50, 53, 58–60, 66, 67, 72, 77, 78, 89, 90, 93, 101, 103, 104, 114–116, 125, 126, 131, 132, 134, 136, 137, 148, 152, 155, 157, 158, 163, 176, 180, 185, 197, 199, 220, 258
  value of in teaching methods, 28
videos, 18, 21, 34, 73, 77, 78, 80, 85, 181, 184, 259, 263, 265
  review of teaching, 102, 156, 168, 180, 181, 264
  use in class, 27, 33, 36, 39, 40, 45, 53, 60, 66, 72, 74, 76, 77, 79, 80, 85, 88, 109, 114–116, 123, 126, 128, 131, 133, 134, 139, 149, 150, 161, 163, 170, 171, 176, 178, 219, 257–259
visuals, 21, 111, 119, 120, 128, 134
  design, 1, 16, 17, 19, 20, 23, 37–40, 42–45, 47, 49, 52, 53, 61–68, 70–74, 76, 77, 80, 82, 84, 85, 97, 114, 115, 138, 139, 141, 157, 162, 167, 174, 176–178, 184–186, 197, 198, 202, 259, 263–265
  types, 17–19, 21, 28, 35, 39, 41, 47, 49, 50, 53, 59, 66, 67, 73, 78, 80, 95, 104, 122, 167, 172–175, 177, 179, 180
vulnerability, 16, 177
  student, 3, 5, 7, 9–12, 14–21, 23–28, 30–36, 39–42, 44, 45, 47, 48, 50–52, 55–63, 65–68, 70–78, 80, 83, 85, 87–94, 96, 98–105, 107, 108, 110, 114, 116, 117, 119, 120, 122–125, 127, 131, 133, 135–163, 165, 167, 168, 170, 172–181, 183, 185–187, 197–199, 202, 215, 223, 235, 237, 238, 245, 251, 253, 256–259, 261, 264–266
  teachers showing, 9, 26
wait-time after questioning, 121, 123
webpages, 61–63
writing, 5, 6, 14, 18–21, 30, 31, 33, 35, 37, 39, 41, 42, 54, 55, 59, 62, 63, 65, 66, 73–75, 78, 82, 83, 88, 100, 102, 104, 105, 110, 114, 116, 122–124, 126, 129, 131–133, 139, 140, 142, 156, 157, 159, 168, 170, 171, 173, 181, 182, 186, 187, 192, 196–199, 203, 208, 214, 222, 227, 230, 234, 235, 240, 243, 247, 249–252, 258, 259, 265